Smokestacks
and
Black Diamonds

A History of Carbon County, Pennsylvania

by

Joan Campion

with contributions by
George Harvan, Vince Hydro, Michael Knies,
Lance Metz and Rita Plotnicki

**Canal History and
Technology Press**

National Canal Museum
Hugh Moore Historical Park and Museums, Inc.
30 Centre Square, Easton, PA 18042-7743

Published by Canal History and Technology Press

Copyright © 1997

National Canal Museum

Hugh Moore Historical Park and Museums, Inc.

30 Centre Square, Easton, Pennsylvania 18042-7743

Book design by Ann Bartholomew

Cover design by Stan McKenney

Cover photograph: Late nineteenth-century view of Susquehanna Street in Mauch Chunk, from the Raymond E. Holland Regional and Industrial History Collection.

Library of Congress Cataloguing-in-Publication Data

Campion, Joan.
    Smokestacks and black diamonds : a history of Carbon County, Pennsylvania / by Joan Campion ; with contributions by George Harvan ... [et al.].
        p.   cm.
    Includes bibliographical references and index.
    ISBN 0-930973-20-8 (lib. bdg. : alk paper). — ISBN 0-930973-19-4 (soft cover : alk. paper).
        1. Carbon County (Pa.)—History.   2. Anthracite coal industry—Pennsylvania—Carbon County—History.   I. Title.
    F157.C2C18 1998
    974.8'26—dc21
                                                    98-9593
                                                    CIP

Manufactured in the United States of America

Canal History and Technology Press

Contents

Part Two

Acknowledgments

Smokestacks and Black Diamonds has had a long and tempestuous journey into print. It was on the verge of publication in 1993 when, for reasons that can only be speculated upon, the sponsoring organization suddenly withdrew its support.

In despair, I decided at that time that it was best to destroy the manuscript and forget about the project. Fortunately, my admired, supportive friend and former colleague, Shirley Collins, persuaded me not to do this; so to her is owed the physical survival of the work.

The Canal History and Technology Press expressed an early interest in taking up the torch and publishing the work. Delays followed, mostly owing to the effort to bring the magnificent new National Canal Museum in Easton into being. Steve Humphrey, Lance Metz, and Ann Bartholomew are to be commended for their patience and dedication in working with me at a time when I was not especially easy to work with — not to mention that the finished project owes a great deal to the extraordinary knowledge of regional history exhibited by Mr. Metz and Mrs. Bartholomew. Having survived as a manuscript, *Smokestacks and Black Diamonds* may be said to have been saved as a published work by a passing canal boat.

Too much can hardly be said for the gifted historians who have contributed to this work. When I was given the assignment I had only one year to complete it. I also knew there were people out there who knew far more about many aspects of Carbon County history than I could hope to learn in the allotted time; so I took the logical step of inviting some of them to contribute to the work. They have done a superb job, all of them — Vince Hydro, Michael Knies, Lance Metz, Rita Plotnicki, and that superb historian with a camera, George Harvan.

Although an index comes last in a book, it is certainly far from least — especially for those seeking information quickly. Thanks to Caroline Vickrey for undertaking the laborious but vital chore of indexing this work.

My deepest gratitude and admiration to all.

Joan Campion, 1997

Dedication

To Arlene Haupt and Mazie Ziegler

Two remarkable teachers

Crucible

A Capsule History of Carbon County, Pennsylvania

In the eighteenth century the historical phenomenon known as the Industrial Revolution began the process of reshaping methods of production that had been in use for many centuries.

The transformation was swift, as historical processes go. The cottage industry or the small shop with one master and perhaps a few journeymen and apprentices became obsolete in the space of a few decades.

New means of transportation powered by new fuels — most notably trains drawn by steam locomotives fueled by coal — made it possible to concentrate the materials and labor needed for production at carefully chosen spots, where densely populated towns grew up around factories and mills. In these vast, usually unhealthy structures, the workers themselves made little or nothing. Instead, they attended — and their lives were regulated by — gargantuan machines which did the actual manufacturing. These machines had, too, the capacity to maim or kill any worker who misstepped around them; industrial accidents did in fact take the lives of many.

This new system of manufacture had both advantages and disadvantages. For millions it made possible a higher material standard of living than the world had ever seen before. On the other hand, it ate up the lives of millions of workers; and it encouraged pollution and the wholesale pillage of natural resources.

Beginning in Western Europe, most notably in Great Britain, the Industrial Revolution rapidly spread to the United States. There it was to find perhaps its fullest expression and have its greatest effect on the world. American steel, to name one example, still is to be found in many of the world's most famous structures, although this clearly will not be true with regard to future construction.

It is hard to imagine a place more closely bound to the history of the Industrial Revolution than Carbon County, Pennsylvania. Indeed, it might be said to be the crucible of the American Industrial Revolution; the historian Alfred D. Chandler places the beginning of that era in American history in the year 1820, when 365 tons of anthracite coal reached Philadelphia from the coalfields of the future county.

Anthracite, the first fossil fuel to be heavily exploited for industrial purposes, became essential to the economy of the nation. It fueled the great iron furnaces of the Lehigh Valley and beyond, and provided the impetus for the first railroad networks to be developed. The cheap iron that could be produced in hitherto unimaginable quantities with this plentiful fuel hurtled the nation into the Industrial Revolution, changing the way of life for all.

Demographics changed as families moved from farms to towns and new, different kinds of jobs. A cash economy developed. Agriculture changed as new implements were invented. Home life changed as new appliances were marketed. Anthracite, the fuel of the wide array of new manufacturing industries being developed throughout the Northeast, was also the fuel for home use in heating and cooking, for steam and power plants, and for powering ocean liners and cargo ships. Nowhere was better anthracite found than in Carbon County.

The stamp of destiny was on the place from the moment Philip Ginder, a miller from the Mahoning Valley, discovered anthracite on Sharp Mountain (now the site of Summit Hill) in 1791. The new fuel did present certain problems, however. It was so hard to ignite that it seemed unsuitable for widespread use for industry or home heating. And, in the case of coal from the Carbon County area, it was hard to get to market economically.

Both these problems were solved by two Philadelphia entrepreneurs, Josiah White and his partner Erskine Hazard. The first turned out to be the easier problem of the two; one of White and Hazard's workers at their wire and nail mill accidentally discovered that if a draft were forced through the coal it would not only ignite, but would burn for hours with a steady white-hot heat. White and Hazard saw anthracite as the fuel of the future, and bought large tracts of coal-bearing land in the upper Lehigh River valley.

The second problem, transportation to market, involved achieving some measure of control over the recalcitrant Lehigh River — a challenge that had previously frustrated such entrepreneurs as Col. Jacob Weiss of Weissport and Jacob Cist of Wilkes-Barre. White and Hazard experimented with a series of sluice dams and "bear trap" locks to control the flow of the water, but with limited success.

Seeking a better solution, they came up with a plan to make the Lehigh and the Delaware rivers navigable by steamships as far as the coalfields by building massive dams on the rivers — in effect giving the anthracite region an opening to the ocean. For a variety of reasons, mainly political, this audacious scheme was never attempted. They then decided to build a two-way canal, with locks, along the river. The canal, which became known as the Lehigh Navigation, was built by the Lehigh Coal and Navigation Company. White and Hazard had formed this company in 1822 by combining two predecessor companies, the Lehigh Navigation Company and the Lehigh Coal Company.

The first section of the canal, from Easton to the new town of Mauch Chunk, was completed between 1827 and 1829. The so-called Upper Grand Division from Mauch Chunk to White Haven, with a further downstream-only section to Stoddartsville, was an even more massive engineering achievement. Built between 1835 and 1838, it was destroyed in the great flood of 1862 and was never rebuilt.

White and Hazard built several feeder railroads to bring the "black diamonds" to their canal. One of these was the Summit Hill to Mauch Chunk Gravity Railroad, later called the "Switchback Railway," which brought coal from the Sharp Mountain mining operation to Mauch Chunk. Another was the Room Run Railroad, a gravity line from the Room Run mines near Nesquehoning to the Lehigh River at Lausanne. A third was the Lehigh and Susquehanna Railroad between White Haven and Wilkes-Barre, which gave the LC&N access to the coal of the Wyoming Valley. It included the famous steam-powered Ashley Planes, which operated until 1949.

Perhaps not unreasonably considering their achievement, Josiah White and his colleagues could not or would not see that an all-rail transportation system would be far more efficient than the canal-feeder railroad combination. One who did see this was Connecticut-born Asa Packer, one-time canal boat contractor for the LC&N. From 1851 to 1855 Packer pushed through his Lehigh Valley Railroad from Easton to Mauch Chunk. It soon had taken away a sizeable chunk of the Lehigh Navigation's freight haulage, and it went on to be a famous regional carrier of passengers as well as freight.

Not until the 1862 flood had wiped out the Upper Grand Division of the Lehigh Navigation did the LC&N begin to respond seriously to Packer's challenge — and then, most likely, only because they were forbidden to rebuild the Upper Grand Division. After the flood the Lehigh and Susquehanna Railroad was extended from White Haven to Mauch Chunk, and by 1867 to Easton. The railroad was leased in 1871 to the Central Railroad of New Jersey, and as a result became known to Carbon County residents as "the Jersey Central," or simply "the Central."

The Lehigh Valley and the Central were the best-known railroads serving, or at least passing through, Carbon County. There were others, among them the Beaver Meadow Railroad, dating from 1833, which eventually was absorbed into the Lehigh Valley RR. It began life as a feeder railroad, bringing coal to the Lehigh Navigation from the Banks Township area; it was famous for its technological innovations. Another was the Lehigh Coal and Navigation Company's Bethlehem-based Lehigh and New England, which in 1912 ran a line through East Penn Township's Lizard Creek Valley to Tamaqua.

While anthracite mining was easily the dominant industry in Carbon County during its "prehistory" and early years, it was by no means the only one. Until about the time of the Civil War lumbering was also a very sizeable enterprise. However, the practices of clear-cutting and of letting forest fires burn out of control wiped out the forest resources. What we see when we look at the large wooded areas of the county today are new-growth trees.

There was also a certain amount of quarrying of sand, building stone, and even slate. Much of this was concentrated in the so-called Stony Ridge that runs east of Palmerton, but other outcroppings were found and worked throughout the county. So were deposits of ocher, a kind of iron ore used in the manufacture of paint.

Toward the end of the nineteenth century, textile mills such as the Dery Silk Mill in Mauch Chunk, offered employment to significant numbers, chiefly women and children. A little later garment factories began to appear, with ever-greater work opportunities.

Carbon County's last acquisition of truly heavy industry occurred in 1897, when the New Jersey Zinc Company established a major manufacturing facility near the Lehigh Gap and built a model company town called Palmerton after company president Stephen S. Palmer. The company came to employ thousands at its two Palmerton plants.

The growth of industry led inexorably to the growth and diversification of population. During the eighteenth century European-stock settlers north of the Lehigh Gap had been relatively few, both because the land was not especially good for agriculture and because for some decades there was a danger of such hostile attacks as the one which in 1755 destroyed the Moravian Church's Gnadenhuetten mission in the Mahoning Valley at present-day Lehighton.

Following the American Revolution more people of European stock moved into the future county. The earliest coal miners were in large part Pennsylvania Germans from nearby farms. Soon the coal entrepreneurs advertised for expert miners from Wales and England; these men often became mine bosses or supervisors.

As early as the construction of the Lehigh Navigation a new ethnic factor was introduced, for Irish laborers helped build the canal. Fleeing persecution and hard times in their homeland, the Irish were to become a growing presence in the future Carbon County, especially as miners in the coalfields. They brought with them not only a new point of origin, but a religion new to the region and one the subject of much bigoted speculation. There can be little doubt that anti-Irish bigotry played a part in the memorable 1870s tragedy of the Molly Maguires.

Having achieved considerable economic clout through its industry, Carbon County was formally established in 1843. At that point, though, the full extent of its ethnic diversification had barely begun. The period 1880-1910 saw a major influx of peoples from all over central, eastern, and southern Europe — Slovaks, Russians, Poles, Hungarians, Ukrainians, Italians, Jews of various nationalities, and others. They brought with them additional religions — Judaism, Eastern Orthodoxy, Eastern Rite Catholicism. In many cases they had been sent for by the corporations who ran the county's industries, from coal companies to New Jersey Zinc.

They did not necessarily get along at once, nor did they at once find common ground with the groups that had preceded them. But out of their common experiences all these peoples began to forge a community as time went by. The crucible of industry also was a melting pot of peoples.

With firm economic bastions like anthracite, zinc, the canal and railroads, and the garment industry to rely on, it must have seemed that Carbon County's future was assured. But the twentieth century saw those bastions crumble one by one.

The old Lehigh Navigation was the first to go. It closed officially in the 1930s, a belated victim of its own technological limitations.

For some years the lordly trains continued to sweep by the once-proud ditch. Through World War II, their contributions to the nation's wellbeing — indeed, to its survival — were regarded as vital.

But they, too, were being challenged by newer forms of transportation — trucks, automobiles, airplanes. When in the 1950s the federal government made a major commitment to the building of interstate highways, the glory days of railroads came to an end at last. The New Jersey Central, bankrupt, consolidated its railroad operations in Pennsylvania — which included the Lehigh and Susquehanna — with the Lehigh Valley Railroad in 1972. The Lehigh Valley Railroad became part of ConRail (Consolidated Railroad Corporation) in 1976. Today, only a relative handful of ConRail trains can be seen rolling on what remains of Carbon County's once-thronged rail network.

As to the famous "black diamonds" of the region, if anything in the economic life of Carbon County seemed secure, surely it was anthracite. Since before the county itself came to be, its chief product had been smelting iron, powering industries, and heating homes throughout the Northeast. It had fueled the ironclads of the Union Navy during the Civil War, and had been a mainstay of the United States Navy through World War I. But after that it lost ground fast, mostly to a far more flexible fuel — oil. As this is written in 1997, it is hard to find homes and industries even in the former anthracite region that are heated or powered by anthracite.

Near the Lehigh Gap, the plants of the New Jersey Zinc Company of Pennsylvania continued to roll out zinc products, seemingly remote from the troubles that beset the anthracite region. An economic and environmental turning point was probably reached, though, when the company ran out of its fabulously pure Franklinite zinc ore from the Sterling and Franklin mines in New Jersey and had to import lower-grade ore from farther afield. Moreover, in the aftermath of World War II, new materials such as aluminum and plastics were being used for products that had formerly required zinc in their manufacture.

By 1997 the zinc manufacturing facilities in Palmerton had changed ownership several times. Most of the west plant had been razed, and the zinc industry, in the form of Horsehead Industries, was little more than a vestigial presence in the town it had founded. An angry and divided citizenry debated the existence, scope, and significance of environmental problems arising from decades of zinc manufacture.

The last, probably smallest, and certainly least dramatic mainstay of the old economy was the garment industry, with its many small shops dotted across the landscape. As the twentieth century waned it declined too, as many large buyers decided to buy from manufacturers using cheap foreign labor.

Carbon County had been one of the first American communities to pass into the Industrial Revolution. It was also the first, perhaps, to go through the whole historical epoch and come out the other side. As the twenty-first century approached the crucible had cooled, the fires had gone out.

Like the rest of America, only more so, the county faced the task of forging a new future. Hopefully it will be aided in this effort by a just and accurate understanding of its past.

part one

Prologue:
St. Anthony's Wilderness

Nicholas Ludwig von Zinzendorf, count of the Holy Roman Empire, was a man resolute and pious, a man of high standing in his own world, and not lacking in courage. A Lutheran minister, he had provided refuge for an entire persecuted sect, known as the Unitas Fratrum (Unity of the Brethren), on his estate in Saxony in the eastern part of what is now Germany. Theologically, the group traced its lineage to Jan Hus, a proto-Protestant Bohemian church reformer who was burned by the Council of Constance in 1415; but persecution over the course of several centuries had reduced its numbers until extinction seemed likely to be its fate.

On Zinzendorf's broad lands in Saxony, the group had established a village called Herrnhut, or "Shelter of the Lord." They were popularly known as "Moravians," because many of their original members had come from that portion of modern-day Czechoslovakia known as Moravia. The count himself had become their leader, their second founder. They had chosen for themselves an historic missionary role, to bring Christianity to those who had not yet heard its message. The Americas looked like a good field for their missionary activity. There they seemed likely to be relatively free from persecution themselves; and there they would find thousands who needed them — not only unchurched whites, but also African-American slaves, and — the largest group for sheer numbers — the many nations of American Indians.

After an abortive effort to set up a mission in Georgia, the Moravians succeeded in founding two settlements in the Pennsylvania wilderness — Nazareth in 1740, Bethlehem in 1741. Bethlehem became the foundation for an impressive, decades-long effort to evangelize the American Indians, an effort that ended in tragedy through circumstances the missionaries could not control.

It was in an attempt to get this evangelization underway that, in 1742, Count von Zinzendorf journeyed into what later became Carbon County. The negotiations he would conduct with Indian leaders on this trip would, among other things, lay the groundwork for the founding of the ill-starred Gnadenhuetten (Huts of Mercy) mission along the Mahoning Creek, on the site of what is now Lehighton.

Passing through the imposing Lehigh Gap, the count and his party found themselves in a beautiful but desolate landscape — desolate, that is, where signs of humanity were concerned. Here, ridge succeeded rugged, densely forested ridge, and the most pervasive non-human sounds must have been those of bird song and the waters of the tumbling, rushing Lehigh River, sometimes called the Lechau, sometimes the West Branch of the Delaware. There were few habitations even of Indians; for the Indians native to the region, the Lenape or Lenni Lenape (the name means "the real people") were pretty much a settled, agricultural people, and the thin soil of the region beyond the Lehigh Gap offered them scant opportunities for agriculture. The Indians had built a trail that led from the Forks of the Delaware at Easton to the upper reaches of the Lehigh, then cut across the hills and down into the Wyoming Valley and the banks of the Susquehanna River. That, basically, was what they did with this vast, forested wilderness — they passed through it.

As to the newcomers from Europe who had recently been arriving in the area, according to lines drawn on maps in faraway cities like London they were the real owners of the land. At the time of Zinzendorf's visit, the area beyond Lehigh Gap was a part of Bucks County, a subdivision of the proprietary colony of Pennsylvania. In 1752 it fell under the jurisdiction of newly created Northampton County.

The count was impressed, even shaken, by what he saw beyond the Gap. We may deduce this by the name he gave to the region. He called it St. Anthony's Wilderness.

The St. Anthony he meant was not the medieval Franciscan friar St. Anthony of Padua, who is characteristically depicted with the Christ Child in his arms; that St. Anthony would have been too exclusively Catholic to appeal to the Protestant count. His reference was rather to a much earlier Anthony, St. Anthony the Hermit, who, like Jesus — and like thousands of his fellow Christian hermits — was subjected to temptation in the desert. In the old sense of the word, "desert" was simply a place without people. What was to become Carbon County certainly fit that description when Zinzendorf visited it, and for decades thereafter. "St. Anthony's Wilderness" was not a name that clung to the land, though a related Indian word did. That word was "Towamensing," meaning, simply, "wilderness."

When Zinzendorf visualized the area north of the Lehigh Gap as the setting for temptation, he may have been seeing into the future. In the decades following his visit, the temptation most frequently encountered there was that of violence and bloodshed. More often than not, it proved irresistible.

The groundwork for violence had been laid before the count ever visited the territory, in the dealings of other Europeans with the native population. William Penn, the Quaker proprietor of Pennsylvania, had tried to deal fairly with the Indian nations of his gigantic American estate, buying the land from them at a fair price. It is doubtful, though, whether even Penn's integrity could have resolved all the potential problems between Europeans and Indians, for the Indians had no conception of land ownership in the European sense.

By the time Penn paid his two visits to America (1682-1684 and 1699-1700), at least some of the Indians had had previous experience dealing with other Europeans — the Swedes and the Dutch, who had founded early colonies near the mouth of the Delaware, and whose chief interest had been trade in furs. This trade, pursued also by the French and the English, was to ruin the native peoples and set them at war with each other.

The purchase of their lands, even by so high-minded a negotiator as Penn, could have no other effect than to drive them from their homes and into the interior — which is why the Lenni Lenape (also called Delaware) Indians of the Delaware Valley eventually wound up as far afield as Ohio, Ontario, and even Oklahoma.

Unfortunately, not every negotiator was on the moral level of William Penn. Under the great proprietor's sons and successors, Thomas, Richard, and John Penn, there occurred the infamous Walking Purchase of 1737. This resulted from efforts by Thomas Penn and the acting governor, James Logan, to obtain the remainder of the Lenni Lenape land in the Forks of the Delaware area.

By an agreement of 1686, the Englishmen were allowed to claim as much additional land, going north from Wrightstown, Bucks County, as a man could walk in a single day. When this agreement was finally put into effect in 1737, Thomas Penn and James Logan selected the three most powerful walkers they could find — Solomon Jennings, James Yeates, and Edward Marshall. These three set out to cover as much territory as possible, though Jennings gave out before the Lehigh River had been reached. He returned to his farm along the Lehigh River between Allentown and Bethlehem. On the morning of the second day, Yeates collapsed at the foot of the Blue Mountain; his would-be helpers found that he had gone blind. He died several days later.

Marshall alone completed the "walk," having come a distance of somewhere between 55 and 86 miles. He ended well north of the Blue Mountain — possibly in the vicinity of Tobyhanna Creek, part of the present-day line between Carbon and Monroe counties. To compound the trickery, the northern boundary of the Walking Purchase territory was drawn, not straight east to the Delaware River as the Indians wished, but at a diagonal reaching toward the northeast from the point at which Marshall had stopped. Thus did the colonists lay claim to thousands of additional acres of Indian land.

Disgusted, but under pressure from the powerful Iroquois Confederacy to comply with the agreement, the Lenape burned their homes in the Forks of the Delaware area and retreated toward the Wyoming Valley. But the Walking Purchase, just a few years before Count Zinzendorf's visit to St. Anthony's Wilderness, became one more strand in a net of grievances that was to entangle guilty and innocent alike.

When, in 1746, the Moravians established their Gnadenhuetten mission, settlement of the Carbon County area by people of European stock was already beginning. Around 1750, English people with names like Thomas, Custard, Washburn, Meyers, Johnson, Rhoads, Tipple, and Pearsoll began to appear in the Lizard Creek Valley of what is now East Penn Township. A few families also were to be found in today's Franklin and Mahoning townships, while about the same time Nicholas Opplinger settled at the mouth of the Aquashicola Creek in the Lower Towamensing area. Other early settlers in that area included the Mehrkems, the Strohls, the Boyers, and the Baumans or Bowmans. These and other homesteads of European colonists were scattered lightly and precariously over the landscape. Many would not survive the storm that was to come.

Since the beginning of the eighteenth century, England and France had been arrayed against each other in a series of dynastic wars. On the European continent these wars featured a kaleidoscope of shifting alliances. Because both countries had colonial interests, their struggle also had repercussions as far afield as India, and in North America the two European powers were locked in a bitter struggle for control of the rich new continent.

The earlier colonial wars of the century had left the eastern part of Pennsylvania relatively unscathed, but by about 1750 things had changed. Embittered by their dealings with the proprietary government of Pennsylvania and its representatives, many regional Indians were now ready to side openly with the French. In 1755 British General Edward Braddock was ambushed with his army as he approached the French Fort Duquesne, on the present site of Pittsburgh. Braddock was mortally wounded; but one young Virginia militia officer in his suite, George Washington, survived to make a larger impact upon history.

News of Braddock's defeat was spread up and down the Pennsylvania frontier with fire and blood. On November 24, 1755, the peaceful mission at Gnadenhuetten was attacked by Indians. Ten men and women died at once, while another woman, taken away as a captive, did not long survive. All the victims were white.

Gnadenhuetten was not the only tragedy involving white settlers in the Carbon County area to occur during the period of the French and Indian War. With the eruption of fighting in 1755, the settlers in the Lehigh Gap area had built themselves a stockade called Fort Lehigh, on the present site of Palmerton. The presence of the fort did not prevent an Indian attack on a family called Boyer, whose members lived nearby. During the raids, the father of the family was shot and scalped, and his daughters and son Frederick were carried away into French-held Canada as prisoners. On the march, Frederick and his sisters were separated; he never saw them again. He himself survived five years of captivity, and eventually returned to claim the family farm.

These attacks were just two of many on outlying farms and outposts. Not surprisingly, a large number of the white settlers then in the Carbon County region fled, never to return.

The provincial government's belated response to the frontier in flames was to appoint two commissioners of defense, James Hamilton and Benjamin Franklin — the latter, like George Washington, destined to play a larger role on the world stage.

Passing through Bethlehem and through the dangerous Lehigh Gap, Colonel Franklin and the force he had raised came at last to New Gnadenhuetten, the Moravian mission which stood across the Lehigh River from the old mission where the massacre had occurred. New Gnadenhuetten had been built even before the massacre, since the Moravians had been in the process of transferring the original mission to this new location.

There, on the site of present-day Weissport, Franklin built Fort Allen, the largest and most important in a line of fortifications designed to help restore stability and peace in the area. Named after Judge William Allen, noted provincial jurist and father of James Allen, Allentown's founder, the fort was abandoned in 1761.

The French and Indian War (or Seven Years' War, as it was known in Europe) ended in 1763, with a British victory that meant the effective end of French hopes for dominating North America. But in 1763-1764 the famous Indian chief Pontiac staged an uprising that kept the frontier a-quiver; as a result there was no immediate large movement back into St. Anthony's Wilderness on the part of European-stock settlers. A few hardy souls had always remained, despite the risk of attack. A relative handful of new families moved in between the end of Pontiac's Uprising and the start of the American Revolution.

One such was the Benjamin Gilbert family, originally of Byberry, Pennsylvania, although they had also lived for a time in Quakertown and Makefield, Bucks County. The family were Quaker, or members of the Society of Friends; and Benjamin Gilbert was a staunch pacifist who had written several works advocating a pacifist stance. One of them was a 1749 tract in which he protested the killing of Lenni Lenape Indians, in particular by the Presbyterians of the frontier.

It is possible that, in moving to the Mahoning Valley in 1775, Gilbert was trying to protect his family from the American Revolution, which was then brewing. This would make sense, although his choice of relocation sites proved singularly unfortunate. But Dennis Lynch of Laurel, Maryland, thought the situation was more complex than that. A genealogist, Lynch is a descendant of Joseph Rakestraw, who married Rebecca Gilbert, a survivor of her family's captivity.

Benjamin Gilbert, who was 64 years old when he located in the Mahoning Valley, was the father of two families, Lynch explained in a letter to the author dated 22 September, 1997. As such, "He needed to provide property for the four children of the second marriage and some of the eight children from the first marriage." Lynch also wrote of Gilbert, "His undoing was that as a Quaker, he expected that the Indians would not bother him."

On the morning of April 25, 1780, British-allied Indians swooped down on the Gilbert homestead and captured Gilbert himself, nine members of his family, a servant named Andrew Harrigar, and Abigail Dodson, the fourteen-year-old daughter of a neighbor, Samuel Dodson. The raiders also stopped at the nearby farm of Benjamin Gilbert's stepson, Benjamin Peart. There they added that young man, his wife, and their infant child to their string of captives.

The prisoners were dragged away toward Canada, which at this point was British-held. Andrew Harrigar managed to escape very soon. Benjamin Gilbert's son Joseph also eventually escaped. The elder Gilbert died in captivity. Abigail Dodson was separated from the rest of her party and adopted by Indians. In 1786 she was found by her cousin, Thomas Dodson, and returned to her family.

It is not, perhaps, surprising that the Gilbert family survivors should have chosen not to remain in the Mahoning Valley. Instead, they returned to Byberry.

It should not be thought that all the atrocities of this era were perpetrated by Indians upon whites. One of the worst white crimes against Indians occurred in 1782, on what was then the far western frontier. Moravian missionaries, following their Indian converts into the west, had established a new Gnadenhuetten mission on a new Mahoning Creek, this one in eastern Ohio. In what amounted to a mirror image of the original Gnadenhuetten tragedy, whites commanded by Colonel David Williamson and including the famous "Indian fighter" Lew Wetzel, fell upon the Christian Indians there and slaughtered ninety of them, mostly women and children. This second Gnadenhuetten Massacre stands today as one of the grimmer episodes in whites' dealings with the peoples they supplanted.

This spirit, though reduced in scope, was represented in the Carbon County area by an earlier incident at Fort Lehigh. In 1763, during Pontiac's Uprising, the fort was under the command of Captain Jacob Wetherhold. An Indian named Zachary, his wife and child and another Indian woman named Zippora, were granted shelter in a hay barn near the fort. During the night, however, the soldiers attacked them and killed them all.

By the early 1780s, Zinzendorf's St. Anthony's Wilderness was a wilderness still, and one stained with blood. The land, abandoned both by its original inhabitants and by their supplanters, awaited rebirth. That rebirth, when it came, would not be without its own measure of pain and irony.

The Lehigh in Flood

The Lehigh River that drains Carbon County has historically been the area's most important transportation link with the outside world, as traffic moved to a limited extent on the river itself and to a greater extent on the paths, canal, railroads, and highways that came to parallel it. But, soiled as it has been by generations of industry along its banks, the Lehigh still is nothing more than a glorified mountain stream.

Like all such streams, it is a tempestuous thing. During dry weather it is possible to cross it in many places by stepping from stone to stone. But there have been many times when prolonged rains have caused the river waters to rise and come barreling through the upper gorges with enormous force, spreading destruction, death, and indelible memories of horror from the source all the way down to Easton, where it pours into the Delaware. These floods and their aftermath have affected the lives of thousands of county residents in every generation. For decades the Lehigh's fury was heightened by the effects of logging, the old

The dam at Lehigh Tannery, at 34 feet, was the highest on the Upper Division. This part of the canal was not rebuilt after the devastating freshet of 1862.

Logs and log rafts can be seen stranded on the top of the dam. The damage in the valley of the Lehigh River was so severe in this flood because hundreds of thousands of logs had been impounded behind sawmill dams. When they broke loose, they destroyed everything in their path as they surged downriver.

Following the flood of February 28, 1902, the Lehigh Navigation was closed for two years for repairs.

(Below) The aftermath of the 1902 flood in Weissport. *Courtesy, Raymond E. Holland Collection.*

method of logging that left the hillsides denuded and allowed the rain water to pour down the slopes and into the river without impediment.

Colonel Jacob Weiss, the prominent entrepreneur, and his wife Elizabeth were nearly caught in a Lehigh flood on October 6, 1778, soon after he and his family had moved to the site of present-day Weissport. The flood was unexpected, and was heralded at the last moment by a cry of "We are surrounded!" Mrs. Weiss was carried to safety in an armchair borne by some of the settlers, while her husband rode out on horseback.

A neighboring family named Tippey did not fare so well. Mr. and Mrs. Tippey and their two children were in their home when floodwaters swept it off its foundations. When the house struck a tree, the children were carried away by the stream and were never seen again. The parents later were rescued by one of Colonel Weiss's servants. Because of their tragedy, the flood went down in local memory as "Tippey's Flood."

The freshet of June 9, 1841, destroyed the Mansion House Bridge at Mauch Chunk, and also cost the lives of Mauch Chunk resident Adam Beers and his family.

The great flood which began on June 4, 1862, wiped out the Upper Grand Division of the Lehigh Navigation from White Haven to Mauch Chunk, once considered a marvel of engineering, and resulted in the drowning of some one hundred fifty people throughout the Lehigh Valley. The upper part of the canal was never rebuilt; and two to three thousand men and six hundred horses needed more than four months to repair the section from Mauch Chunk to Easton.

The 1862 flood was made more devastating by the impact of the timber industry, which was then operating on a large scale in the region. Several hundred thousand logs happened to be impounded behind booms at White Haven. When the booms gave way, each log became an individual battering ram, carried down the river at terrifying speed. It was, in fact, these logs which were responsible for destroying the Upper Grand Division of the Lehigh Navigation, and much other property besides.

The Lehigh Valley Railroad suffered heavily in this flood, which also is noted for the near-miraculous escape of Leonard Yeager. Yeager was a Mauch Chunk resident who was swept down the river from his Susquehanna Street place of business. Around Packerton, he spotted a loose canal boat, and managed to clamber aboard it. It bore him over flooded Weissport, and on down the river. Near Parryville he grasped an overhanging tree limb, pulled himself up, and succeeded in returning to dry land at last.

Two floods struck in 1901. In the first of these, on August 24, the Mauch Chunk Creek rose under Broadway in Mauch Chunk and swept away four men — Patrick Johnson, Jesse Struthers, William J. Morgan, and Henry Haggerty — to their deaths. In the second freshet of the year, the Mansion House Bridge was once again wiped out, and railroad traffic was paralyzed.

Mauch Chunk scene following the flood of August 24, 1901, in which four men died. Courtesy, Raymond E. Holland Collection.

The Mauch Chunk Creek was responsible for the damage seen in this series of photographs of the flood of 1934. The creek, which had been channeled and placed underground, regularly burst its banks and flooded Broadway until Mauch Chunk Lake was constructed.

All photos, courtesy Raymond E. Holland Collection.

A flood on February 28, 1902, was even more destructive than the one just two months earlier, in December of 1901. The Lehigh Navigation suffered massive damage, and was under repair for two years.

An unexpected 1942 freshet put an end to what little was left of traffic on the Lehigh Navigation. The canal had been closed, officially, in 1932. At this point, nothing was moving on it except in the area between Treichlers, Lehigh County, and Parryville. The only product carried was coal silt dredged from behind the dam breasts along the river, especially at Treichlers. This was taken to Palmerton, where it was formed into briquettes and used by the New Jersey Zinc Company as fuel for its furnaces.

When the 1942 flood came on, only one boat was on the canal. It was raining, but the two crewmen on board were not expecting serious flooding. At Walnutport, they decided to stop at the Diamonds firehouse for a beer. They then moved on to another establishment. They had not been at their new location long when they were aroused by a pounding at the door. The pounding was accompanied by shouts of "Come and get your mules! The water's rising!"

By the time they returned to the towpath, the mules were standing in water up to their belly bands. The two managed to release and rescue the animals, but the boat swirled off on the angry waters. Thus ended, unfinished, the very last commercial trip on the Lehigh Navigation System, not counting excursions of various types.

The flood generated by Hurricane Agnes in 1972, which so devastated the Susquehanna Valley, wreaked havoc in the Lehigh Valley as well. But for Carbon County, and especially for the town of Jim Thorpe (as Mauch Chunk had since been renamed), the outcome of this catastrophe was qualified good news.

What is now recognized as the town's historic district had at that point lain derelict for many years, just because of its flood problem. Whenever there were floods, Mauch Chunk Creek, which had been routed under Broadway and Race streets, overflowed, flooding all the buildings in the area and causing many deaths.

On the occasion of the Hurricane Agnes flood, the dam impounding the waters of the creek and forming Mauch Chunk Lake had just been completed. In this, its first emergency, the structure held, and did its job of regulating the creek waters. Far up the Lehigh another dam, named for former Congressman Francis E. Walter, also held. Flooding in downtown Jim Thorpe was for the first time kept to a minimum. At that point, community leaders like Agnes McCartney and Joe Boyle understood that they could go ahead and develop the town's tourism potential. The rest is — well, history.

Stereo view of the Lehigh River and the canal, which provided the original transportation system for anthracite coal, the railroads on both sides of the narrow river valley, the thriving towns of Mauch Chunk in the foreground and East Mauch Chunk in the background.

The Lure of Black Diamonds

The central fact of Carbon County history is the discovery of rich deposits of anthracite coal in the northern part of the county, and in neighboring counties such as Schuylkill and Luzerne. Without this discovery, it is impossible to imagine the history of the area taking shape as it has.

Without the lure of "black diamonds," the transportation system serving the region would have been far slower to develop, and would have had a different focus. County towns like Mauch Chunk (Jim Thorpe) and Lehighton, if they had been founded at all, would have been way stations along railroad rights-of-way, rather than the important destinations they once were.

Without the prospect of jobs in the mines to draw them, representatives of a wide range of ethnic groups — Germans, English, Welsh, Irish, Italians, Croats, Slovaks, and many more — never would have come and enriched the fabric of regional life — learning slowly, in the process, to tolerate and even to like each other.

Without coal, and the railroads and canal that served it, many other aspects of economic and social life could not have developed as they did. It is even highly doubtful that, lacking this resource, New Jersey Zinc would have located in the southern end of the county and built Palmerton. Important as the zinc industry became, there is no doubt what had to come first.

The discovery of anthracite coal in Carbon County and the surrounding regions had a transformative effect on life in the county, at least after the problems of mining the coal, shipping it to market, and making effective use of it were solved. From being a forest-shrouded wilderness almost devoid of human inhabitants, the northern part of the region became within a few decades a place virtually bare of trees, pocked with the scars of mining, and bustling with people. The streets of the little settlement of Mauch Chunk, founded by Josiah White and Erskine Hazard of the Lehigh Coal and Navigation Company, teemed with entrepreneurs and speculators. Men streamed in to work in the coal holes and mine tunnels — first, Pennsylvania Germans from nearby farms, later, immigrants from a range of foreign countries stretching from Ireland to Russia.

In the northeastern United States homes began to be heated, and industries to be run, on Pennsylvania anthracite. As the U.S. Navy made the switch from sail to steam its ships' bunkers, too, were filled with anthracite — at least through World War I. Later, as the Navy's range of activities expanded, petroleum made it possible to eliminate the need for coaling stations, and the anthracite industry lost one of its major markets.

Certainly, without coal, the land would not have its present contours, with ridges meeting the sky in crazy angles even where trees have grown on black culm banks.

For better or for worse, then, we have been shaped by this underground presence — and still are being shaped by it, even though coal output has dwindled to a tiny fraction of its former volume.

The next several essays provide an overview of the discovery of coal, some of the entrepreneurs who promoted it, the transportation system that was built to move it to market — and that almost coincidentally moved thousands of people as well — and the life that grew up in the coal regions. The final pieces in this section will take a brief look at one of the most difficult and tragic episodes in county history, the story of the so-called Molly Maguires.

The Discovery of Coal

In 1991 the Pennsylvania Historical and Museum Commission dedicated one of its distinctive markers at the site of the Ginder (also spelled Ginter, Gintner and Ginther) monument in Summit Hill, commemorating the Mahoning Valley millwright's discovery of "stone coal" or anthracite on Sharp Mountain two hundred years earlier. The marker repeated local folklore by stating that Ginder was hunting on Sharp Mountain when he stumbled upon the black stone that burns, an event that set the stage for the development of the anthracite industry in what would later become Carbon County.

This story is part of an oral tradition that has become legend in Carbon County. Through the centuries the Ginder myth has evolved from the simple discovery of stone coal on Sharp Mountain to the claim that Ginder made the first discovery of anthracite in Pennsylvania. This latter claim has resulted in much controversy.

The story of the discovery of anthracite coal in the various regions of Pennsylvania is shrouded in mystery, lore, and questionable facts. Each of the Pennsylvania anthracite regions has its own folk hero who accidentally discovered stone coal and changed forever the course of Pennsylvania history. Some of the folk stories have striking similarities, such as the Philip Ginder and Necho Allen stories. The story of Philip Ginder's discovery was preserved purely as the result of an error, a wrong turn on one of the back roads of the Pennsylvania wilderness.

The Lausanne Connection

It was the year 1804. A Philadelphia obstetrician by the name of Thomas Chalkely James was on his way to the upper Lehigh region with his friend and brother-in-law, Anthony Morris, also of Philadelphia. The two men were traveling on horseback, and the object of their trip was some land, jointly owned and located at the mouth of the Nesquehoning Creek on the Lehigh River, a location known as "The Landing at the projected village of Lausanne."

Once through the Lehigh Water Gap, the pair rode to the land of Jacob Weiss over a state road constructed by Nicholas Kern, Jr. But, instead of turning north after they crossed the Lehigh River near Weiss's, the men headed west, into the Mahoning Valley. They soon realized that they were lost, and that night was approaching. Luckily they arrived at the home and mill of Philip Ginder. Ginder put them up for the night, promising to take them to their property the following day. This he did, but a detour took them by the Sharp Mountain quarry, operated haphazardly by the Lehigh Coal Mine Company.

> We were kindly furnished by our host with lodgings in the mill, which was kept going all night; and as the structure was not of the most firm and compact manner, we might almost literally be said to have been rocked to sleep. However, after having been refreshed with a night's rest, such as it was, and taking

breakfast with our hospitable landlord, we started on the journey of the day, preceded by Philip, with his axe on his shoulder, an implement necessary to remove the obstructing saplings that might impede the passage of our horses, if not ourselves; and these we were under the necessity of dismounting and leading through the bushes and briars of the grownup pathway, if pathway had ever existed.

It probably was not simply to brag about his discovery that Ginder took the men to see this property, for Dr. James was a stockholder in the Lehigh Coal Mine Company, and also a speculator in coal lands.

During their visit to the open quarry, Ginder related the story of his discovery to James and Morris:

> He said, when he first took up his residence in that district of country, he built for himself a rough cabin in the forest, and supported his family by the proceeds of his rifle, being literally a hunter of the backwoods. The game he shot, including bear and deer, he carried to the nearest store, and exchanged for the other necessaries of life. But, at the particular time to which he then alluded, he was without a supply of food for his family, and after being out all day with his gun in quest of it, he was returning towards evening over the Mauch-Chunk mountain, entirely unsuccessful and dispirited, having shot nothing; a drizzling rain beginning to fall, and the dusky night approaching, he bent his course homeward, considering himself one of the most forsaken of human beings. As he trod slowly over the ground, his foot stumbled against something which, by the stroke, was driven before him; observing it to be black, to distinguish which there was just enough light remaining, he took it up, and as he had often listened to the traditions of the country of the existence of coal in the vicinity, it occurred to him that this perhaps might be a portion of that "stone-coal" of which he had heard.

Ginder carried his samples of coal back home with him to the Mahoning Valley where his blacksmith friend George Neyer was able to ignite the rocks in his forge.

It wasn't until many years later, on April 19, 1826, that Dr. James fished the story out of his mind, dusted it off, perhaps embellished it a bit, and related it to members of the Historical Society of Pennsylvania, who published it in the *Memoirs of the Historical Society of Pennsylvania*. In 1829 the story was reprinted in Samuel Hazard's *Register of Pennsylvania*, and so saved for posterity. (Samuel Hazard was the brother of Erskine Hazard, co-founder of the Lehigh Coal and Navigation Company.) Dr. James's story of Ginder's discovery apparently initiated the mythological "poor hunter" motif.

In the book *Black Rock*, Pennsylvania folklorist George Korson related his meticulous research that shows that Ginder was not poor, nor did he make his living as a hunter. While it is possible that Ginder hunted from time to time, he didn't rely on the kill to feed his family. Instead, he was a prosperous farmer and millwright with several hundred acres of land, as well as an established mill. According to Korson, Ginder was on Sharp Mountain that fateful day, searching for a suitable "grinder."

Sharp Mountain was a great place to look for such stones, being littered with boulders of the Pottsville Conglomerate, also known as "pudding rock." These stones had a reputation for making excellent millstones.

Digging Coal along Room Run

It was no accident that Ginder took his find to Colonel Jacob Weiss at his place on the Lehigh River. Weiss, a veteran of the Revolutionary War, was established near the mouth of the Mahoning Creek, at the previous site of Fort Allen. But, in spite of local legend, Weiss was not surprised to see samples of stone coal.

Prior to Ginder's discovery, Jacob Weiss not only knew about "stone" or hard coal, but he burned it and even sent some of his laborers to dig for it. This conclusion is based upon entries in Weiss's account book, preserved by the Lehigh County Historical Society, showing that he had employees digging coal for him several years prior to 1791.

During his research for the book *Philadelphia's First Fuel Crisis*, Dr. Benjamin Powell studied the Reading Howell map of 1792, which shows a road leading from Weissport through Beaver Meadow to Berwick on the Susquehanna River. Because of the existence of this road, Powell speculated that Weiss obtained his coal from a mine that had been opened at Beaver Meadow by Nathan Beach. Other evidence suggests a different theory.

Charles Seng of Penn Forest Township also studied the Jacob Weiss papers, and learned that Weiss was using coal as early as 1787, a good four years before Ginder stumbled across his find on Sharp Mountain. Seng was quick to realize the significance of this, namely that Ginder couldn't have been the first to discover coal in the Lehigh anthracite region.

The credit for discovering that Jacob Weiss had discovered this coal — not on Sharp Mountain near present-day Summit Hill, but in the headwaters of Room Run, to the southwest of present-day Nesquehoning — goes to Christopher Baer, assistant curator of manuscripts and archives at the Hagley Museum in Delaware. The outcrops were later "re-discovered" by Isaac Abel Chapman, who mined coal at Room Run and shipped it from Lausanne during the War of 1812, and even later by Josiah White, an event that led to the construction of the Room Run Railroad and the laying out of the village of Nesquehoning.

According to an unpublished paper by Christopher Baer:

> Sometime in the year 1786, not long after he had established himself and brought his family up from Nazareth, Weiss or someone in his employ discovered coal in the upper reaches of Room Run where the outcrops had been cut by the action of the stream.

Jacob Weiss informed Tench Coxe of Philadelphia about his find. Coxe later was a member of the "Society for Promoting the Improvements of Roads and Inland Navigation," and a stockholder of the Lehigh Coal Mine Company. He asked Weiss for samples of this coal.

In April of 1787 Weiss directed some of his laborers to dig this coal, but the samples would not burn, possibly because they were recovered from the slate roof of the coal seam — material known as bony coal.

Apparently nothing further came of his discovery at this time, but Weiss tried to protect his find. On November 11, 1786, Weiss purchased several hundred acres of land surrounding the spot where the coal had been discovered and placed it in the name of his wife, Elizabeth. Later, after Ginder's discovery on Sharp Mountain, when the Lehigh Coal Mine Company was busy buying up the land surrounding the mountain, Weiss kept the Room Run property from the LCMC. Josiah White and Erskine Hazard later acquired this property and transferred it to the Lehigh Coal and Navigation Company. It may have been Robert McMullin or Seth Chambers who dug the Room Run coal for Weiss. These were two of the many laborers employed by the colonel for such odd jobs as farming, stone work, rafting, and carrying chain for surveyors.

Weiss also had dealings with Alexander Dunn, who lived in the Nesquehoning Valley. The 1792 Reading Howell map of Pennsylvania shows the location later called Nesquehoning as "Dun's." Weiss's account book, in which he meticulously recorded the time spent and tasks completed by each of his laborers, shows the following:

> Sept. 18, 1786, Seth Chambers, employed by Alexr Dunn and Took J. Weiss's waggon up to Nesquehoning

> April 28, 1787, Robert McMullin digging coal

Weiss had more important things on his mind than a few outcrops of coal of questionable quality. He was deeply involved in the lumber business and in land speculation, and also in the construction of the Nicholas Kern and Evan Owen roads that led from the Lehigh Water Gap through Lausanne to Berwick on the Susquehanna River. When Philip Ginder approached him with some excellent samples of Sharp Mountain coal that he had seen burn in Neyer's Mahoning Valley forge, Weiss was savvy enough to know that something good was afoot. The site where Ginder came across the coal turned out to be a unique location where the Mammoth vein, the motherlode of all coal veins, was found. To make matters even better, the vein had been folded back upon itself many times, increasing the thickness. The seam also was easily accessible, being located on top of a mountain peak, covered by only a thin layer of loose dirt. Mining this coal would be much easier than mining at Room Run, a circumstance turned to advantage later by the Lehigh Coal and Navigation Company. It is even likely that Weiss had told Ginder to keep an eye out for coal. In the Weiss account book, Robert McMullin, on August 11, 1787, "went of inquest of P. Gintner." Ginder's discovery eventually led to the formation of the Lehigh Coal Mine Company and beyond that, the Lehigh Coal and Navigation Company.

Philip Ginder Memorialized

In the year 1890, as the one hundredth anniversary of Ginder's discovery approached, some residents of Carbon County felt that he had not been honored for his contribution to the area's heritage.

In July of that year, "prominent" citizens of Summit Hill planned to celebrate the centennial of Ginder's discovery with a large demonstration to be held in September of 1891. The announcement of the proposed celebration brought praise as well as criticism. The problem was that citizens of Summit Hill did not merely credit Ginder with the discovery of coal in Carbon County, but called him the "Columbus of Coal," declaring that Ginder made the first discovery of coal in the state of Pennsylvania. Although this claim had no basis in fact, it was repeated in the *Mauch Chunk Coal Gazette*.

The following response from the *Wilkes-Barre Record* was typical of the reaction:

> His [Ginder's] exploit must have been a mere local event, for anthracite was known to exist in Wyoming Valley a quarter of a century earlier.

The *Mauch Chunk Coal Gazette* conceded somewhat by stating:

> ... The Gazette, with everyone else connected with the Ginter Monument project and the proposed commemoration celebration, will cheerfully waive, for the present, all discussion as to priority of discovery, etc. Such matters will no doubt all come out in the exercises that will be connected with the celebration, and in fact this celebration may be the very means of settling once and for all who is who and what is what in the discovery and development of the anthracite coalfields of Pennsylvania.

After making the concession, the *Gazette* claimed that, even though he was not the first to discover coal in Pennsylvania, it was Ginder's discovery that awakened capitalists to the value of stone coal as a commodity, especially as Ginder was credited with the discovery that stone coal would burn. Other newspapers responded to the proposed celebration, including the *Allentown Chronicle*, the *Scranton Truth*, the *Hazleton Plain Speaker*, and the *Bethlehem Times*. The proposed celebration was expanded to include the erection of a memorial in tribute to Ginder.

A special planning meeting was held at the Eagle Hotel in Summit Hill on Monday evening, August 18, 1890. In attendance were chairman Colonel T.L. Mumford, one of the operators of the Switchback Railroad, and secretary James W. Malloy, editor of the *Lansford Record*. Invitations were sent to several important people, including coal baron Eckley B. Coxe and the Hon. Allen Craig, lawyer, state legislator, and judge.

The meeting resulted in the creation of an executive committee, consisting of the Summit Hill Town Council, which would have immediate supervision of the event, and a general committee which was to include representatives of the anthracite coal region and the Lehigh Valley. Lansford resident William D. Zehner, superintendent of the Lehigh Coal and Navigation Company, was appointed chairman of the general committee. Other members of the executive committee, called "alive, wide awake, progressive citizens" by the editor of the *Coal Gazette,* included James McCready, the chief clerk in the Lansford office of the Lehigh Coal and Navigation Company. McCready was made president of the council. Ex-county treasurer Samuel Rickert and William Schneider, both prominent merchants in Summit Hill, also were among its members. The remaining members included Edward Miley, William C. Miller, Thomas Lynn, and contractor H.W. Storch.

The Summit Hill meeting directed that a future meeting be held at the Mauch Chunk courthouse on Thursday, August 28. The meeting was never held. No further mention of the event or the Ginder Monument was made in the *Mauch Chunk Coal Gazette* until March 27, 1891, when the newspaper reported that Senator William Rapsher had initiated a bill for the appropriation of one thousand dollars for the erection of the Ginder Monument.

The *Coal Gazette* editorialized about the previous project, saying that it, "proving to be too vast for a handful of men, limited in means ... was allowed to drop and nothing has been heard of it since."

Upon receipt of the news of the financial appropriation, the *Hazleton Sentinel* proposed what they considered a fitting inscription on the monument:

To the Memory of

PHILIP GINTER,

Whose discovery led to the establishment of

a business which made HARD TIMES

an eternal possibility in the

Coal regions.

The editor of the *Coal Gazette* indignantly called upon Ginder's ghost to "rise from thy resting place and whack the unappreciative writer of the above senseless squib over the head."

In April of 1891, after passing a second reading in the Senate, the appropriation bill was amended to increase the amount of authorized money from one thousand dollars to two thousand dollars. This was a sure sign of the impending legislative failure of the bill. Instead of simply voting against the bill as it stood, some politico increased the amount requested, probably in an attempt to make the bill harder to pass the House of Representatives. The bill finally passed the Senate sometime in late April 1891. But it was most likely quenched in the House of Representatives, for the *Mauch Chunk Coal Gazette* dropped the issue as fast as if it were a red-hot lump of stone coal.

It wasn't until 1941 that a monument commemorating Ginder's find was erected just east of the old abandoned Sharp Mountain quarry where Ginder had, by an accidental discovery, changed the course of the history of the region later to be called Carbon.

The Ginder monument in Summit Hill, with lumps of coal painted black in the centre.

Colonel Jacob Weiss

At the base of the park in Lehighton, gazing out over the traffic on First Street with a lordly air, stands a statue of a man in a Revolutionary War uniform. The man is Colonel Jacob Weiss, who donated the land on which the park stands, and who lent his name to the town of Weissport, just across the Lehigh River. Few local residents know more than that about him, if indeed they know that much.

Born in Philadelphia, Weiss was the son of a physician of German origin. As the Revolutionary War brewed, the sympathies of the family were with the Colonists and against their British rulers.

Jacob Weiss was known for his outstanding business abilities. During the Revolution he served in an important noncombatant post, that of deputy quartermaster general. As such, he bore much of the responsibility for seeing to it that Washington's ragtag army had enough supplies and equipment to hold the field against the British.

Following the war, Weiss performed additional service in Northampton County. Then he decided to move to present-day Carbon County. He bought land from the Moravian Church — he himself was a Moravian — and settled at the site of Benjamin Franklin's Fort Allen, once also the location of the New Gnadenhuetten mission. It was not long before the settlement began to be known as Weiss's Mill. After the Lehigh Canal was built, it became Weissport.

When Philip Ginder stumbled upon his famous piece of black rock while wandering on Sharp Mountain, it was inevitable that he would show it to Weiss, who was easily the most sophisticated and knowledgeable businessman in the region. Blacksmiths in the colonel's employ seem to have been using anthracite, dug in the Lausanne area, as early as 1785 or 1786.

Weiss is buried in the so-called "Bunker Hill" cemetery, just east of the canal in Weissport. He was slightly ahead of his time; the "stone coal" of the region could not be fully exploited until the problem of getting it to market was solved — not to mention the additional challenge of getting it to burn efficiently. But his early role in promoting the new fuel nevertheless makes him one of the true architects of Carbon County's history.

Isaac Abel Chapman:
The Unsung Hero of the Lehigh Coal Region

Some names are familiar to almost anyone who lives in Carbon County, regardless of the extent of their interest in local history.

One such name is Asa Packer, the Connecticut Yankee who marched into Mauch Chunk determined to make something of himself in the booming anthracite business. Packer created the Lehigh Valley Railroad, which eventually grew to be a major competitor of the Lehigh Coal and Navigation Company's canal. His mansion still perches on a hillside overlooking the town of Jim Thorpe.

The county is indebted to at least one other Connecticut man, whose work set the stage for what Packer and others would accomplish after him, but who is almost forgotten today.

This man was Isaac Abel Chapman.

It appears that no likenesses of the man were ever drawn, or have survived the passage of time. He was described as "a man of most pleasing and agreeable manners, and in his dress and habits, the very embodiment of cleanliness and neatness."

A versatile, self-educated man, Chapman has received little, if any, credit for the accomplishments that led to the development of Carbon County and its expansion into a center of the anthracite coal trade. His work laid the solid foundation upon which rested the successes of many people, including Josiah White, Erskine Hazard, and the Lehigh Coal and Navigation Company.

Chapman was born on March 23, 1787 in Norwich, Connecticut. Like Asa Packer, he journeyed to what is now Susquehanna County, Pennsylvania, when still a small boy. Along with his brother, he spent his youth clearing forests by day and, by the light of a blazing night fire, studied whatever books he could scrounge from nearby neighbors. It didn't take long for both men to become excellent mathematicians, surveyors and draftsmen. Isaac Chapman also touched on poetry and landscape painting in his education.

When he had saved enough money to buy a compass, Chapman traveled to Luzerne County to work as a surveyor. In Luzerne County he met Jacob Cist, and the two became great friends, for they had much in common.

Jacob Cist was the son of Charles Cist of Philadelphia, a noted printer and publisher, and the nephew of Jacob Weiss, the man who had bought land from the Moravians and settled near Fort Allen. Jacob inherited his father's shares in the Lehigh Coal Mine Company, and from an early age took an interest in the Sharp Mountain mines.

Jacob's destiny led not to the Lehigh coal region, but to Luzerne County, where he married the daughter of Mathias Hollenback, one of the wealthiest men in the region. He retained his interest in the anthracite trade, particularly in the Lehigh mines.

In 1813, after forming a company with Charles Miner and John Robinson, Jacob Cist leased the Lehigh coal lands from Jacob Weiss's Lehigh Coal Mine Company and hired his friend, Isaac Chapman, to be his right arm.

Chapman set up his base of operations at Lausanne, the small settlement at the mouth of the Nesquehoning Creek. There he established an ark yard and supervised the opening of mines at Sharp Mountain and also at Room Run. He constructed arks and was responsible for mining coal and getting the coal onto the arks and down the Lehigh River.

During the War of 1812 (1812–1814) Chapman's hard work helped Cist's company make money. But he didn't spend all of his time at Lausanne in the coal trade. He was one of the earliest postmasters for the village of Lausanne. He also spent time keeping up a daily journal and, during the British invasion of Baltimore, suspended his coal operations long enough to organize a relief company. He headed for the besieged city, returning to Lausanne after learning that his services were not needed.

The group was able to make money during the War of 1812 due to the high cost of fuel in the port city of Philadelphia, but after the war ended the venture became unprofitable.

Following the end of the war, Chapman headed north again, taking over Charles Miner's Wilkes-Barre newspaper, the *Gleaner*, in 1816. He also found time to study law, write a book on the history of Wyoming, which was later published, and also experiment in the growing of vegetables.

Before he left the Lehigh region, Chapman spent at least some time advising Josiah White on the state of the Lehigh coal trade. In early 1818 he met with White and Hazard at Hagenbuch's tavern in Lehighton to discuss the region's potential, a meeting that was recorded in his journal. He soon returned to his role as a surveyor, working for the Pennsylvania Land Office. In this role he hiked along the Sharp Mountain and Locust Mountain ranges between the Lehigh and Little Schuylkill rivers. Along this hike he may have discovered coal outcrops along the Sharp Mountain range, which would lead to Josiah White's decision to drive the Hacklebernie Tunnel in 1823.

Chapman's early studies prepared him to become an accomplished map maker. His early map of Lausanne is still in the collection of the Mauch Chunk Historical Society. He also drew what is probably the earliest map of the Great Coal Quarry at Summit Hill, which details the quarry directly after the construction of the Mauch Chunk and Summit Hill gravity railroad. This map is in the collections of Lehigh University.

In 1816 and 1817, while working for the Pennsylvania Land Office, Chapman drew some of the earliest maps of Northampton, Luzerne and Susquehanna counties. These maps are still preserved at the State Archives in Harrisburg. He also wrote extensive articles on the geographical features of these counties, which were later reprinted in the *Lehigh Pioneer and Mauch Chunk Courier* as well as in *Hazard's Register of Pennsylvania*.

Travels in his capacity as a surveyor for the Land Office took Isaac Chapman to all parts of the coal region. One of his abilities, that of a locator of coal outcrops, came into play during these travels, when he discovered coal outcrops along Room Run, a stream that once flowed southwest of the village of Nesquehoning. These are noted in his map of Northampton County, drawn in 1817. In 1829 and 1830 Josiah White would receive the credit for the discovery of these coal outcrops.

Chapman also discovered coal on Buck Mountain. He persuaded Asa Lansford Foster, a friend who was married to his niece, to enter into a partnership with him and purchase the land containing the Buck Mountain outcrops, which had become available at a tax sale. These purchases later led to the formation of the Buck Mountain Coal Company and the construction of the Buck Mountain gravity railroad.

Isaac Chapman was responsible for bringing Asa Lansford Foster to Mauch Chunk. Foster ran the Mauch Chunk store for several years before taking interest in the Buck Mountain mines. Following the January freshet of 1841, which destroyed the Buck Mountain coal-loading facilities at Rockport, he briefly returned to Mauch Chunk. He later moved to the Panther Valley and was responsible for the driving of Tunnel No. 2, "Foster's Tunnel," along with Robert Q. Butler. When the patch towns of the Panther Valley were consolidated into one town, it received the name of Lansford, after Asa Lansford Foster.

In 1806, while surveying the headwaters of the Nescopeck, Isaac Chapman had discovered a valley extending to the Lehigh River, through which he believed a canal might be constructed. In 1821 he mentioned this to Josiah White, and in November of 1824 performed a survey of the possible canal route. In the battle between the proponents of canals and railroads, Josiah White took his stand in favor of canals. He was intensely interested in a possible canal route between the Susquehanna and the Lehigh, and was interested in Chapman's suggestion.

Nothing ever came of the idea for a Susquehanna and Lehigh Canal. Instead, an alternate route was eventually traversed by the Lehigh and Susquehanna Railroad, connecting White Haven and Wilkes-Barre. This railroad was eventually extended through Mauch Chunk to Easton. In the 1870s, it was leased to the Central Railroad of New Jersey.

Chapman wrote informative letters to White up until mid-1826, when White offered him a position in Mauch Chunk. The verbal employment contract included $800 a year in salary, a company house, and free coal. He arrived in Mauch Chunk on June 29, 1826, and was immediately put to work surveying the Lehigh River between Mauch Chunk and Easton. In August of 1826, after his survey of the lower section was complete, he surveyed the Lehigh River between Mauch Chunk and Stoddartsville, also the Delaware River between Easton and Philadelphia.

In September of 1826, Chapman was put to work on Josiah White's pet project, the survey of the proposed route for a gravity railroad between the Summit Hill mines and Mauch Chunk. The route followed the original route of the company's stone turnpike as far as about two miles from Mauch Chunk. Near the end of its run, the railroad passed directly below the cemetery that the Lehigh Coal and Navigation Company had established in 1823.

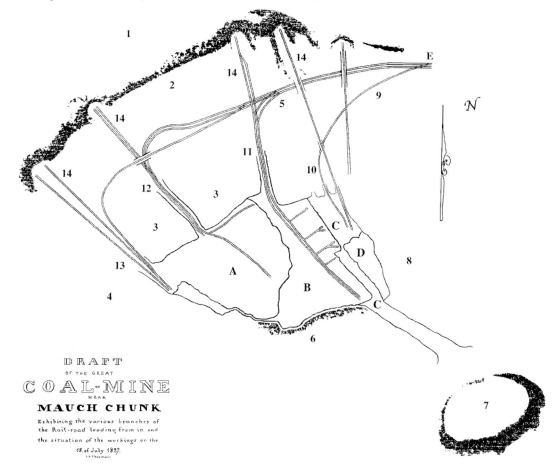

DRAFT
OF THE GREAT
COAL-MINE
NEAR
MAUCH CHUNK
Exhibiting the various branches of
the Rail-road leading from in and
the situation of the workings on the
18. of July 1827.

Chapman also assisted Josiah White with the laying of a test track for the gravity railroad along what is today the west end of Broadway in Jim Thorpe. Here experiments were performed with wagon and brake designs. Chapman invented a hydraulic brake with Josiah White, although White later claimed this as his own invention. The brake design, although never used on the Mauch Chunk gravity railroad, was used on the Pennsylvania Portage Railroad as well as on the Ashley planes of the Lehigh and Susquehanna Railroad.

When the first official trip of the Mauch Chunk railroad took place, on Saturday, May 5, 1827, Chapman rode with Josiah White in the first coal wagon over the company's railroad, which was later called the Switchback.

In the fall of 1826 Isaac Chapman was assigned as supervisor on the driving of the Lehigh Coal and Navigation Company's "Old Tunnel," now known as the Hacklebernie Mine. This assignment supposedly led to his death, around which there appears to be some mystery. The tunnel work was suspended in June of 1827, after the completion of the Mauch Chunk gravity railroad. Sometime prior to this, according to a short biography written by George W. Gustine, Chapman caught a cold in the tunnel. This cold developed into typhoid fever, which led to his death on December 8, 1827. Typhoid fever is usually associated with the gastrointestinal tract and the drinking of water tainted by human waste. How a common cold could develop into typhoid fever is unknown.

At the age of forty-one, Isaac Abel Chapman died and was buried in the cemetery in Upper Mauch Chunk, near the edge overlooking the railroad which he had leveled only one year earlier. It is only fitting that he receive some acknowledgment for his accomplishments, and that his name be listed side by side with those of Josiah White, Erskine Hazard, and Asa Packer in the annals of Carbon County history.

Opposite: Chapman's 1827 map of the great coal mine at Summit Hill. Legend:
1. *A mound of loose earth and decomposed coal, which originally covered the mine and from which it has been removed.*
2. *Spoil bank — formed of earth which covered the coal.*
3. *High bank containing a Stratum of Sand Stone called the "North Fort."*
4. *On this side of the main opening the coal is covered in a similar manner to that on the East side and extends to an unknown distance.*
5. *To this intersection all the road lines descend, and here the horses are attached to the waggons to haul them to the summit at Slush hill whence they descend by gravity to Mauch Chunk.*
6. *On this side is a narrow sandstone, forming the boundary of the present opening, called the "South Fort." From this line the ground gradually descends to the North & to the South.*
7. *Spoil bank. Composed of loose earth which formerly covered the mine whence it has been removed.*
8. *On this side of the main opening the coal is covered with earth, varying in thickness from __ to __ feet. Its depth and extent are unknown.*
9. *This line descends to the first intersection at E.*
10. *First Entrance No. 1.*
11. *Second Entrance No. 2.*
12. *Third Entrance No. 3.*
13. *Fourth Entrance No. 4.*
14. *Uncovering lines.*
A. *This part of the mine forms the bottom or floor of the present workings.*
B. *This bench is about 15 to 112 feet above the bottom floor marked A.*
C. *This bench is about 16 feet above the bench marked B.*
D. *This bench is about 10 feet above the bench marked C.*
E. *Main line of Rail Road leading to Mauch Chunk.*

The Three Partners

For their roles in building the Lehigh Navigation System canal and in founding the Lehigh Coal and Navigation Company, Josiah White and Erskine Hazard have earned an important place in the history of the American Industrial Revolution. Their partner, George Frederick Augustus Hauto, is a much more obscure figure, yet interesting in his own way — a way very different from that of White and Hazard. Like other early figures in the history of the county, the three partners have largely faded from public memory. A brief sketch of their lives and careers therefore is in order.

Born to a New Jersey Quaker family in 1780, Josiah White was apprenticed to an ironmonger when he was fifteen years old. Later, in 1802, he went into the hardware business, in which he made a fortune.

From his earliest years White had been interested in mechanical devices. His success in the hardware business allowed him to pursue these interests, as he was able set aside the substantial sum of $500 a year for conducting mechanical experiments. White became interested in designing a waterpowered machine to roll and shape iron, and in March of 1810 he received a patent, the first of several he was to acquire, for a machine for rolling iron.

In 1810 White purchased a site along the Schuylkill River at the falls, intending to develop its waterpower potential. In 1812 he entered into a partnership with Erskine Hazard, who had studied at Princeton College (later University), Harvard, and abroad in Europe. He was a member of a prominent Philadelphia family; his father, Ebenezer Hazard, was the former Postmaster General of the United States.

Erskine Hazard, eight years younger than Josiah White, was mechanically inclined, intellectually adventurous, and, like White, possessed of an entrepreneurial spirit. The two formed a partnership and friendship that was to last a lifetime.

The White-Hazard enterprise was creative, developing new manufacturing techniques for nails and wire, techniques that were regarded as innovations when they were rediscovered fifty years later. For five years, from 1810 to 1815, they operated their wire and nail mill at the Falls of Schuylkill. During the blockade of the War of 1812, when English and Virginia soft coal became unavailable in Philadelphia, the two partners accidentally discovered how to make effective use of anthracite coal from the upper reaches of the Lehigh River, which they had purchased as an experiment. They decided to become involved in mining such coal and marketing it in Philadelphia.

The only known photograph of Erskine Hazard was taken shortly before his death in 1865. Courtesy, James Cox.

That was when George F.A. Hauto entered the picture. Hauto was cutting a fairly wide swath through Philadelphia society. He spoke German and several other languages fluently, and claimed to be a member of a wealthy German noble family. He seems to have been learned, charismatic, and a complete charlatan. Hauto managed to convince White and Hazard that they needed him, not only for the immense sums of money he said he was able to raise for their project, but as an intermediary with the largely German legislature. He did actually succeed, in 1818, in persuading the lawmakers to grant the partners the right to improve the navigation of the Lehigh River — an essential step if they were to bring coal to market. The rights granted by the legislature were extraordinary, giving them virtual ownership and monopoly control over the river provided they completed the improvements. The risks they undertook were immense; "We granted them the privilege of ruining themselves," one lawmaker said at the time.

But the money Hauto promised to raise was not forthcoming. Instead, he seems to have spent with a liberal hand what few funds the partnership could scrape together. White angrily reported an episode in which Hauto bought the contents of a bakery and distributed sweets to all the neighborhood children. They hailed him as "Belsnickel," the Pennsylvania Dutch version of Santa Claus.

His partners were not amused by such public relations-style gestures. In 1821 they urged him to go to Germany and raise money from his alleged noble relatives. He refused, saying he did not want to arrive in Europe poverty-stricken. At that, White and Hazard bought him out, although their own financial status was precarious at the time.

So Hauto virtually disappeared from history. His own side of the story may never be fully understood, since as far as is known he left no document, not even a single letter, to explain or justify his conduct. His name remains on the regional landscape, though, in the town of Hauto and the Lake Hauto area. Josiah White, too, won a kind of geographical immortality; his name is attached to White Haven.

The loser in the place-name game has been Erskine Hazard. There once was a village called Hazard, complete with post office, just up the Lehigh River from present-day Palmerton; Hazard Road is the name of the Palmerton street that led to the village. But New Jersey Zinc decided the place would be a good site for its original Palmerton plant, later called the West Plant. Gradually the village was swallowed up by the growth of the plant, and Hazard's name disappeared from local maps; it survives only in Hazard Park in Jim Thorpe.

Asa Packer

Coal, canals, railroads, industry — these were the major forces that transformed life in Carbon County during the nineteenth century. These were also the forces that shaped the life of Asa Packer, a carpenter who came to Mauch Chunk in 1833 to pilot one of the first coal-laden canal boats to Philadelphia. By the time of his death in 1879, coal, canals, railroads, and industry had made Packer one of the richest men in the country.

The nineteenth century saw the glorification of "the self-made man," the entrepreneur who recognized opportunity, took risks, and rose from humble beginnings to great fame and fortune. Packer's life was a textbook example. Born in 1805 in Mystic, Connecticut, he received a rudimentary education in the local schools. As a youth he was apprenticed to a tanner and also tried farming. But opportunities were hard to come by in the region and his family apparently had little money to help him.

Packer walked to Susquehanna County, Pennsylvania, in 1822. There he served an apprenticeship with a relative who was a carpenter. Settling on a farm in Springville, he met and married Sarah Minerva Blakeslee in 1828.

Packer was one of many brought to Mauch Chunk by the marriage of coal and canals. From piloting, he turned to construction and merchandising, building, and repairing boats. He also persuaded a brother-in-law, James I. Blakeslee, to join him in running a general store. With his younger brother Robert, Packer branched out into the transportation, leasing, and mining of coal, and was reputed to be the first to send coal in unbroken loads from Pottsville to New York.

During those early years as an entrepreneur, Packer began to develop the pattern of his business ventures — identifying opportunities, finding promising associates and entrusting

Asa Packer as a young man

them with specific projects, and, eventually, running a vast number of enterprises through a small, close-knit group of managers. He began to leave his mark on Mauch Chunk and Carbon County. In 1835, he joined his friend and religious mentor, William Sayre, Sr., as a founding member of St. Mark's Episcopal Church; he was a generous benefactor of the parish throughout his life. He also obtained the charter for the Mauch Chunk Water Company and was active in the Masonic Order.

While serving in the legislature from 1841 to 1843, he helped engineer the separation of Carbon County from Northampton County and its incorporation in 1843 with Mauch Chunk as its county seat. He also served a five-year term as an associate judge of the new county, acquiring the title of "Judge Packer," which would remain with him for the rest of his life.

Even as the canals were thriving, a new form of transportation, the railroad, was beginning to show its tremendous potential. The Beaver Meadow Railroad and Coal Company, the first steam railroad in the anthracite region, began running in 1836-1837, and other small lines followed in the next few years. Legend has it that Packer urged the directors of the Lehigh Coal and Navigation Company to build a railroad, but they refused. He then joined with another group to obtain a charter for a line along the Lehigh on the opposite bank of the canal. Though the charter for the Delaware, Lehigh, Schuylkill and Susquehanna was granted in 1846, nothing was done until 1851, when the charter was about to expire. Packer became a member of the company's board of managers, bought much of its stock, and did the grading necessary to save the charter.

With Sayre's son, Robert, as chief engineer in charge of building, Packer began construction of the Lehigh Valley Railroad in 1852. All of the wealth he had acquired in his many business ventures was put into the railroad. The new line hauled its first load of coal from Mauch Chunk to Easton on September 15, 1855, with borrowed equipment. The Lehigh Valley Railroad quickly became profitable. Asa Packer, wealthy small-town businessman, by the 1870s became Asa Packer, nationally known railroad magnate.

Late nineteenth-century view of Mauch Chunk. The Lehigh Valley Railroad tracks, depot, and warehouse can be seen above the canal, downriver and across from the town. The bridge in the center of the photograph in front of the Mansion House hotel connected the Lehigh Valley depot to the town. Trains can be seen on the tracks of the Lehigh and Susquehanna Division of the Central Railroad of New Jersey along Susquehanna Street.

During 1853 to 1857 Packer served two terms in the U.S. House of Representatives, but he was often absent because of his business interests. Historian W. Ross Yates wonders what Packer gained from his stint in Washington, since he served on obscure committees at a time when Congress took a laissez-faire attitude toward railroads, and he made no recorded speeches. Then, as now, the corridors of power emanated from Washington, and Packer could well have added a new circle of national government and business contacts to his railroad associates and his Harrisburg connections.

The Lehigh Valley Railroad became the lodestone of Packer's interests. He bought coal lands and began the mining operations of the Lehigh Valley Coal Company to ensure a source of cargo. When he needed a source of iron rails, he and his associates helped reorganize the Bethlehem Iron Company in 1860, and brought in the pioneering ironmaster John Fritz to build the furnaces and the rolling mill. The company eventually grew into Bethlehem Steel Corporation, one of the nation's leading steel producers. Recognizing that the expanding railroad and iron industries would soon need men with advanced technical training to run the operations, he approached the Right Reverend William Bacon Stevens, Episcopal Bishop of Pennsylvania, with the idea of endowing a university. The first thirty-nine students began classes at Lehigh University in South Bethlehem in September of 1866.

Packer even organized his estate to ensure that the railroad would remain intact and under the control of the managers he selected. Only his wife Sarah could have any part of the estate that she wanted outright. The other beneficiaries, including his children, received income from the estate.

Packer the entrepreneur, Packer the visionary, Packer the philanthropist won lavish praise from his contemporaries, but there is little information on Packer the human being. His few surviving letters deal mainly with business. When he spoke in public, his remarks were summarized rather than quoted. His associate, A.K. McClure, wrote that "he had no taste for society; indeed all formal duties were extremely irksome to him. His greatest pleasure was to have three friends join him in the evening at his Philadelphia residence, play euchre (a card game, similar to bridge) until about half past ten, and then join him in a drink of good old rye and adjourn."

Why he was a favorite-son candidate for president at the Democratic convention of 1868 and accepted the Democratic nomination for Governor of Pennsylvania in 1869 remains a mystery. Although he did little campaigning, he lost the governorship by fewer than five thousand votes.

Entrance to Asa Packer's mansion in Mauch Chunk, which is now owned by the borough of Jim Thorpe and maintained by the Jim Thorpe Lions Club and is open for tours. Photo by Joseph Elliott

In comparison to the showplaces built by many other industrial magnates, the mansion he built in Mauch Chunk was restrained. He made one trip to Europe in 1865, possibly for his health, and returned home with few artifacts and paintings. Many of the furnishings used to redecorate the mansion for the Packers' golden wedding anniversary in 1878 came from the 1876 U.S. Centennial Exposition, of which Packer was a commissioner.

Like most nineteenth-century entrepreneurs, he showed little sympathy for organized labor. Packer personally led a group of strikebreakers to Easton in 1843 to break up a strike of canal boatmen, and was thrown into the canal by the strikers.

In this period of individual enterprise, he did offer opportunities to those with talent and initiative through his companies and through Lehigh University, which he founded for "the intellectual and moral improvement of the young men of that region." Beginning in 1871, he covered the entire operating costs of the university, making the school tuition-free to those who qualified to attend.

Packer died on May 17, 1879, after suffering a fall in Philadelphia. Sarah's death followed in 1882. Of their four children who reached adulthood, one — Lucy Packer Linderman — had died in 1873, leaving Packer with his only heirs. The two Packer sons, Robert and Harry, died in 1883 and 1884. Only one daughter, Mary Packer Cummings, remained. She continued many of her father's charities, especially the Episcopal Church and Lehigh University. When she died in 1912, she left the Packer mansion and its furnishings to the borough of Mauch Chunk.

The Lehigh Coal and Navigation Company

Now that it no longer exists, it is difficult to imagine the ascendancy the Lehigh Coal and Navigation Company once had over the economic life of the upper part of Carbon County. The company was founded in 1821, as a merger of two companies begun several years earlier by Josiah White and Erskine Hazard. One, the Lehigh Coal Company, was established to mine the coal and to build a road from the Lehigh River to the newly opened mines at Summit Hill. The other, the Lehigh Navigation Company, was intended to provide for the transportation of the coal to market by way of the Lehigh River.

Early accomplishments of the LC&N included the building of the Lehigh Canal, officially named the Lehigh Navigation, and two gravity railroads. One brought coal from Room Run near Nesquehoning to the canal at what was then Mauch Chunk; the other ran from Summit Hill to Mauch Chunk. The Room Run Railroad was abandoned in the 1870s after a railroad tunnel was cut through to the Panther Valley, while the Summit Hill line evolved into the famous Switchback Railroad.

By 1839, the Philadelphia-based LC&N had expanded its holdings considerably. It owned some 8,000 acres of coal lands — the eastern end of Pennsylvania's southern anthracite field. Its coal operations were run by a subsidiary, Lehigh Navigation Coal Company, known as "the Old Company" and headquartered in Lansford. Nesquehoning, Lansford, Coaldale, and Tamaqua were this firm's company towns.

Official traffic on the Lehigh Navigation System ended in the early 1930s — with the exception of transportation of coal silt, dredged from behind dams, to Palmerton: this lasted until 1942, when trucks took over the hauling. Holdings of LC&N included the Lehigh and Susquehanna Railroad with its famous Ashley Planes extending beyond White Haven, and the Wilkes-Barre and Scranton Railroad, a joint venture with the Delaware and Hudson. These two railroads stretched from Scranton to Easton, and were leased on a long-term basis to the Central Railroad of New Jersey.

The company also owned and operated another railroad, the Lehigh and New England, which it organized in 1895 through the merger of new lines with the existing Lehigh and Lackawanna Railroad. Headquartered in Bethlehem, and serving both the cement industry and the anthracite industry, by 1904 it had been turned into a functioning railroad. It reached from Tamaqua to Allentown to Maybrook, New York, and was the most consistently profitable of LC&N's operations from its formation until the late 1950s.

In addition, LC&N owned 45,000 acres of forested land, which it had purchased to control the headwaters of the Lehigh River and to assure itself a supply of timber. Much of this is in what is now a prime resort area, and was managed by a subsidiary of the Lehigh Navigation Coal Company known as the Blue Ridge Real Estate Company. On part of it, Split Rock Lodge (now Split Rock Resort) was built at Lake Harmony, originally as a retreat for company executives; it later became a resort for the public.

The LC&N Company used its control of watershed lands to provide water to coal-region towns through the Panther Valley and Nesquehoning water companies. It owned a considerable interest (700,000 shares) of the National Power and Light Company, later Pennsylvania Power and Light, through its sale to the company of the Hauto power plant, which it built in 1911.

Through its Lehigh Navigation Coal Company subsidiary, the company was of course the predominant employer in the Panther Valley area. It also supported many community projects, and paid some 60 percent of the real estate taxes.

St. Mark's Episcopal Church as it appeared in the 1870s from across the Lehigh River. Stereo view by M.A. Kleckner. Courtesy, Raymond E. Holland Collection.

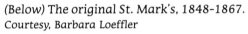

(Left) The chancel, altar, and reredos of St. Mark's. Courtesy, Barbara Loeffler

(Below) The original St. Mark's, 1848-1867. Courtesy, Barbara Loeffler

To list these holdings and activities is merely to mention those that most directly affected the life of Carbon County. The decline of anthracite production in the Panther Valley, and then the discontinuance by the company of underground mining in 1954, were bound to have a devastating effect on the economy. Indeed, it could be argued that full recovery has never been achieved.

The Lehigh Coal and Navigation Company ended its long corporate existence in the early 1980s as a candy manufacturer. The most conspicuous reminders of its one-time dominance of the county scene today are the canal whose ruins still wind parallel to the Lehigh River, a fine office building in the historic district of Jim Thorpe (now apartments), and the continued existence of the Blue Ridge Real Estate Company, which was spun off as an independent entity before the parent company's dissolution. The company that now operates under the name of the Lehigh Coal and Navigation Company is unrelated to the historic Old Company.

St. Mark's Episcopal Church

One of the first things a traveler approaching Jim Thorpe from the direction of Lehighton will notice is the elegant profile of St. Mark's Episcopal Church, nestled at the foot of Flagstaff Mountain. Designed by Richard Upjohn, Sr., with later additions by Addison Hutton, the building has been called the finest Gothic Revival church in Pennsylvania. It is a measure of the wealth the coal and transportation industries once brought to certain segments of the population of Carbon County.

William H. Sayre, as a lay reader, first brought Episcopal worship to old Mauch Chunk. He was joined by, among others, Asa Packer, who soon would employ Sayre's son Robert as chief engineer of the Lehigh Valley Railroad. Today it is the Packer family which is most indelibly connected with the history of St. Mark's.

The present church is the second on the site. Unlike the first structure, which stood from 1848 to 1867, the current one makes dramatic use of its cramped, steeply pitched location.

Inside, the building is full of artistic treasures. The downstairs chapel is decorated with "ordinary" Tiffany glass but the real Tiffany treasures are upstairs in the main sanctuary, in the form of two windows called "The Breadth of My Love," and "The Road to Emmaus." In the first of these, the color is so subtle that Christ's flesh can be seen beneath his robe. It is such works that demonstrate the true genius of Louis Comfort Tiffany.

The altar in the sanctuary is of Italian marble. The reredos is made of Caen soapstone, carved on-site. Its panels were copied, with the permission of Queen Victoria, from the reredos of St. George's Chapel in Windsor Castle, England. Other features of St. Mark's include floors of English Minton tile, and a fine Austin organ. The splendid murals that so much resembled those of a medieval English parish church have been covered over in recent years.

Today, the church remains a center of Episcopal worship. Not surprisingly, it is a magnet for visitors of all faiths who admire beauty.

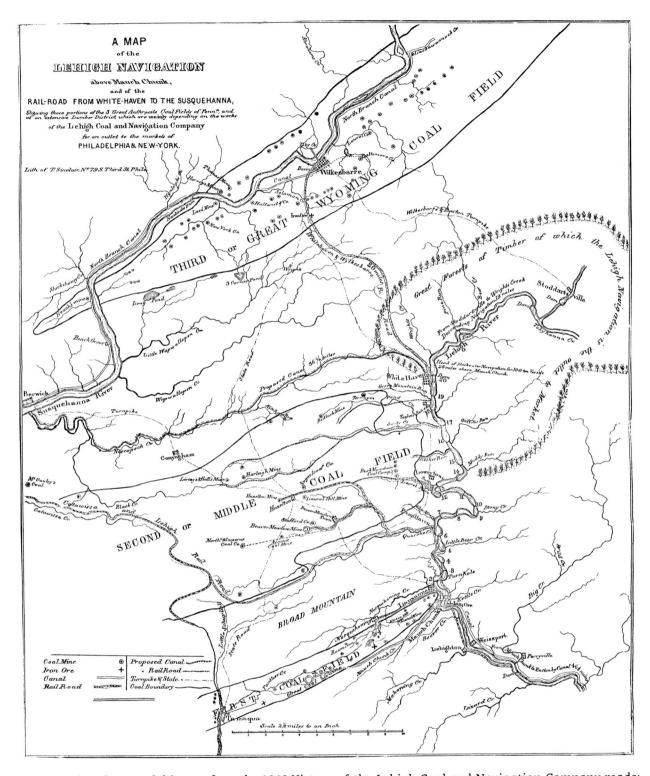

The legend at the top of this map from the 1840 History of the Lehigh Coal and Navigation Company reads: "A map of the Lehigh Navigation above Mauch Chunk, and of the rail-road from White-Haven to the Susquehanna, shewing those portions of the 3 Great Anthracite Coal Fields of Penn[a], and of an extensive Lumber District. which are mainly depending on the works of the Lehigh Coal and Navigation Company for an outlet to the markets of Philadelphia & New York."

Early Days in the Coalfields

At the beginning of the nineteenth century the eastern cities of the United States were on the verge of a fuel crisis. Domestic and industrial consumers relied on wood for most energy needs but supplies were becoming tight and prices rose. Bituminous coal, imported from Virginia and England, began to take the place of wood. Anthracite had been discovered by the Moravians in the 1750s but had not been utilized to any great extent.

In 1791 Philip Ginder, a miller and millwright, discovered an outcrop of anthracite on Sharp Mountain approximately nine miles west of the Lehigh River and about forty miles north of Allentown. Ginder, like other Pennsylvania Germans, had settled on the fertile farmland in the valleys south of Sharp Mountains, but no one lived among the steep, rocky mountains and valleys to the north. In the 1790s only hunters, prospectors, and explorers visited that area. Ginder was probably all of the above.

Ginder knew that he had found anthracite, and he knew that Colonel Jacob Weiss, living at the site of Fort Allen, was very interested in the stone coal. Weiss, deputy quartermaster general during the Revolution, had moved to the wilderness along the Lehigh River to operate a timber business.

The colonel had been hoping for a significant anthracite find; he had dealt with Ginder in the past and trusted his information. Weiss took the samples that Ginder provided to Philadelphia, where other investors were interested in a potential anthracite trade. These included Michael Hillegas, first United States treasurer, John Nicholson, a land speculator, and Charles Cist, a publisher. Hillegas was Weiss's cousin, and Cist was married to Weiss's sister. From their meeting the Lehigh Coal Mine Company was formed; it was formally organized on February 13, 1792.

The company sold stock and hired Weiss's workmen to explore the area. They located coal in a number of places, but the largest quantity was at the outcrop that Ginder had found. Ginder, an older man, did not get involved with the new company. Problems developed immediately. The coal was nine rugged miles from the river. Weiss built a road, but it was a long, expensive, bone-jarring trip to the Lehigh. Farmers dug some coal part-time; no one lived at the Summit mines on Sharp Mountain. They did manage to get some coal to the river, but the Lehigh was unimproved, very rocky, and quite shallow most of the year. It cost more to ship coal from the Summit mine to Philadelphia than from England to Philadelphia.

In 1798 the company directors told Weiss to find coal closer to the river. He found a considerable coal deposit at Room Run, a small stream that fed into the Nesquehoning Creek. This deposit was only four miles from the river, but the coal was harder to mine than the coal on Sharp Mountain. Since the mines near the Nesquehoning Creek were an additional mountain away from the miners' homes in the Mahoning Valley, a few huts were built near Hell's Kitchen Run to house the men.

Transportation costs were devastating, and the Lehigh Coal Mine Company failed. The venture ruined many of the investors, and only Weiss lived long enough to see it succeed. The company did acquire a considerable amount of land, ten thousand acres in all, extending fourteen miles from the Lehigh River on the east, nearly to Tamaqua on the Little Schuylkill on the west. The holdings were four miles wide, and included the sites of what would become Summit Hill, Lansford, Coaldale, and Nesquehoning.

The company leased some of its holdings to those willing to assume the risks involved in getting anthracite to markets, but the land basically remained unused from 1803 until 1813, when the War of 1812 stopped coal shipments from England and Virginia. Jacob Cist, son of original investor Charles Cist, decided to reopen the mines in the hope that the war's fuel shortage would make Lehigh anthracite economical. It did, but only for the length of the war. Cist and his partners, Charles Miner, Isaac Chapman, and John Nicholson, had more success than their predecessors. They managed to send regular shipments to Philadelphia and developed a limited industrial market for anthracite. Josiah White and Erskine Hazard, who operated a wire mill outside of Philadelphia, were among those who used the stone coal.

While the high cost of transportation devastated Cist's operation, White and Hazard planned their own entry into the anthracite trade. They were originally interested in the Schuylkill region, but when political objections arose to White's involvement, they turned their attention to the once-again-abandoned Lehigh coal fields.

In 1818 White and Hazard began operations along the Lehigh River at a site that would give birth to the town of Mauch Chunk. They formed two separate companies, the Lehigh Coal Company and the Lehigh Navigation Company, later combined and incorporated as the Lehigh Coal and Navigation Company — widely known as the LC&N. White's priority was a good wagon road from the Summit mine to the Lehigh River at Mauch Chunk. It took much effort to level this rocky landscape, but it was accomplished. Next, the rocky Lehigh River would be altered and its uneven water flow regulated. In 1820 the entrepreneurs delivered three hundred sixty-five tons of stone coal to Philadelphia. Production increased yearly, and by 1824 the general public had been convinced that stone coal could be used in the home. The corner was turned; anthracite would be a success.

Engraving of the coal mine at Summit Hill, first published in 1873.

The mine that produced this fuel was a simple pit. George Hauto, an early partner of White and Hazard, described it as an "inconsiderable opening, like a moderate-sized stone quarry" when the LC&N acquired it. It expanded quickly, however. By 1825 three acres had been uncovered; and by 1830, according to Yale geologist Benjamin Silliman, who visited that year, over eight acres had been uncovered — in some places to a depth of nearly one hundred feet. The LC&N believed that the anthracite field covered one hundred acres. The coal seams were from twelve to forty feet thick and produced three hundred forty tons per day, according to Silliman. The coal was simply dug by pick and shovel, later with the assistance of gunpowder, then loaded into wagons and hauled by horses or mules to the wagon road.

The company transformed the wagon road into a gravity railroad in 1827. Mules hauled empty cars up to the mines on the tracks, and then returned to Mauch Chunk in their own car with a trainload of coal in front. Tourists came to visit the great mine at Summit Hill, as the growing mine patch was called. Victorians marveled at industry, and visitors showed great interest in the coal quarry. The view at Summit Hill also was noteworthy. Travel writer Anne Royall wrote:

> The whole country around seems to be one continuation of mountains; and the view from the mines is very extensive and beautiful, presenting an endless representation of high ridges and deep valleys.

In 1821 James Broderick, a manager for the LC&N, moved to Summit Hill and became the first resident notable enough for local historians to remember. As late as 1826 there was very little settlement there. Only one house existed within the limits of what would become the town. A few log structures stood at the mine, at the western end of the town. Some of the workers lived in them; but, since over fifty men worked the quarry, it seems that some still walked from their farms and homes in the Mahoning Valley. James Leamon, the mine supervisor, had the only two-story dwelling, which he had to share with boarders.

Thomas Kelley built the first house in Nesquehoning in 1824. Samuel Holland also was one of its first settlers. A long-time LC&N employee, Holland had most recently been superintendent of the Summit Hill mine. By the late 1820s the work force at Summit Hill had grown to eighty men. The company divided the workers into two groups of forty, each with a foreman. Holland conducted the entire operation but when the company decided to work the Room Run field he was transferred to Nesquehoning to supervise.

The LC&N provided a triangular lot for a church and school in Nesquehoning and soon provided a lot for a burial ground. Regular lots cost one hundred dollars each and corner lots were priced at between $120 and $150. By September of 1831, twenty houses had been constructed on seventeen lots. Nesquehoning grew quickly, and staged a Washington's birthday celebration in 1832 that attracted visitors from the neighboring towns of Mauch Chunk, Lehighton, and Lausanne. The editor of the Mauch Chunk paper commented on the "neat cluster of white buildings." The townspeople were erecting dwellings and shops constantly.

Expansion and Competition in the Coalfields

By 1830 the LC&N and Mauch Chunk were well established. A slackwater navigation system had been completed, and the coal business was booming. Until this time the LC&N had owned all the property in Mauch Chunk, and controlled the town like a feudal settlement. Economic prosperity allowed more independence, and the company decided to sell individual lots beginning in January 1831.

In the meantime a new part of the LC&N property had come to life. In 1830 White decided to reopen the mines previously worked by Cist at Room Run. A valley surrounded the Nesquehoning Creek, and it was well disposed for settlement. Nesquehoning was included in the decision to sell individual lots; Summit Hill was not. The LC&N laid out a town plot in Nesquehoning and advertised it extensively as an extremely promising site near one of the best coal fields known. The company made one hundred lots available for purchase, but reserved the area around the Room Run and Hell's Kitchen mines and along proposed railroad rights-of-way.

It was more difficult to mine coal at Room Run than at Summit Hill. There was less coal on the surface there than at Summit Hill, so the LC&N used slopes and drifts. (Slopes go into the earth on a downward angle, and drifts go uphill.) But there was a lot of coal at Room Run and it was closer to the river than Summit Hill, so Room Run became an important LC&N mining site.

The LC&N began construction of a gravity railroad at Nesquehoning in 1830 and opened it in 1833. It built three self-acting planes, rising about one foot in each ten feet. The planes worked by gravity, descending coal cars pulling the empty ones back to the mines. At the top of the third plane, branch railroads ran to each mine. The railroad was five miles, sixteen hundred feet long, covering a 562-foot vertical ascent. Samuel Barber engineered it, while Samuel Holland ran the mines.

Summit Hill also expanded during the 1830s. The LC&N permitted the mine contractors to build ten houses at Summit Hill in 1833 for rent to the miners. In 1836 the board directed that "10 cheap tenements be erected in lieu of the old buildings to be removed." The editor of a Mauch Chunk newspaper called these small houses "hardly fit for human habitation." The oldest miner shacks were one story high, and only eight by ten feet. By 1845 the board wanted "more cheap dwellings for the workers," and these much larger houses received the approval of the editor. The new houses in Summit Hill and Nesquehoning were sixteen by twenty-five feet, and two stories high. They would be rented at ten percent of construction cost. Empty lots could be leased for one dollar a year for a ten-year lease.

The residents built more than homes. Tourism and business attracted visitors, and lodging was needed. Both Summit Hill and Nesquehoning gained hotels during the 1840s and 1850s. In Summit Hill, Mrs. Simpson ran a temperance lodging and Abram Harris was building a large brick hotel to be called the "Eagle." Nesquehoning featured Dennis McAlear's Hotel and Wilhelm's Hotel. Alexander Lockhart and Merritt Abbott built a foundry in Summit Hill in 1851.

The Lehigh Coal and Navigation Company was not the only coal company operating in Carbon County. Further north, in what was to become Banks Township, the Beaver Meadow Railroad was looking in the 1830s for ways to transport coal from the Beaver Meadow coalfields. The company faced one obstacle after another, due to the control the LC&N had over the Lehigh River. Josiah White and Erskine Hazard had suffered much financial and personal hardship to build the LC&N, a company that had opened an entire region to settlement and employed five hundred people. The company certainly did not want competition from other coalfields and was not enthusiastic about providing inexpensive transportation on their canal to newcomers trying to capitalize on the coal market LC&N had created.

As soon as the Beaver Meadow Railroad began work in the valley, the LC&N began to interfere, or to defend its rights. In the abstract, the point of contention concerned the placement of the railroad bed in the right-of-way of the canal towpath. The LC&N argued that the BMRR grade was too close to the river and would interfere with the construction of the upper section of the canal; it wanted the roadbed raised to a higher point along the mountain.

In the field, the point of contention concerned two contractors who would not get paid if their crews did not work. In late July of 1835, LC&N contractor Calvin Barker and his crew erected a shanty and began work near Bear Creek on the Lehigh. On August 16 the BMRR crew arrived to begin work on the railroad. But lack of space along the river bank prevented both crews from working at the same time.

Samuel Ingham, president of the BMRR, ordered his construction crew to get to work immediately and if the LC&N crew interfered, Ingham, who would be present, would have them arrested. The LC&N crew responded by cutting trees and digging rocks for canal construction. The trees and rocks just happened to be on the bank above the river and were thrown down onto the path, effectively preventing the BMRR crew from working. The BMRR took the LC&N to court in Easton for obstruction, but lost its case. Eventually an agreement was worked out for cooperation on the river.

Early in October of 1835 the LC&N received an unsigned proposal from the BMRR: the LC&N could complete the canal as planned, and if the towpath interfered with railroad construction, the BMRR could remove it as long as they would rebuild it without damage to the canal. The railroad could run on LC&N property as long as it had a thirty-foot clearance from the canal. Both sides agreed that this agreement would end the dispute. They were wrong.

By November 23, 1835, the BMRR had completed the twelve miles of railroad from their mines to the Lehigh at the Penn Haven Junction, where Quakake Creek empties into the river. As the 1836 construction season commenced trouble began anew. E.A. Douglas, who had been hired by the LC&N to complete the Upper Division, insisted, according to Ingham, that the BMRR would have to wait until the LC&N was finished. Once again a BMRR crew entered the valley near the LC&N crew and once again the LC&N crew just happened to be felling trees and clearing rocks from the bank directly above the BMRR crew. Once again the BMRR workers ran for their lives.

On August 5, 1836, according to the *Mauch Chunk Courier*, an armed posse led by Ingham arrested the LC&N contractors, Mssrs. Daugherty and Baldwin, and their assistants and took them to Beaver Meadow. Daugherty and Baldwin wisely refused to post bond and were transfered to the county jail in Easton, a city friendlier to LC&N interests. The LC&N contractors, in turn, filed a suit for false arrest against the BMRR. Douglas denied the accusation: "There is not one word of truth in the whole [charge] and [they] know it...."

Edwin A. Douglas

Both actions were settled out of court in a new attempt at a comprehensive agreement. The LC&N would complete its canal to Quakake in one month, the BMRR would then extend its railroad south, and if the BMRR needed to use the canal towpath it could but was required to build another towpath for the canal. The engineers for both companies met to arrange their schedules so that crews would not come into conflict. The BMRR was given free transit through any LC&N property provided its railroad was kept at least thirty feet above the canal, and any bridge provided sufficient clearance. It was the same agreement that the opposing parties had reached in October 1835 but now, a year later, Ingham and his chief engineer, Ario Pardee, accepted the proposal because they had no other choice — the courts had sided with the LC&N.

Gravity Railroads and Inclined Planes

Gravity and inclined plane railroads were built by various mining companies throughout the anthracite coal regions between 1826 and 1862 to transport coal from the mines across mountains to the canals. The first significant one was the nine-mile gravity line between Summit Hill and Mauch Chunk, built in 1827 by the Lehigh Coal and Navigation Company. During the next two decades the company completed several other gravity lines.

(Above) The eighteen-mile railroad that brought anthracite from Summit Hill to the canal at Mauch Chunk and took the coal cars back to the mine. (Below) The hoisting equipment in the engine house at the top of the Mount Pisgah plane on the backtrack, used to pull cars up from Mauch Chunk.

Once the coal cars had been unloaded onto canal boats, the problem of returning empty cars to the mines remained. Originally, mules had pulled the empty cars back to the mines. Increased production overwhelmed this system. White proposed expansion as early as 1830, but company finances and limited demand for coal prevented such an undertaking. In 1844 the company decided to expand its gravity railroad network and construct a backtrack with inclined planes to cope with the increased demand for anthracite. That year it installed two steam and counterbalanced inclined planes on its Summit Hill to Mauch Chunk gravity line to haul cars back up Mount Pisgah. These planes were part of a larger system that used both steam and gravity as motive power, and would put over three hundred LC&N mules out of work.

The expanded system was designed as a figure eight and enabled the company to use one track exclusively for transporting coal to Mauch Chunk and the other for returning the cars to the mine in Summit Hill. The four-hour round trip on the old railroad was cut in half. An inclined plane, 2,223 feet long, was built from the head of the chute to the top of Mount

Three of the planes built by the Lehigh Coal and Navigation Company as part of the inclined-plane and gravity railroad that carried coal from the mines to the Lehigh River were the Mount Pisgah plane (above), the Penn Haven planes (right), and the Mount Jefferson planes (below).

(Right) At Penn Haven two sets of planes descend to the river. The Beaver Meadow planes are on the left; on their right are the planes of the Hazleton Coal Company. Both were completed in 1851.

Both the Mount Pisgah and the Mount Jefferson planes were part of the famous "Switchback Railroad," one of the tourist attractions in the Mauch Chunk area. The Switchback carried both coal and tourists until 1872, passengers only until it closed in the 1930s.

Pisgah, a 664-foot vertical rise from the chutes and 900 feet from the Lehigh River. Two stationary engines, each of 120 horsepower, hauled the cars up the plane.

The steam engines powered a 27-foot-diameter drum, which pulled the cars up the plane with riveted wrought-iron bands that would unwind like a clock spring. The bands were attached to a safety car that pulled the coal train up from behind. The safety, or barney, car was able to pull a train of sixteen cars up the plane in six to eight minutes. An additional engine was later added to each plane to speed the ascent.

From the top of Mount Pisgah the cars ran by gravity on a grade averaging fifty feet to the mile for six miles to the base of Mount Jefferson, below Summit Hill. Another stationary engine raised the cars 462 vertical feet on a 2,070-foot plane. From the top of the Mount Jefferson plane the cars coasted a mile into Summit Hill and on to the mines.

Sunday outing to the Lehigh Coal and Navigation Company's first tunnel, driven in 1844 at the Summit Hill mines.

The LC&N board of managers argued that construction of the backtrack would allow a new arrangement for coal mining. The LC&N could now lease smaller mines, which could be run by smaller companies and produce still greater quantities of coal. Employees would have more opportunity to advance in responsibility and provide themselves with more income. This is essentially what happened.

The Summit Hill mine was still primarily a quarry, but with a few tunnels, drifts, and slopes driven into the walls of the pits. The LC&N divided the Summit mine district into four sections, each under the charge of a different contractor: Old Summit Mines, Springdale Tunnel, North Mines, and South Mines. A separate contractor was responsible for collecting the coal from different stands, transporting it to Mauch Chunk, running the breaker, and depositing the coal into canal boats. In 1845 the company expected a total of 210,000 tons from Summit Hill and 80,000 from Room Run.

The LC&N expanded coal mining into the Panther Creek Valley where George Belford, contractor for LC&N, struck an immense vein in August 1845. This was the famous "Mammoth Vein," the largest known vein of anthracite in the world. It had taken Belford a year and a half to drive a rock tunnel 600 feet into the Hauto Mountain on the Panther Creek, or north, side of the valley before hitting the vein. The LC&N surveyed the valley and selected sites for further mines.

The ingenious "switchback" system provided access to the Panther Creek Valley anthracite field. The descent into the Panther Creek Valley, averaging 221 feet to the mile, was far too steep for a direct gravity railroad. The company devised a means of using a gravity descent that also controlled the speed of the cars. The cars descended a stretch of track for a certain number of feet. They would then begin an ascent on an uphill segment of track designed to slow the cars by gravity. At the end of the segment the cars would again move downhill, until they reached another branch of the switchback. This zigzag movement kept the cars under control. Stationary steam engines hauled full coal cars up to Summit Hill. The cars were then

(Above) Lehigh Coal and Navigation Company's No. 13 Breaker, which operated from 1883 to 1910.
(Below) Coal dock in the #7 section of Lansford in 1892, opposite the Hauto Tunnel. Driving the team of mules is George Kneiss. The Panther Creek Railroad merged with the Lehigh and New England in 1913.

sent by gravity to Mauch Chunk where the coal was loaded into canal boats and the cars were returned to the mines.

Contractors who worked in Summit Hill moved down into the Panther Creek Valley, but with some changes. George Belford remained affiliated with Mr. Weiss in Summit Hill but took William Sharpe as his partner in Panther Valley. Captain McClean and David Williams were partners at the Springdale Tunnel in Summit Hill but it was McClean and Kelso in the

The 200 block of East Bertsch Street in Lansford in 1881. Housing for miners' families, owned by the Lehigh and Wilkes-Barre Coal Company, lines both sides of the street.

Valley. Williams was the first Welsh contractor employed by the LC&N. In 1850 McClean and Williams opened Slope No. 1 in Summit Hill, and worked it until it caught fire in 1858. This burning mine became a tourist attraction.

New contractors also made a start in the Panther Creek Valley, and many failed. James Steel abandoned No. 8 and James Andersen abandoned Tunnel No. 6 after suffering "grievous losses due to faulty workings." Both were in debt and needed help to pay their obligations.

The restored Welsh Congregational Church in Lansford, formerly Ashton.

The contractors, or the LC&N, would erect ten or more double houses at each mine tunnel. They would then rent the homes in these patches to the miners. When Steel and Andersen went under, the LC&N bought the patches as an investment, and also to help the contractors out of debt.

Ashton, the new village in the Panther Creek Valley, was more than a mine patch; the LC&N provided lots for schools and churches. Jonathan Krist rented a sixty-acre farm for one hundred dollars a year. The LC&N continued its pattern of renting lots for one dollar a year. In 1847 the LC&N began to sell lots in Summit Hill, but not yet in Ashton. The company reserved mineral rights, of course. Another mine patch gained prominence in the valley. It was called Storm Hill, allegedly because the home of Peter Fisher was blown down during a storm. These two communities later become Lansford when the patch towns were consolidated in 1877.

Stereoscopic view by M.A. Kleckner of the Panther Creek Plane from the 1880s series "A Trip Around the Switch Back R.R." This plane rose 225 feet in 1800 feet. Courtesy, Raymond E. Holland Collection.

The first church in Ashton was the Welsh Congregational Church, erected in 1850. It was restored during the 1980s, and is used for a variety of cultural activities. Surprisingly, Summit Hill did not gain a church building until 1847, when the Presbyterian congregation outgrew the school house that it used for services. In 1850 the Episcopal congregation of Summit Hill built a Gothic-style church.

The towns may have been prospering, but not all was well. Labor problems came quickly to the valley. In 1847 workers on the Panther Creek Railroad turned out for higher wages. The contractors were not impressed. (The Panther Creek Railroad was an ever-changing system of inclined planes and backtracks that moved coal from the Panther Creek Valley to the summit of Sharp Mountain, where the coal cars were shunted onto the original gravity railroad to be sent to Mauch Chunk and the canal.) The Mauch Chunk newspaper stated that the contractors would pay wages owed and dismiss the strikers. The paper commented that the railroad workers were being paid more than the miners in Summit Hill, and that the contractors had turned down many job applicants. Furthermore, the flood of Irish immigrants promised to lower wages across the board.

Miners at the entrance to No. 3 Mine on Sharp Mountain. The photographer was C.A. Staudt of Summit Hill.

Mining accidents were common. Coal gave off firedamp, or methane, during mining, and this explosive gas was a constant danger to the miners. Various means of diluting the gas were used, including large furnaces that heated the mine air to create drafts and increase circulation by bringing in surface air through convection. This worked to some extent, but could be dangerous if a sufficient concentration of methane found the fire. The miners later used giant fans to circulate the air, but methane remained a problem. The first firedamp explosion in the valley occurred in 1838 in Nesquehoning, when two men were slightly injured by the "fulminating damp," as it was also called. The worst firedamp explosion in the history of the anthracite coal fields took place at Avondale, near Wilkes-Barre, in 1869. There, one hundred and eight men and boys died when a circulation fire was relit following a strike, creating an instantaneous explosion of methane. The fire caught the shaft, then the headframe of the only entrance into the mine. This collapsed into the mine, trapping the miners.

On August 17, 1854, two firedamp explosions in Nesquehoning claimed four lives and seriously injured eight. The cause of the first explosion was unknown, but it resulted in only minor injuries. However, the force of the explosion caused a door to jam and blew out the safety lamps of the miners behind the door. A rescue team went for a sledge to force the door; one miner, James Stevens, stayed behind and decided to provide the

Nesquehoning (Room Run) Shaft No. 1, which at one time was the worst deep mine in the state of Pennsylvania for firedamp explosions. Courtesy Jay Frantz.

trapped miners with a light. He stuck a lighted candle under the jammed door, and this ignited the firedamp trapped with the miners. Stevens died instantly, and three other miners died from their injuries over the next few days.

Not all mining accidents occurred underground. In 1849 a coal and rock bank in Summit Hill collapsed on two workers; James Callahan died, and Michael Diver sustained a broken arm. Twenty men dug the victims out, and moments after they were removed a second and much larger bank collapsed, just missing the rescue team.

Perhaps the most gruesome accident occurred in 1851 when sixteen-year-old Daniel McConoway fell into the coal breaker at Mauch Chunk. He was horribly mangled and torn to pieces. James Curran, age twenty-two, was returning from McConoway's funeral when he tried to catch a ride on a coal car, missed his jump, fell underneath it and died a horrible death. The *Carbon Democrat* reported that the car "passed over his body, mutilating it in a terrible manner."

Some accidents were less tragic. In 1843 a Summit Hill coal train collided with a two-hundred-pound "porker." There were no injuries, except for a dead pig, but sixteen cars derailed, and four were smashed to bits.

Because of the hard work, because of the danger, because of their cultural background, most miners drank. The LC&N disapproved. It disapproved at first because Josiah White was a Quaker and frowned on alcohol. Whiskey was reluctantly permitted on the canal. The work was hard, but not technically difficult, and standing in a river all day required a belt now and then. The canal boatmen drank also. Driving a canal boat isn't that dangerous, but it is boring. The company disapproved, but looked away. The mines were different. The work was hard, technically demanding, and very dangerous. The LC&N did all it could to prohibit alcohol in the mines and the mining villages. It failed, of course.

In 1829 contractor Samuel Holland asked the board for permission to open a public house in Summit Hill. The board replied that "from a fear that injurious consequences would flow from the proposed establishment the managers are compelled by a sense of duty to decline."

Holland also managed the company store, and was censured by the company in 1836 for selling liquor to persons living or working at the mines. The board told him to find another operator for the store, someone not connected to the contractors or to the miners. The board worried that the contractor as store owner had become dependent on the miners. The board does not explain that paradoxical remark. We normally think that the company store took advantage of the miners, not the other way around. Perhaps the miners threatened a work slowdown or vandalism in order to coerce Holland into supplying liquor. An independent store owner could not be pressured like that.

At some point the LC&N gave in and a tavern was opened in Summit Hill, but not for long. In 1844 the board directed that the "tavern house at SH be cleaned and put in decent order as soon as it is cleared of occupants so that John Simpson can have the said building as a Temperance accommodation for travelers."

The company and those concerned with morality placed great hope in the temperance movement. In 1840 the temperance pledge was introduced at the Catholic church in Summit Hill, since the Catholic Irish were considered the hardest drinkers. Sixty-nine parishioners signed the pledge, but they were not going cold turkey. Owing to their former habit, they were allowed one and one-half gills in twenty-four hours. The organizers hoped the miners and families would soon take the "teetotal" pledge and abstain from alcohol completely.

Some miners did abstain completely, but they were not the ones who made the headlines. In 1845 Levi Smith was convicted, fined thirty dollars and court costs, and placed on probation for a year for operating an illegal tippling house. Smith maintained a "grog shop in the vicinity of the old mines at which it has been the custom with the miners to congregate for the purpose of drinking and carousing." Smith survived his punishment, but killed himself a few years later.

Even worse, liquor led to adultery and murder. On January 1, 1844, William McKay left for work. He arrived at the mine to find it closed. Why he went to work on New Year's Day is an unanswered question. He returned home about 11 o'clock in the morning to find his drunken wife with Henry McCloskey, also drunk. He attempted to enter the house but could not; so he went to a neighbor, Mrs. Owens, where he had a few drinks and complained about his wife. At about noon he returned to his house but still could not open the door, so he entered a window. He found his wife and McCloskey lying together on a bench, both nearly unconscious from alcohol. McKay assaulted McCloskey, who was apparently too drunk to fight back. From the gory courtroom testimony provided by Benjamin Rush McConnell, the mine doctor, we find that McKay plunged a knife into the ribs and intestines of his wife's lover, causing McCloskey's guts to spill out on the floor and ending his life in short order.

McKay ran into the streets screaming that he was a murderer. The neighbors rushed in to find Mrs. McKay cradling McCloskey's dying body in her lap. When asked what happened, she replied, "It is a small loss." McKay was convicted of second degree murder and sentenced to ten years solitary confinement at Eastern Penitentiary in Philadelphia.

Some crimes were of a lighter variety. The *Mauch Chunk Gazette*:

> It appears that the commonwealth has no mercy even on females, for almost the first action brought at the present session was on the charge of assault and battery against Mrs. Julianna Puff. Mrs. Julianna came into court with an almost Amazonian stride and took her seat beside her counsel who appeared quite proud of the fine appearance made by his client. In the course of the evidence it was shown that Mrs. Bridget Cunningham's child and the child of Mrs. Julianna Puff were quarreling, when the mothers interfered, and Mrs. Julianna took first a fishing pole and then a billet of fire wood to illustrate her affection for her offspring over the shoulder of her neighbor. This mode of showing the strength of maternal love was thought rather active by the court who sentenced Mrs. Julianna to pay the cost of prosecution, a $5 fine and stand committed till sentence be complied with.

Although violence flared for any number of reasons, the various ethnic groups got along reasonably well during the early period. In typical paternalistic style, the Nesquehoning contractors Barber and Holland treated their eighty employees to a roast beef and plum pudding dinner in 1833. The various immigrant miners, Welsh, English, Germans, and Irish, all toasted their native lands. They sang songs and went home well pleased.

It pays to remember that the English and Irish traditionally did not get along. In the mines the English and Welsh had the better-paying jobs as miners, while the Irish worked as miners' helpers or laborers. The Welsh and English also were able to make the transition to jobs outside the mine, while most Irish remained in the mines for life. The Welsh had a history of mining, but the Irish were farmers until forced to emigrate by the potato famine, religious persecution, and personal and political oppression.

Tensions flared after the Irish began to emigrate to America in large numbers during the 1840s. The local papers attacked the Irish Catholics for their beliefs and their lifestyles. A small number of Irishmen attacked the Welsh Congregational Church in Ashton in 1850. Enraged Irishmen jeered, cursed, threw rocks and broke windows during services.

There was a lighter side to life in the coal regions, despite the sectarian violence, hard work, alcoholism, crime, and industrial disaster. There were parades and celebrations. New Year's Day, Washington's Birthday, St. Patrick's Day and July Fourth were usually celebrated. The 1852 Fourth of July Temperance Celebration proceeded like this:

> The participants gathered at the Summit Hill Temperance Hall and then marched to the Presbyterian Church for hymns and prayers. The parade featured the following: The Mauch Chunk Brass Band, the Cadets of Temperance, and The Sons of Temperance. Upon exiting the church, they marched through Summit Hill and Ashton and returned to Mrs. Simpson's Temperance Hotel in Summit Hill for dinner. The brass band played, and J.H. Chapman read the Declaration of Independence.

A less religious celebration occurred on the fortieth anniversary of the Battle of New Orleans. The Carbon Guard of Summit Hill invited the Cleaver Artillerists and the German Jaegers of Mauch Chunk to participate in a parade and military demonstration. The Mauch Chunk militia groups marched to the Carbon Guards armory building in Summit Hill, where Nathan Patterson gave a patriotic speech. The companies paraded and manoeuvered in the streets of Summit Hill. The militia groups then had dinner at Abram Harris' Eagle Hotel, and the officers spent an hour drinking toasts.

The baseball team from Weatherly. The town had a variety of industries, including Lehigh Valley Railroad shops, and a silk mill. Courtesy, Raymond E. Holland Collection.

(Above) Safety practices were taken seriously by coal companies and other industries from the early part of the twentieth century after the "Safety First" movement started.

(Below) The Lehigh Valley Railroad's pay train at the Weatherly yards in the 1880s. The train traveled from location to location to pay railroad workers and miners. NCM; gift of Jack Koehler.

Sometimes a celebration became violent. A brawl started at the premises of Henry Houser, probably an illegal tippling house, on July 4, 1849. Porter bottles and revolvers were freely used, according to the news account. The melée resulted in two dead and several wounded.

Sports also were popular. The workers enjoyed boxing, foot racing, and cockfighting. Cricket became popular, but after the Civil War the new sport of baseball won the hearts of the mine workers.

The area continued to grow throughout the nineteenth and early twentieth centuries, as the coal trade gained importance.

In 1871 the Lehigh Coal and Navigation Company drove a railroad tunnel through the Hauto Mountain on the north side of the Panther Valley. The tunnel provided an easier and more direct route to ship coal from the Panther Valley mines to the Lehigh River by way of the Hauto Valley and Nesquehoning. The gravity-switchback railroad was no longer needed for coal transport. The switchback portion was decommissioned, but the gravity railroad between Summit Hill and Mauch Chunk remained in use as a tourist ride.

Ashton and Storm Hill grew into one town, and were incorporated in 1877 as Lansford, after Asa Lansford Foster, an officer of LC&N. Lansford and its neighboring community of Coaldale became the centers of the company's mining operations during the last decades of the nineteenth century, and LC&N moved its coal-mining administrative functions to Lansford, where it built a large office building. The building was abandoned in the late 1950s, when the company closed its deep mines, and was destroyed by a spectacular fire in 1975. Summit Hill and Nesquehoning declined in importance as the company shifted its operations to the deep mines in Lansford, although underground mines continued to be operated at Nesquehoning and an enormous stripping operation occupied the site of the original LC&N mine at Summit Hill.

(Above) The Hauto washery in 1917.
(Below) The "Big Office," the Lehigh Navigation Coal Company's office in Lansford, built in 1873. Courtesy, Clarence Hendricks.

Breaker in Beaver Meadows burned by strikers. Courtesy, Pennsylvania Historical and Museum Commission. Charles H. Burg collection.

Both Summit Hill and Nesquehoning remained prosperous communities until the general decline in the anthracite trade during the twentieth century.

Anthracite declined for a variety of reasons. Alternate fuels, particularly oil and natural gas, became feasible for home heating during the 1920s. Furthermore, oil and gas furnace manufacturers initiated and sustained a vigorous marketing campaign for the new fuels. Anthracite companies were much slower and less cooperative in their marketing attempts to save their market.

Underground sit-down strike by miners during the 1930s.

Labor strife was a continual problem during the first decades of the twentieth century. While public opinion had supported the miners during the critical 1902 strike, by the 1920s the public had grown tired of the recurring problems between labor and ownership. The longest strike in anthracite history occurred in 1925 when the miners struck for 170 days. During and after this strike, the public seriously began turning to the new fuels.

As the market declined, the companies instituted cost cutting measures, primarily by closing the most costly collieries. This fomented more labor problems as miners argued that all collieries should remain open and work should be equalized between the collieries. This equalization movement was particularly assertive, and successful, in the Panther Valley.

Furthermore, advances in mining technology increased productivity, thereby requiring fewer miners. Finally the companies began implementing surface, or strip mining. Strip mining can out-produce underground mining by three to one, thereby eliminating more jobs. Strip mining also has given the area much of its devastated appearance.

But as the market for coal continued to decline, neither equalization, improved technology, nor strip mining could save jobs or the industry. A succession of warm winters in the late 1940s severely hurt the industry. The LC&N stopped mining coal in 1954; the company completely went out of business in 1985.

A few attempts were made by private parties to reopen the mines in the late 1950s but these also failed. A strip-mining operation remained in the 1960s that was eventually taken over by Bethlehem Mines, a division of Bethlehem Steel. This operation was sold to a newly created LC&N in 1986 and remains in operation.

An abandoned stripping operation in the Mammoth Vein in 1992. Earlier workings are clearly visible where old tunnels have been exposed. Photo by Joseph Elliott.

Stripping operations in the Mammoth Vein, west of Lansford, 1992. Photo by Joseph Elliott.

Deep mining in Panther Valley had an interesting return during the 1960s. In 1960, a group of laid-off miners leased the Number 9 mine and began underground mining operations. This employee-owned Lanscoal company remained in successful operation until 1972 (in the midst of Hurricane Agnes), when state mine regulations forced the company to close because it could not afford to purchase new fans.

By then mining was quickly becoming forgotten in the Panther Valley. Many men commuted to Bethlehem, Allentown, or Reading to work in plants and factories, preferring to raise their children in the small towns, and to remain close to elderly parents. The towns of the Panther Valley suffered high unemployment during the 1970s and consequently a significant exodus of young people.

Little has changed in the ensuing decades, except that newly retired city folk are viewing these small coal-mining towns as inexpensive and safe retirement communities.

Summit Hill celebrated the bicentennial of the discovery of anthracite in 1991. Mauch Chunk, now called Jim Thorpe, is once again a tourist town; Lansford has a successful bed and breakfast. Scholarly interest also is growing. The *Valley Gazette*, a monthly local history publication, is thriving. There are even signs that the economy is reviving.

When Old Mauch Chunk
Was Young

Mauch Chunk was one of America's original company towns. During its first thirteen years, from 1818 to 1831, the entire town was owned by the Lehigh Coal & Navigation Company; homes and businesses were leased by individuals.

Until Josiah White and Erskine Hazard started developing Mauch Chunk, there were three stone, six frame, and eight log houses located northward from the Lehigh Gap, the present site of Palmerton, to Lausanne — a total of thirteen miles. There was nothing at Mauch Chunk. The first house in Mauch Chunk was built at the lower end of the creek for Nicholas Brink, the company steward. Brink, his wife Margaret, the first woman in town, and their four children lived in one end of the house, while Brink had his bakery in the other end. A long house was built adjoining the dwelling, which served as a mess hall and barracks for up to six hundred workers, with Margaret in charge. The long house also contained a company store and offices. Nicholas was in charge of procuring provisions from Lehighton and Lausanne, as well as trekking to the post office eight miles away. A few log and frame shanties were erected soon after and a post office was opened in town in 1819.

When George Hauto made his last trip to Harrisburg as a company representative in late 1819 he delivered a report on the progress at Mauch Chunk to the Pennsylvania legislature. In the report, which was published in the *National Recorder* of February 19, 1820, he stated:

> We have erected about forty buildings for different purposes, among which is a saw-mill (driven by the river), for the purpose of sawing stuff for the use of the navigation; ... one other saw-mill (driven by Mauch Chunk Creek), a grist-mill, a mill for the saving of labor for the construction of wagons, etc. (also driven by the creek), smitheries (with eight fires), workshops, dwellings, wharves, etc. We have cut about fifteen thousand saw-logs and cleared four hundred acres of land.

Unfortunately, this early and seemingly authoritative account may be wildly exaggerated. According to Eleanor Morton, White's biographer, White was concerned about Hauto's tendency to overstate the progress made at the site. According to White, only a few log and frame shanties were erected during 1819. Hauto's mention of forty buildings seems too high based on the number of buildings that can be estimated in a drawing from 1832 as well as the fact that only one dwelling, the long house, was known to exist in 1820. Nonetheless, one might assume that the number of mills mentioned is approximately correct, since some were absolutely necessary. Hauto's account also includes the lumber camp upriver of Mauch Chunk at Lowrytown, now Rockport.

Opposite: Engraving of Mauch Chunk published in the 1872 edition of "Picturesque America."

(Left) Early engraving of Mauch Chunk, following construction of the canal and the Gravity Railroad but before the backtrack was built.

(Above left) "Canal-boats receiving Coal." Engraving from Picturesque America, 1872. *Courtesy, Ann Bartholomew.*

(Above right) The home of Samuel Leisenring, which was originally built for Josiah White and his family. *Courtesy, Raymond E. Holland Collection.*

(Left) 1852 engraving of the developing town of Mauch Chunk from Eli Bowen's Pictorial Sketch-Book of Pennsylvania.

By the start of the third decade of the nineteenth century, Mauch Chunk was beginning to take shape. In 1820, this new-born settlement was christened by the birth of its first child. Born to Nicholas and Margaret Brink, the child was named Josiah White Erskine Hazard George F. Hauto Brink, in honor of the founders of the town. A party followed his birth:

> The forest was illuminated with pine torches, plenty of good old and pure whiskey was drank, and the noise and dancing were so great that it seemed as if the very tops of the pines had caught the infection and kept time with it by waving to and fro.

The multi-named lad later became an employee of the LC&N.

In a series of articles published in the *Mauch Chunk Coal Gazette* during 1892, Samuel Lippincott, Jr., reminisced on the early days of the settlement. He wrote that his father, Samuel Lippincott, started work for the LC&N as chief clerk, bookkeeper and cashier on July 1, 1821. (He actually started on March 25, 1822.) He had been one of the original stockholders and had devised a bookkeeping system for the company. He was hired for only two months at $50.00 a month to implement his system. He never left. By 1827 he was making $1,200.00 per year as bookkeeper and was responsible for installing and updating one of the most advanced accounting systems in ante-bellum business. Later he became a prominent lumber merchant in town.

Samuel Jr. recalled that Josiah White had a house built for himself in 1821 on the hill to the north overlooking the town. According to Lippincott, Hazard's house was built at the base of the hill with steps connecting the two dwellings. There is, however, no visual evidence or LC&N documentation confirming Hazard's house. Samuel Jr. stated that he remembered staying at the White house for a few weeks in 1822 until the Lippincott residence at Number One Broadway, at the point where Race Street now meets Broadway, was completed.

The LC&N Board of Manager's minutes of March 11, 1822, show acceptance of a plan for White's house. It was to be a frame two-story plain but substantial dwelling, 20' by 33' with a staircase and a two-story kitchen attached. There is no mention of a house for Hazard, although White wrote to his wife on September 25, 1821, "The house for Erskine and Mary will be ready next summer. We are building one room of what may be a fine house as Erskine feels this one room will suit him well now. We are now plastering the stove and building a nice stairway to what will be the upper story. Starting in this way they can fix the whole to suit their plans."

Erskine Hazard moved into his new house in Mauch Chunk with his bride, Mary, in 1822. Josiah White's family moved from Philadelphia to join him in Mauch Chunk soon after. His children stayed in Philadelphia with an aunt and uncle during the school year, but his wife, Elizabeth, remained in Mauch Chunk until 1830, when she returned to the city.

An entry in the minutes of May 7, 1822, noted that the Acting Manager's (White's) house and the townhouses were to be finished shortly. The townhouses referred to were sixteen stone houses constructed on Broadway starting at, and including, Lippincott's and moving down toward the river. They were built on both sides of Broadway, below the "willow tree" and were finished in 1823, although Lippincott's may have been completed earlier. A July 7, 1823, citation shows that the LC&N had received $1069.27 in rent from the houses at Mauch Chunk. White's house cost $1745.00, according to Mathews and Hungerford's 1884 *History of the Counties of Lehigh and Carbon*.

Although Lippincott's dates cannot be trusted (he seems to be consistently one year early for most of his attributions), his description of the town is interesting and one of the very few surviving accounts from the 1820s. He described Mauch Chunk as

... [a] primitive city in those days, with a single zig-zag, crooked windy street, commencing at the river, crossing the creek at the head of what is now Broadway, carving around by the Bear Trap shop, and Jimmy McCrae's wheelwright shop up to Fatzinger's foundry. The creek at the time ran down behind the row of stone houses, and emptied into a mill pond, about where the public square now is. A mill race was afterwards dug on the side of the mountain, and the water to run the mill carried over the road leading to the hotel, the pond filled up, and the public square built up.

The mill was a stone grist mill, with two run of stones, built between 1821 and 1825 on the present site of the Hooven building, at the intersection of Race Street and Berwick Street, now called Susquehanna Street. This building would later become the site of the first indoor wire-rope factory in the United States. In 1823 the LC&N started construction of the Mauch Chunk Inn, later called the Mansion House Hotel; the building was finished in 1824 but was often altered. It was built on the south end of Berwick Street and was the first building encountered upon entering town from the south on the old turnpike road. The LC&N owned the hotel and leased it to various proprietors over the years. It was used for many LC&N functions and later housed the offices. The first landlord, James Atherton, was quickly succeeded by Edward Kimball.

Mauch Chunk in 1826, map drawn by Josiah White's nephew, Solomon White Roberts. The legend bottom left reads:
"Dwelling houses 111
Saw Mills 5
Blacksmith's Forges 19 or 20
Shoe Manufactories 3
Foundery
Boat Shed &c"
Courtesy, Raymond E. Holland Collection.

Also in 1823, a lease was granted to Messrs. Hay and Holland to build a brewery along Mauch Chunk Creek. It is uncertain whether it was ever built. White, a strict Quaker, disapproved of alcohol consumption but could not suppress it. Due to the general labor shortage of the antebellum period, the workers' demands for whiskey were met. While building the canal, the workers were granted a ration of whiskey every day. During work on the canal a stiff drink was probably necessary, now and then, to keep the workers standing waist deep in the Lehigh. The old ballad below relates that six measures of whiskey a day were granted (probably at least six ounces) and, consequently, many alcoholics resulted. Samuel Lippincott, Jr., wrote that only two cups were given daily and that very little drunkenness was seen. Regardless, the company offered each employee more than the cost of the whiskey in cash, if they would refrain from strong drink during working hours. The lease for the brewery may have been aimed at getting the workers off whiskey by offering them beer, which was considered less debilitating and sinful. Whether or not the brewery was built, it was no longer in existence by 1836 when a Mauch Chunk newspaper, echoing the town temperance movement, hoped that a brewery could be built, so that the men could have the option of drinking a good English draft ale instead of whiskey.

The following verses were prepared by Rev. Mr. Webster for a temperance celebration some years later, on July 4, 1842:

When old Mauch Chunk was young,
J_____ [Josiah White] used to say,
A man that labored hard should have
Six "Billy Cups" a day.
And so, with an unsparing hand,
The whiskey flood was flung,
And drunkards they were made by scores
When old Mauch Chunk was young.

When old Mauch Chunk was young,
At noon they blew the horn,
And, gathering thick, came gangs of men,
And so at eve and morn.
With grace and promptitude and skill
They moistened lip and tongue,
And went to work in rain and mud,
When old Mauch Chunk was young.

When old Mauch Chunk was young
Lehighton was in prime,
And fights and frolics frequently
Were had in olden time.
Like short-tailed bulls in fly-time,
They at each other sprang,
And many a battle there was fought
When old Mauch Chunk was young.

When old Mauch Chunk was young,
And Captain Abels preached,
The top notch of intemperance
By many a one was reached;
And dark the cloud of sorrow
O'er many a dwelling hung,
With deep disgrace and poverty,
When old Mauch Chunk was young.

When old Mauch Chunk was young
A treat was no great shakes
Unless before the company
Was set a heap of cakes.
And never better cakes were eat,
Or better song was sung,
Than this which we are laughing at,
When old Mauch Chunk was young.

The phrase "Billy cups" in the ballad above is derived from the name of William Speers, the "jigger boss," who was employed by the LC&N with the sole duty of regularly dispensing a jigger full of whiskey to the laborers.

While the LC&N attempted to moderate its workers' vices, it also promoted valuable social institutions. From 1821 school had been held in a log building owned by the company. It was financed in part by the LC&N, with the remainder coming from tuition. Since there was only one child in Mauch Chunk in 1820, age one, the need for a school one year later is evidence of rapid population growth. This growth was not only of single men willing to work in the wilderness but also of families and perhaps single women. There is nothing in the company records to indicate that families were sought, but White did believe that women civilized men and there would be less alcohol abuse and violence once the workers were married and settled down.

On August 25, 1823, the company decided to erect a "school building on an economical plan" as soon as business permitted. It was built on upper Broadway, near the site where Fatzinger's foundry would be constructed. James Nowlin, the "eccentric 'Irish schoolmaster'" taught at this school through 1841. In September 1829 he advertised himself as a specialist in geometry, trigonometry, and navigation as well as grammar and history. Some residents of Mauch Chunk apparently found this hard to believe and William Abels challenged him, in the newspaper, to solve some rather complex math problems to prove his competence as a teacher. Nowlin responded by having one of his private students, Patrick Sharpage, age 12, solve the problems. Nowlin was called "incompetent" and "irresponsible" for not solving the problems himself. He weathered the controversy and went on to teach the fundamentals of science to many second-generation Mauch Chunk engineers, such as Robert Sayre, the future chief engineer and general superintendent of the Lehigh Valley Railroad.

The date on this family record sampler, stitched by a nine-year-old in 1834, indicates that fine needlework skills were being taught very early in the young settlement. It reads: "Abigail Farr is my name, single is my station. Mauch Chunk is my Dwelling Place, Christ is my Salvation." *Courtesy, Ben and Carole Walbert.*

Nowlin was considered a strict disciplinarian in the classroom, meting out a crack on the knuckles for incorrect answers and disobedience. He was, nonetheless, friendly outside of the classroom and regularly played games with the children; he was beloved by his students, according to Mathews and Hungerford, who implied that his discipline was somewhat old-fashioned. He received $2.50 per pupil, per quarter. Another school was built in 1824, closer to the business district on Broadway, near the present site of the YMCA building. It was a slab building but was later lathed and pebble-dashed. Margaret Maline Brooks Dalton Sanders was the teacher.

Education was important to the paternalistic LC&N; cultural and religious activities were also encouraged. White, in his 1832 *History given by himself,* wrote:

> The first shew of fine arts in Sundry paintings was exposed to View, for 12 c ea in our Wheelwright shop at M Chunk in 11 mo 1823. [Unfortunately, no information was included concerning where the paintings came from.] ... The first Preaching at a Public Meeting in Mauch Chunk was by Henry Clark a Baptist Minister in the Wheelwright Shop at M Chunk 3 mo 12, 1823.

Quaker services had been, and continued to be, held in White's house.

In 1824 nineteen log buildings were erected above the Bear Trap on Broadway. Postal service was expanded to twice a week and the foundry mentioned above was built on upper Broadway. The foundry was run for many years by John Fatzinger and Jacob Salkeld. They rendered invaluable service to both the LC&N and the town by providing everything from steam engines to church bells.

After Charles Miner left the Lehigh coalfields and his association with Jacob Cist, he moved to West Chester, Pennsylvania, and began publishing the *Village Record*. During the summer of 1825 Miner revisited the valley in which he had expended so much effort a decade earlier. His chronicle provides a major source of information on Mauch Chunk during the 1820s. His judgement and observations seem to be dependable, although perhaps too laudatory of the LC&N achievements.

Not only did Miner provide a great amount of information on the industrial development of the upper Lehigh Valley, but he also gave an account of the town evoking its atmosphere as well as enumerating its accomplishments. He offers a romantic description of the scenery:

> [the lower Lehigh Valley presents] a scene of rural beauty and substantial wealth; while ... far ahead, the Blue Mountain rears its barren back to clouds, presenting a scene where desolation reigns in lofty and solitary grandeur.

After recounting, briefly, the tale of the LCMC and his venture with Cist, Miner begins his description of Mauch Chunk. Cist and company had used Mauch Chunk to load their arks but had made no improvements:

> We left not there a single roof of any description; we abandoned it a solitary waste, the trees grew near to the river's brink; the mountain, high and rocky, pressed so close on the Lehigh, as only to leave a narrow way for a road above and below the Mauch Chunk Creek ...

Miner sketches the short journey from Jacob Weiss's house over the bridge up past Lehighton and around the turns of the "rapid [and] roaring" Lehigh complete with dams and sluice gates, and in the distance he detects the sounds of hammers and saw-mills.

Appropriately, for the sake of travelers and tourists, the "first large and elegant building" that Miner sees upon rounding the last turn before Mauch Chunk is James Atherton's hotel, with foundation laid upon the rocks of the mountain and just enough room for a road between the building and the river. It was three stories high with double piazzas (verandas, actually):

> We found the house excellent; the beds good, the table well spread ... The lower rooms are devoted to business men chiefly — the sitting parlor and dining room are on the second floor. As we had been detained by business on the road, it was near sunset before we arrived, but our impatience to see would admit of no delay, and we walked up through the town. Several hundred buildings gradually open to your view — the streets are thronged by a multitude like a crowded wharf — the rapid dash of the saw mills; the hammers of the boat builders; the "Gee-Bright" of the lumber carters — the "Who-e come hither" of the coal haulers, & a combination of a thousand other sounds "stun the glad ear" and you stand and gaze, and wonder if it be possible that all of this can have been created within seven years.

"A Mauch-Chunk Highway." Engraving from *Picturesque America*.

Miner recounts the excitement felt upon speaking with former associates from his days on the Lehigh:

> "Don't this beat all!" said one exultingly, as he shook my hand. — "Ich dom for me," cried Totten, "Did you ever dream such a thing?" "Well Charley," said my old friend Klotz, "did you ever see the like?"

Miner would later comment that the upper Lehigh Valley "was doomed by God and Nature to an eternal solitude but is now doomed by the LC&N to eternal noise."

The year 1825 featured an incident that nearly aborted the LC&N story. White maintained a wild animal park behind his home in Mauch Chunk. Miner states that it had thirty or forty fenced-in acres containing several deer and a pair of elk. According to Miner, the elk were obtained from a "Caravan of Animals" touring the country. After the Miner visit, while entertaining friends, White tangled with an elk and sustained serious injuries. In the effort to save White, Hazard was severely bruised. The elk was killed in the struggle and was found to weigh more than 350 pounds. It was mounted and displayed for many years in the company store. White and Hazard were out of commission for several weeks.

Buildings

Miner's report includes a numerical account of the buildings in Mauch Chunk in 1825. There were seventeen stone dwellings including a large tavern, twelve of frame, sixty-six of log, twelve of plank and six of slab for a total of one hundred and thirteen, but of these, twenty-one were in the Pine Forest where the lumber camp was located. Finally, there was a school house with dimensions of 20 feet by 40 feet.

Miner provides a more detailed account of the buildings used by the company:

> Headquarters, stone office and store 36 by 50 feet, 2 stories — stone store house adjoining — two frame granaries — grist mill — three saw mills each with two saws, cutting regularly about ninety thousand feet per week — log pen large enough to hold a stock of ten thousand logs — Powder Magazine — Foundry and appendages, in which about two tons of Iron and brass machinery per week has been cast with Lehigh coal only — six smith shops 15 fires ... two wheel-wright six carpenter and other work shops — three large barns — stabling for 100 horses and oxen — boat houses — machinery for building boats — mill for breaking stone for repairing the coal road — perpetual lime kiln, 7 feet diameter 12 feet high, in which ten bushels of the fine refuse screenings of coal burn sixty bushels of lime daily.
>
> The immediate neighborhood of Mauch Chunk is nearly all barren mountains, possessing scarcely any value except for the coal, with but little good timber — hence the company have [sic] to go further up the river for a supply, and have made a settlement in the Pine Forest, 15 miles above, for chopping, hauling, sawing, boat building, rafting, &c. &c. Improvements as follows — store house — grist mill — two large barns — stabling for thirty horses and sixty oxen — two smith shops — wheelwright and carpenter shops — two saw mills cutting regularly about 50 thousand feet per week — one other saw mill — boat house and machinery for building boats.

On December 26, 1825 the board of the Lehigh Coal and Navigation Company decided to take out insurance on the hotel, grist mill, saw mills, White's house, all stone dwellings on Broadway, and other buildings not specified. The company was concerned for its property, but there was little chance of a major chain reaction fire during this period since there were many open lots and space existed between the buildings. Although the town was safe in the 1820s, the 1840s would see the threat of fire grow, since more and more open lots were being filled with wooden structures, and culminate in a spectacular blaze that destroyed the Broadway business district in 1849.

In 1827 the company built a fire-proof office (or so they thought), constructed their first bridge over the Lehigh and bought a hand-pumped fire engine, with hose and buckets, for $696.00. They continued their fire insurance at the Pennsylvania Fire Insurance Company. Seven years protection on their stone buildings cost $9,200.00 at 2½% deposit and seven years protection for their frame buildings cost $7,300.00 with a 3% deposit. During 1827 the LC&N collected $1,927.86 for rent in Mauch Chunk.

A new company storehouse was built on the present site of the courthouse in 1828. It was a two-story stone building and cost $4,562.00. When Carbon County was organized in 1843 the store was given to the county to serve as the courthouse, which it did until 1849 when it was destroyed by fire with the rest of lower Broadway, known as Market Square.

Miner provided detailed census information through 1824. There were 96 families, 106 male adults and 142 female adults, 185 boarders-working hands, 41 male and 30 female children over ten. There were also 95 males and 83 females under ten. Thirty-six births were recorded in 1824 and 30 children had already been born by July of 1825.

At the end of 1824 there were 734 people and 470 arrived since the beginning of 1825, making a total population of 1,204 at the beginning of July. This is a tremendous population increase considering that White and Hazard began operations with twelve hands in August of 1818 and there was only one woman and one child in town in 1820. Mauch Chunk certainly drew population from the surrounding area but the town also drew people from the lower Lehigh Valley. Some immigrants arrived, although most of the foreigners came later. According to census information published by White in *Hazard's Register* in May 1828, Mauch Chunk and its dependencies had 395 citizens in 1822. By 1827 the population had expanded to 1,343. Both Miner's and White's accounts provide a total for the entire township, not just Mauch Chunk.

A tax assessment list of 1828 for Mauch Chunk contains 272 names and shows that the LC&N paid $91.80 of the total levy of $160.44. The tax was assessed "on over four thousand acres of land, a grist-mill, three saw-mills, a store-house, tavern, furnace, sixteen stone dwellings, sixty-nine log and frame dwellings, forty-two horses, thirty-six oxen, and thirty-six mules," according to Mathews and Hungerford.

On May 5, 1829 the *Lehigh Pioneer and Mauch Chunk Courier* began publication, providing a new and, at times, detailed source on the development of Mauch Chunk. The paper was subsidized by the LC&N and served as an unofficial company mouthpiece. The paper was owned by Asa Lansford Foster, manager of the LC&N company store, with Amos Sisty serving as editor. It provided a forum for the company's position on social, political and economic matters, as well as providing general news, entertainment and advertisements.

The first editorial comments concerning the town contained glowing praise for the company-owned Mauch Chunk Hotel. It was described as having fifty-three "commodious" rooms and a French cook. The hotel was called, in typical nineteenth-century hyperbole, the epitome of "taste and judgement." A "handsome and expensive" gravel promenade was laid out behind the hotel where part of the mountain had been leveled; the promenade was 200 feet long and 30 feet wide. It commanded an "excellent" view of the railroad termination and coal chutes. "The Mauch Chunk Hotel vies with those of the city, but in addition it

provides the beauties of nature in their wildest garb that will gratify the restless mind." The editor appealed to tourists to visit the coal quarries by way of the gravity railroad. Mauch Chunk had begun its dual role as both an industrial-transportation center and a tourist resort.

This is an example of the common early-Victorian attitude of glorifying industrial development. Whereas later twentieth-century society condemns strip mining for leaving scars upon the landscape, the nineteenth-century mind wondered at the quarries as glorious examples of man's achievements in contest with an uncompromising nature. Much like Renaissance art where nature perfected was preferred to nature wild, nature tamed and serving the will of man was favored by the nineteenth-century mind. After millennia of mankind living in fear of nature (there was no feeling of harmony with nature until industrialism made it safe and scarce), this enthusiasm at finally being in some control became so pervasive that it was even sentimentalized. For example, on June 26, 1830, an engraving was made available at the Lehigh Pioneer and Mauch Chunk Courier office of a child's view of the coal mine, and a later generation of Mauch Chunk residents would see the young men of town taking their favorite girls on afternoon outings to the coal quarries for romance.

View up Susquehanna Street from the porch of the Mansion House in the 1860s.

Mauch Chunk, as an important mining and transportation town, was quickly becoming renowned for its industry and for its scenery and it began to attract important visitors. During October of 1828, the town received a visitor who, from her upper-class, skeptical and well-educated perspective, provided information different and more critical than that available from other observers. Mrs. Anne Royall was the widow of a wealthy Virginia gentleman-farmer, William Royall. After his death in 1813, Anne took his fortune and began traveling the United States. Her in-laws were scandalized by this woman wandering America alone, squandering her late husband's fortune. By 1823 they had his will declared void and Anne, at age fifty-four, was penniless. From the notes she took during her earlier travels she wrote a travelogue, published in 1826, that was well received but controversial due to her critical views and anti-clerical beliefs. In 1828, with a second volume published, Anne decided to tour eastern Pennsylvania.

She visited Philadelphia and the Lehigh Valley and, after a less than lovely stay in a poor hotel in Bethlehem, Royall boarded a coach for Mauch Chunk and the "celebrated" Lehigh coal mines. She began her account with the customary remarks about the scenery but quickly turned her attention to a less-picturesque aspect of the developing upper Lehigh Valley, the Irish canalmen or the "Teagues" as she called them. Her words are a combination of pity and disdain. The poor Teagues were "scarcely alive, stupid from drink."

The state of the Irish was the result not of company policy or working conditions but rather of wealth. The Irish had fled oppression and poverty. In America they worked hard and had enough money to get drunk, constantly. Royall reports that they generally lived only about eighteen months after arriving in America. Their mortality was due not as much to hard work in severe conditions as to alcohol abuse with its accompanying poor diet. This was not a universal problem among the canal workers, however. The English and Germans on the canal did not waste their time in drunkenness but took their wages home and created a comfortable existence. Royall's pity ended when a drunken, stinking, mud-covered Teague boarded her coach. The teenaged driver was unable to roust the fellow so Royall walked the last half-mile to Mauch Chunk.

The Lehigh Coal and Navigation Company attempted, as discussed above, to moderate alcohol consumption on the grounds of both Quaker morality and productivity by offering cash substitutes for whiskey, but there was such a labor shortage in the early antebellum period that a dissatisfied employee could easily find a new job, particularly on the canals, and Royall notes that many Irish canal workers were quite mobile. Whiskey was demanded and the LC&N provided it.

Upon walking into Mauch Chunk, Royall took a room at the Mauch Chunk Hotel. There were few other guests at the hotel, three ladies and two gentlemen from Philadelphia, and a handful of company clerks who boarded there. At dinner Royall was shocked to find the wife of the landlord eating with the guests. She had never seen this happen in America but attributed this breach of manners to the fact that the landlord was a hireling of the company and therefore less concerned with appearances. She found the woman crude, ugly, neglectful of her proper role and worst of all, religious, a proselytizer and head of the Tract Society in Mauch Chunk. Royall, a noted deist, quickly entered into an argument with her over the virtues and evils of the missionary movement. Royall was amazed that the company would endanger the prosperity of their establishment, quite crowded during the summer, with such a useless woman.

The visitor was the center of attention because her travelogues had been published before and were well known. This was much to the dismay of the mother who had brought her daughters to the hotel in the hope of attracting husbands. This was a common strategy in the world of Victorian resorts. The hotels were designed to help the mating ritual along by providing verandas, called piazzas, large enough for promenading and for mother to keep a watchful eye. However, Royall noted that the bachelors of Mauch Chunk were familiar with the game and "avoid them as carefully as though they were just so many wild cats."

Royall provides a brief and general description of the scenery of Mauch Chunk, offering few details but noting that it is a place

> of little beauty, the mountains approaching too near — it only pleases from its surprise, novelty, and wildness, which is unequalled by any mountain scenery I ever met with, and it will forever be what it is now, as these rocky steeps defy, alike, the hand of art and the hand of taste. Wildness, therefore, will forever reign sole monarch of Mauch Chunk, unconquerable and unsubdued.

She found the gravity railroad delightful, smooth, comfortable, scenic and thrilling. The "Pleasure Carriages" for tourist rides were privately owned and cost $.75 per ride. They operated only during the afternoon since the morning was reserved for coal transport and, with only one track operating in 1828, coal got priority.

Royall also visited the mines and described the ease with which the huge pits of anthracite were dug and loaded into the wagons that criss-crossed through the pits. The miners were a mix of Irish, German and Yankee who "work, drink whiskey, fight, receive their money in the fall, go home, spend the winter, and return in the spring." She states that they earned 80 to 90 cents daily but adds, probably inaccurately considering Miner's account, that there was no boss and they drew their wages whether they worked or played. She did find the view from the Summit mines to be spectacular.

Royall recounts her meeting with Josiah White and his wife. She was quite impressed with them; White was a man of great courtesy and knowledge, Elizabeth polite and informative. Unfortunately, Royall's visit ended on a sour note. Her bill was the highest she would be charged in America, $3.62½ for two days. The bill was steep due to the immense expense of keeping Mauch Chunk supplied by carriage, its limited accommodations, and its growing reputation as a tourist town.

She took a late carriage out of Mauch Chunk and stayed over in Lehighton. She was quite pleased by the town which had a "flourishing new appearance" and a comfortable tavern with a courteous and pleasant landlord, good fare and low rates.

Anne Royall was by no means the only notable to visit Mauch Chunk during its early period. John James Audubon visited during 1829 but spent most of his time in the pine swamps where he sketched a couple of rare bird species for his folio. Napoleon's brother Joseph Bonaparte visited in August 1829. Prince Maximillian of the west German principality of Wied brought artist Karl Bodmer in August 1832, who painted Mauch Chunk from the east side of the Lehigh River, providing one of the most reliable early views.

The area north of Mauch Chunk also became popular with tourists seeking a new vacation. Furthermore, "men of science" had discovered the Upper Lehigh Valley. The *Lehigh Pioneer and Mauch Chunk Courier* praised the geologists and naturalists who found many wonders to dwell upon:

> The forests which but a few short years past were the resort only of wild beasts, have been filled with an active population and the sound of the axe has driven the bears and wolves in search of less frequented quarters.

According to Mathews and Hungerford, by 1830 the town was growing slowly but still retained

> a very crude and rough appearance, and there was nowhere to be seen any attempt at ornament or the attainment of comforts beyond the commonest. The stone houses were all alike, — small, thick-walled, with a low second story, and they invariably displayed a door and one window below and two windows above. The fronts were finished in what is known as the "rough cast" or "pebble dashed" style.

The town was still struggling with its environment:

> The road and the creek did not occupy the same relative position that they now do [1884], and the ravine in some places was a deep, mirey marsh, thickly overgrown with brush and covered with a tangle of vines, through which a man could not make his way.

Mauch Chunk, in 1830, had 700 inhabitants with a total of 1,348 in the entire township.

On May 24, 1831, a significant change in LC&N policy was initiated. The board of managers instructed White to place advertisements in various papers offering lots in Mauch Chunk for sale, as well as in the other company towns of South Easton and Nesquehoning. A previous advertisement of May 9, 1831, in the *Mauch Chunk Courier* offered leases on the company store with smokehouses next door, and on the LC&N grist mill with two run of stones. On September 19, 1831, the first advertisement offering lots in Mauch Chunk was run in the press. The company was optimistic about the sale and the stockholders report for 1831 noted a good prospect of realizing profit from the sale because the board considered Mauch Chunk the best place in the country for enterprising individuals to establish themselves.

It was more than profit that motivated the company to begin to sell lots in 1831. Mauch Chunk was finally in position to become a self-sustaining community. Contrary to the pattern in the Schuylkill or Wyoming coalfields, where towns like Pottsville and Wilkes-Barre existed before anthracite development and a large number of small, independent coal companies emerged to exploit the market, Mauch Chunk was created only after the coal was discovered and it was built to serve as headquarters for the only company in the field. Consequently, the LC&N took all the risks and stood to gain as much of the profit as it could take.

By 1831 the structure of both the town and the productive facilities of a corporation were in place. Between 1827 and 1829 the LC&N converted the descending navigation into a canal-and-slackwater navigation system. The opening of the ascending navigation provided cheap two-way water transportation, lowering the cost of goods imported from the Lehigh Valley and Philadelphia. It also provided the company with a dependable transportation system and source of income. The gravity railroad had made coal transport economical.

By the mid-nineteenth century, Mauch Chunk had become a substantial town. In this William Rau photo from the 1890s, the conical roof on the far right marks the New Jersey Central station.

The canal brought in tourists and, more importantly, would be the artery to import the immigrant laborers who would work the mines. The mines — open pits and simple drifts — were so bountiful that deep mines would not be needed until 1844. The town now had a newspaper, which made commerce easier and also facilitated the dispersal of town-promoting information.

Perhaps most importantly, the LC&N finally had clear title to the land that it was selling. The company could be certain that it would not be subjected to a myriad of lawsuits by lot owners who themselves had been sued by the pre-LC&N owners of the property. The LC&N could always use the money garnered from lot sales for improvements at its mining and transportation facilities.

As a fitting indication of Mauch Chunk's viability and its change in status from a company town, Josiah White, founder and in essence ruler of Mauch Chunk, relinquished the position of acting manager at the start of 1832 and moved back to Philadelphia (Hazard had returned in 1824).

In the coming decades Mauch Chunk's reputation as an industrial and transportation center and as a tourist mecca flourished. For the next two decades, until White's death in 1850, the LC&N and Mauch Chunk remained at the center of the American industrial revolution. The company survived floods and depressions. The town also survived floods as well as the common enemies of antebellum American cities, fire and cholera.

Even as Mauch Chunk's preeminence as an industrial center waned in the second half of the century, its reputation as a tourist center grew and it became known as the "Switzerland of America." The gravity railroad became known world-wide as a thrill ride and remained operational until the Great Depression of the 1930s. The decline of the railroad in the twentieth century ended Mauch Chunk's tourist fame, but during the 1980s the town, rechristened Jim Thorpe, once again began to attract tourists, capitalizing on its historical significance.

Tourist cars on the "Switch Back" in the 1880s.

Black Rocks on the Black Lick:
The Village of Nesquehoning

Cramped between the Locust Mountain range on the south and the Broad Mountain on the north is the Valley of Nesquehoning, incorrectly believed to be an Indian name for "narrow valley." The Nesquehoning Valley was named by the Lenni Lenapes, not for its size, but for the stream that flows through it, west to east, emptying into the Lehigh River one mile above Jim Thorpe.

The Indians called this stream Neska-Honi meaning black or dirty lick. The stream was black, but it was not the black caused by coal fines that would later pollute the stream. It was so named, as were several other streams emptying into the Lehigh, for the hemlock that dripped from the roots of towering trees, blackening the swift-flowing stream.

Although the village of Nesquehoning resulted from coalmining operations along Room Run, a stream originating in the hills to the southwest of the village, the valley was settled in the late eighteenth century by farmers and lumberers, principally the family of Alexander Dunn. Jacob Weiss, the founder of present-day Weissport, also operated a sawmill at the mouth of the Nesquehoning Creek.

In 1792, when Reading Howell made his survey of the Lehigh River up to the Hetcheltooth Falls in the company of Timothy Matlack and William Dean, they found the valley inhabited by the family of Alexander Dunn. The location was marked "Dun's" on the map that resulted from this survey.

At this point the village of Mauch Chunk was decades from being settled, and the only structure standing at the future site of Lausanne at the mouth of the Nesquehoning Creek was the Union Sawmill. The only other nearby settlement was the land and operations of Jacob Weiss near Fort Allen.

In the year 1785 and again in 1787 workers for Jacob Weiss discovered outcrops of coal along Room Run, a stream that cut through the Locust Mountain, emptying into the Nesquehoning Creek approximately four miles west of its mouth. These coal deposits would later be "rediscovered" by Josiah White in the late 1820s, resulting in the opening of mines in 1831 and the construction of the Room Run Railroad.

The Room Run Railroad was built with stone block and wood rail topped with iron straps. Iron cars were pulled by mule and coasted by gravity, like the Mauch Chunk Railroad built a few years earlier.

The Lehigh Coal and Navigation Company advertised for miners to work in the underground mines at Room Run. The company also attempted to import workers from countries as far away as Belgium. Workers from various nationalities straggled to the valley. But by

(Above) The Nesquehoning Breaker.

(Below) Coalminers' band at Nesqhehoning. *Courtesy, Raymond E. Holland Collection.*

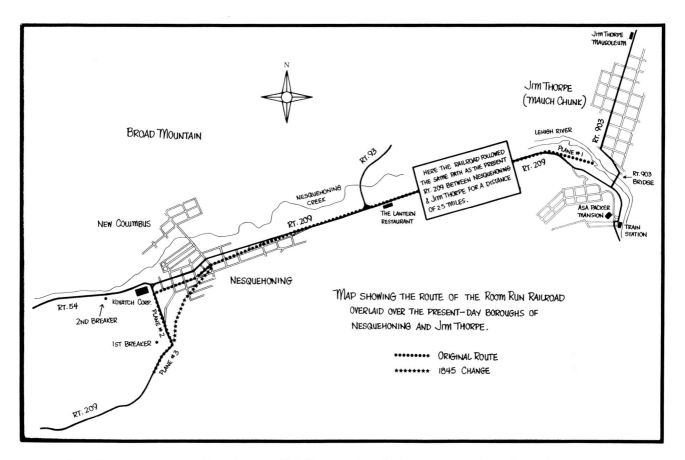

Here the railroad followed the same path as the present RT. 209 between Nesquehoning & Jim Thorpe for a distance of 2.5 miles.

MAP SHOWING THE ROUTE OF THE ROOM RUN RAILROAD OVERLAID OVER THE PRESENT-DAY BOROUGHS OF NESQUEHONING AND JIM THORPE.

•••••••• ORIGINAL ROUTE
✶✶✶✶✶✶✶✶ 1845 CHANGE

1833, when the Room Run Railroad was officially completed, there were only eighty miners living near the mines, principally English, Welsh and Irish. Later, around the turn of the century, people from other European nations including Italy, Poland and the Slavic countries would seek work in the narrow valley.

Josiah White, a stubborn man in some respects, was a man of vision in others. In 1831 White and the LC&N parted ways with the other fledgling coal companies that were springing up throughout the anthracite region of Pennsylvania. In that year the Lehigh Coal and Navigation Company ordered surveys and offered lots for sale in the towns of Mauch Chunk, South Easton and Nesquehoning, preventing the formation of company towns. White believed that by making property available to the common laborer, prosperity would come to the valley. The village plots of these towns, as well as that of Lausanne, were surveyed by Enoch Lewis.

In May of 1831 Josiah White, acting manager of the LC&N, was authorized to lay out and advertise lots for sale in these towns. The first lots were bought by men with names such as Barber, Holland, Allen and Ratcliff, contractors and supervisors at the nearby mines, who built houses and rented them to the miners.

The company also hired a company physician for the Summit and Nesquehoning mines. The first physician in the area was Dr. Benjamin Rush McConnell.

By September of 1831 the village had been laid out into one hundred lots, seventeen of which had been sold at $100 each, with twenty houses erected on the seventeen lots. The remaining lots were priced at between $120 and $150 apiece. These lots were laid out along three streets, Railroad, Catawissa and Mill streets, which ran east to west. The lots were bounded on the east by School Street and on the west by Market Street. Between School

(Above) Nesquehoning (Room Run) Drift No. 1 around the turn of the century.

(Below) Miners and loaded coal cars near the entrance to the Nesquehoning Drift No. 1 after the Tamaqua and Lansford trolley had been extended through Nesquehoning to Mauch Chunk. The trolley bridge appears in the upper left of the picture.

Both photos, courtesy Jay Frantz.

(Above) Clearing a rock fall at the entrance to Room Run Drift No. 1 around the turn of the century. Richard W. Johns is holding the sledgehammer. The man with the beard is Richard (Dickie) Thomas. Courtesy, Winnifred J. Johns.

Street and Market Street lay hills with names such as Ratcliff, Holland and Allen. Railroad Street was named for its nearness to the Room Run Railroad. Catawissa Street was on the public road leading from Mauch Chunk to Catawissa.

The company encouraged settlement by donating land for schools and churches. The first schoolhouse was built in late 1831 on a triangular plot of land donated to the "settlers" in June of 1831. This was on the northeast corner of School and Catawissa streets, at the present-day site of the Corner Store. The "settlers" were also permitted to cut, free of charge, as many logs as were needed in the construction of the planned building. Two years later the company donated land for the construction of a place of worship. This land was located across Catawissa Street from the School House, on the southeast corner of School and Catawissa streets.

In 1839 the Nesquehoning Catholic Congregation decided to construct a church from stone and lime mortar, twenty-eight by forty-three feet. Andrew McCabe was placed in charge of letting contracts for the construction. Nesquehoning's first Catholic church was built on lots 52 and 54 on the north side of Catawissa Street, across from the present site of the American Legion. These lots were deeded to Francis Patrick, in trust for the congregation, for the sum of $230 in July of 1840.

In October of 1844 the LC&N directed that twenty houses, two stories high and measuring sixteen by twenty-five feet, be constructed and rented for ten percent of cost.

By 1845 the town boasted between twenty-five and thirty houses, a store and a tavern. All the buildings in Nesquehoning were whitewashed, presenting a picturesque appearance to travelers descending the Broad Mountain into the valley along the steep Lehigh and Susquehanna turnpike.

The prosperity of the citizens of the Nesquehoning Valley rose and fell with the price of coal. Men such as Asa Packer, Robert W. Packer, Charles O. Skeer and Andrew A. Douglas became rich leasing the Room Run mines from LC&N, while other men struggled to eke out a living in the damp, dark and gassy underground mines. People died in the mines, on the gravity railroad, or from epidemics that swept through the town. Nesquehoning's Shaft No. 1 had the dubious distinction of being one of the worst firedamp mines in the state.

In 1848 a smallpox epidemic swept through the town, thought by some to have been brought into the town in a bag of feathers. The disease killed adult and child alike. The obituary columns of Mauch Chunk newspapers are filled with sad accounts.

By 1850 Nesquehoning had prospered to the point that the village boasted 913 inhabitants. Population of the village would never increase much beyond twice this number.

With the death of King Coal in the mid-twentieth century the death of the village might have been predicted. But it has survived, supported by the hardy stock who immigrated to the town from the Old World, seeking religious freedom and personal liberty and a place where a living could be earned by the sweat of the brow.

Many found their homes in the Nesquehoning Valley.

Moving Coal and Moving People

Anthracite, Canals, and Railroads

The presence of huge deposits of hard coal on the upper reaches of the Lehigh River would have been merely an interesting fact, of no economic consequence, if a way had not been found to move the coal to market. The challenge was met, but not without great difficulty. In this success lay the origins of the Industrial Revolution in America. For Pennsylvania anthracite rapidly became the single most valuable energy source throughout the industrialized Northeast, and was in large measure responsible for this industrialization.

Clearly, a road such as the Lehigh and Susquehanna Turnpike, described by Vince Hydro in "Carbon's Grand Old Highway," could not have withstood the pounding of teams transporting thousands of tons of coal; besides, that road ran nowhere near Philip Ginder's rich anthracite discoveries on Sharp Mountain. Yet to produce and transport the fuel in small quantities would effectively price it out of the reach of many potential users.

In the days before railroads, the most frequent recourse for the transport of heavy goods was the nearest waterway. But the waterway in this case presented unusual problems. The Lehigh River was liable to alternate between spells in which it ran nearly dry and times of rampaging floods — floods that clear-cutting of forests and the coming of industrialization would intensify, until in recent years the regrowth of trees on the mountainsides and the construction of the Francis E. Walter, Beltzville, and Mauch Chunk Lake dams achieved some apparent measure of control over the stream.

Colonel Jacob Weiss and his colleagues of the Lehigh Coal Mine Company failed to solve the problems of making the river a reliable means of transport for coal. It was left to those two distinguished Philadelphia entrepreneurs, Josiah White and his associate, Erskine Hazard, to succeed.

The careers of White, Hazard, and their sometime partner George Hauto have been examined briefly. White and Hazard were running a nail and wire factory near Manayunk at the Falls of the Schuylkill River when, in the late summer of 1814, they bought some anthracite that came from an ark which had survived the trip down the Lehigh and Delaware rivers.

"Stone coal" from Pennsylvania's Wyoming Valley had been used during the American Revolution to help manufacture guns for the Continental Army. Even earlier, in 1746, Moravian missionaries along the Lehigh are believed to have reported the existence of deposits of anthracite near Summit Hill, which were most likely used in the forges of blacksmiths at the Moravian settlement of Nazareth, Northampton County, between 1750 and 1755. By the time the War of 1812 (June 1812 to December 1814) caused disruption in the transport of soft coal from Virginia and England, anthracite was being used in some homes and had become an established fuel in some of the small forges and foundries of the day. It had not yet been used successfully in furnaces.

White and Hazard experimented with this coal from the upper Lehigh to see whether they could use it as fuel in their own business. Their first attempts were not encouraging. Erskine Hazard, writing in 1827, recalled that with one shipment of stone coal

> a whole night was spent in endeavoring to make a fire in the furnace when the hands shut the furnace door and left the mill in despair. Fortunately, one of them left his jacket in the mill, and, returning for it in about half an hour, noticed that the door was red hot, and upon opening it was surprised to find the whole furnace of a glowing white heat.

Thrilled with the new possibilities that opened up with the accidental discovery that a draft of air had to pass *through* anthracite, rather than *over* it, for the fuel to generate the steady, dependable, white-hot heat of which it is capable, White now sought to guarantee a reliable supply of the coal. He thought first of getting it from the headwaters of the Schuylkill River, where large coal deposits also had been discovered. But the new Schuylkill Navigation Company stood in the way of making the necessary navigational improvements to that river. Only then did White turn to the Lehigh. So financially pressed was he at this point that, when he rode up the river in 1817 with George Hauto as his companion, his horse and his surveying instruments were borrowed.

White was sufficiently impressed by what he saw to arrange to take over management of the coal mine at Summit Hill, and to lay plans to improve the road that led from it to the river. The mine had been opened by Wilkes-Barre entrepreneur Jacob Cist, a son of Jacob Weiss's old partner Charles Cist, and a man whose early death probably prevented him from obtaining as commanding a position in industrial history as White himself was to achieve.

On a new road to Summit Hill designed by White, the first properly engineered road in America, White eventually laid the gravity railroad that carried coal from the mine to the newly founded town called Mauch Chunk. This in turn became the precursor of the famous Switchback Railroad, which, after its service as a coal carrier, lingered on for many decades as a tourist attraction. For a time (1833–1870), another gravity railroad brought coal from the Room Run mines southwest of Nesquehoning to the new coal-shipping town on the Lehigh.

Josiah White, Erskine Hazard, and George Hauto formed a company to exploit the coal of the upper Lehigh area, and in 1818 petitioned the state legislature to grant them navigational rights on the Lehigh. At this point Hauto, who later had to be bought out because of his failure to make good on his fund-raising promises, performed perhaps his one and only genuine service to the partnership. He managed to persuade the legislators to grant the navigation rights sought, which gave White and Hazard virtual ownership and monopoly control over the Lehigh River, provided the lower navigation was completed within seven years and the upper within twenty years.

The first improvements on the river, though, did not include the Lehigh Navigation. White, Hazard, and their crew constructed a series of wing dams at intervals from the Nesquehoning Creek down to the Lehigh Gap. The following year, in response to a severe drought, these were widened and equipped with "bear traps," hydraulic sluices which would carry the coal arks from one dam to the next on a rush of water. Additional dams also were constructed that year.

White and Hazard had a crew of some two hundred unruly workmen, many of them foreign-born, who were housed on scows on the river as the work progressed. They got in the water and worked side by side with the men. Sometimes the work lasted as long as seven or eight months a year, every second of it hard, cold, wet, and uncomfortable.

In the end, White beat the Schuylkill Navigation Company, his old corporate nemesis, in bringing coal to market. In 1820 the first regular shipment of coal — 365 tons — arrived in Philadelphia from the upper Lehigh; historian Alfred D. Chandler dates the real beginning of the Industrial Revolution from this point. The Schuylkill company had not yet entered the coal trade.

But there still were problems. The coal came down the river by wooden arks which could not go back upstream; they had to be broken up and sold for lumber in Philadelphia. The crews had to walk or ride back to Mauch Chunk. Moreover, timber to manufacture the coal arks was already running out in the upper Lehigh area.

In 1821 White and his associates combined the two firms they had founded — the Lehigh Coal Company and the Lehigh Navigation Company — into the Lehigh Coal and Navigation Company, a name that would be prominent in the region for well over a century. White and Hazard's 1823 plan to convert the Lehigh and Delaware waterways into a ship canal capable of passing steam tugs, with tows, all the way from tidewater to the anthracite region with a minimum of lockage, died a political death in 1826. In 1827, the LC&N began construction of a navigation system that would allow two-way traffic along the river, and make possible reusable boats.

Mid-nineteenth-century engraving depicting coal arks coming through Lehigh Gap.

By 1829, the 46.01-mile canal, running from Mauch Chunk to Easton, had been completed. It had been built by local Pennsylvania Dutch workmen, "Yankees," and Irish immigrants — perhaps the first Irish to be seen in the region. The new canal was soon linked to Philadelphia by the Delaware Division Canal, and to New York by the Morris Canal across New Jersey.

Soon, in a more awe-inspiring engineering feat even than that represented by the original construction, the Lehigh Navigation was extended along the turbulent upper reaches of the river to White Haven. But as we have seen in "The Lehigh in Flood," this achievement was wiped out in the great flood of 1862.

As means of transportation and hauling, canals had several disadvantages. One was that they had to close down for several months each winter due to ice; at least, that was true for canals in the northeastern part of the United States. In the case of the Lehigh Navigation, there was still another problem: the canal could not go directly to the mines from which it derived most of its freight. It remained necessary to build connecting roads or

Ruins of a high lock south of White Haven. Thirty feet deep, this lock was abandoned when the Upper Division was destroyed in the flood of 1862.

(Above) Boats being loaded at the foot of Mount Pisgah in the late 1860s or early 1870s. These were section boats, designed to be separated in the middle for easier loading and unloading. The tracks of the Lehigh and Susquehanna Railroad run under the trestle so coal cars could be filled at the foot of the plane.

(Below) Mule tender John Grey with his mules at Lock 3, just below Mauch Chunk, in 1916. Boatmen and mules worked long hours during the canal season, from 4 a.m. to 10 p.m. Mules were fed every four hours, and rested only while the boat was going through a lock.

M. W. BALDWIN & CO., Locomotive Builders, PHILADELPHIA.

(Above) Builder's photo of a coal-burning ten-wheeler freight locomotive built for the Lehigh Coal and Navigation Company in 1861.

(Below) 2-4-0 switcher built for LC&N, photographed in 1868 at the Baldwin Locomotive Works in Philadelphia.

railways from the mineheads to points along the waterway. For these reasons, railroads began to be explored as an alternative means of transport. In Carbon County, the coal town of Beaver Meadow near Hazleton became a center of steam locomotive development. The Beaver Meadow Railroad was one of several feeders for the navigation.

The Beaver Meadow Railroad and Coal Company was incorporated in 1830, its aim being to build a 20-mile railroad from the coalfields of Banks Township to the Lehigh River and the new canal. Eventually it and its successor, the Lehigh Valley Railroad, would serve all the towns and mine patches of the area, including Jeansville, Tresckow, Audenreid, Yorktown, Colerain, and others.

But a start was not actually made on the construction of the Beaver Meadow Railroad until 1833, when two famous men surveyed the route. One was Canvass White (not related to Josiah White), the great engineer who had worked on New York's Erie Canal, and who had also made contributions to the success of the Lehigh and Delaware Division canals. The other was Ariovistus Pardee, more commonly known as Ario, a former New York farm boy who was to become possibly the most celebrated of Pennsylvania's hard coal barons and the saviour of Lafayette College in Easton.

The builders of the new railroad found that the canal tolls the Lehigh Coal and Navigation Company wanted to charge them were, by their standards, unreasonably high; so they decided to continue the railroad down to Easton. By the time they came to terms with the LC&N they had built as far as Parryville. From 1836 to 1841, Banks Township coal continued to be carried as far as Parryville by rail, and shipped by canal from there. In the latter year, one of the Lehigh's tumultuous floods washed away the entire track below Mauch Chunk, and from then on the coal carried by the Beaver Meadow Railroad was loaded onto canal boats at Mauch Chunk.

In 1860, another flood carried away some bridges, as well as the railroad's shops at Weatherly and Penn Haven. In 1864 the Beaver Meadow Railroad was absorbed by the Lehigh Valley Railroad.

The early days of the Beaver Meadow Railroad were youthful days for steam railroading in general. Technological innovation was going on everywhere, and the shops of the BMRR were no exception. The railroad's first master mechanic was a gifted Welshman named Hopkin Thomas. Thomas invented advanced mine pumps and machinery, and succeeded in adapting steam locomotives to burn anthracite instead of wood. He also invented the chilled cast-iron car wheel and built the *Nonpareil*, which may have been the first ten-wheel locomotive in the country. Beaver Meadow locomotives were among the earliest to use anthracite instead of cordwood to fire their boilers.

The railroad shops were moved from Beaver Meadow to Weatherly in 1842, following the 1841 flood. Thomas's successor as master mechanic was the revered Philip Hoffecker, who continued on into the employ of the Lehigh Valley Railroad when it took over the Beaver Meadow Railroad. Hoffecker was known for the excellence of his locomotives, and for the quality of the men who served their apprenticeship under him.

The Lehigh Valley Railroad pushed through to Mauch Chunk in September 1855. An account of the origins of this prominent railroad, chartered in 1846, may be read in the chapter on Asa Packer. At first the LVRR was headquartered in Mauch Chunk, and yards were constructed at Packerton (originally Burlington, then Dolonburg) for the construction and repair of cars. Packerton Yard specialized particularly in the construction of coal cars.

Mauch Chunk offered too little space for expansion, and the railroad's offices were moved eventually to South Bethlehem. There a connection was made to Philadelphia via the North

Penn Railroad; and there the LVRR's chief engineer and general superintendent, Robert H. Sayre, took up his residence. Sayre's elegant mansion, restored in the early 1990s as a bed and breakfast inn, was the first of many comparable homes in the Fountain Hill area. It was Sayre, not Packer, who was in control of day-to-day operations of the Lehigh Valley Railroad for many years.

The Packerton yards, the Lehigh Valley Railroad's main repair yard. Courtesy, Raymond E. Holland Collection.

When the LVRR moved to Bethlehem, the Packerton Yard continued in operation. It survived in its original location until 1973, when it was closed.

The Lehigh Valley Railroad acquired the Beaver Meadow Railroad in 1864, and five years later it picked up the Lehigh and Mahanoy Railroad, which ran from Black Creek Junction near Weatherly to Mount Carmel. In 1868 it added the Hazleton Railroad, and in 1890 it built a branch line from Lizard Creek Junction through to Pottsville. The Lehigh Valley Railroad was subsumed into Conrail in 1976. In the course of its colorful history, it was one of the main trunk lines between New York and the Great Lakes region.

Organized in 1861, the Nesquehoning Valley Railroad Company ran from Nesquehoning Junction to Tamamend in Schuylkill County. It was designed to su-

persede the Room Run gravity railroad and the Switchback railroad as a carrier for coal from the mines of the Lehigh Coal and Navigation Company. This railroad, approximately seventeen miles in length, became part of the Lehigh and Susquehanna Railroad — a name relatively few readers will recognize, unless they are railroad buffs.

The Lehigh and Susquehanna Railroad's extension from White Haven to Easton had its origin in the devastating freshet of 1862, that flood which had wiped out almost all of the Lehigh Navigation from White Haven to Mauch Chunk. This section, as we have seen, was never rebuilt. In fact, its reconstruction was forbidden by law, since it was believed that the bursting of the dams on the upper reaches of the Lehigh had contributed to the devastation caused by the flooding in the lower parts of the valley. The appalling damage in this flood was the result of sawmill dams breaking during a heavy rain. The force of this water caused log booms to break, sending hundreds of thousands of logs crashing through the large dams, releasing enormous volumes of water and smashing everything in their path.

To take the place of the Upper Grand Division of the navigation system, the Lehigh Coal and Navigation Company was given a charter to extend a railroad between Mauch Chunk and White Haven. This was the Lehigh and Susquehanna, which had begun as an inclined plane from White Haven to Wilkes-Barre in 1839. On the White Haven end it linked up to

The Reliance was built by Baldwin for LC&N's Lehigh and Susquehanna Railroad in 1865. A wood-burning 0-6-0, it was designed for secondary branch or colliery service, possibly for switching.

Built for the Lehigh and Susquehanna in 1866, the wood-burning, ten-wheeler Wapwallopen was a main-line freight locomotive.

(Right) The advantages of rail transportation compared with canals in the Lehigh River Valley are clearly depicted in this early photograph of a unit train hauling anthracite from Carbon County on the Lehigh and Susquehanna Division of the Central Railroad of New Jersey.

The railbed is above the floodway, so was less prone to damage from flooding and ice, and one train could haul significantly more anthracite than one canal boat. The size of canalboats was constrained by the narrow dimensions of the locks on the state-constructed Delaware Canal.

The Lehigh Navigation remained in operation as long as it did because coal dealers along the Delaware Canal in Bucks County were dependent on boats to deliver anthracite. There was no railroad that followed the Delaware River in Pennsylvania. After roads were improved to withstand heavy traffic, truck hauling supplanted canal boats and the navigation went out of business.

(Below) A symbol (general) freight train on the Lehigh Valley Railroad heading south through Lehigh Gap. Palmerton is in the distance. Ruins of the bridge abutment for the Lehigh and New England bridge can be seen on the hillside.

(Left) The Lehigh and New England bridge across the Lehigh River at Lehigh Gap under construction during the winter of 1911-1912.

(Below) The first trains over the bridge on July 8, 1912.

Both photos, courtesy Raymond E. Holland Collection.

(Above) View across the Lehigh River at Packer's Dam to East Mauch Chunk. The Central Railroad of New Jersey is in the forefront. A train is on the tracks of the Lehigh Valley Railroad on the other side of the river. Upstream were "coal pockets" where coal from mines east of the river was stored, and where canal boats and trains were loaded with anthracite.

(Left) The old Lehigh Valley Railroad station at East Mauch Chunk figured in the story "Last Train From Mauch Chunk" by John O'Hara, a native of Pottstown. During the mid-twentieth century, author Joan Campion sometimes met her grandfather, LVRR locomotive engineer Myron J. Fairchild, here. This building was opened in March, 1902, to replace the station seen below. The station was burned for firemen's practice, and the site is now the parking lot of a supermarket. Photo from the Lud Larzelere Collection.

(Left) The magnificent Victorian station at East Mauch Chunk. This was the third station on this site. It was closed in March, 1902, when the station seen above was opened. 1897 photograph by William Rau, one of the photographers who contracted with the Lehigh Valley Railroad to take pictures of places along its trackage for promotional purposes.

the Ashley Planes, which carried trains via the Wilkes-Barre-Scranton Railroad across the mountains to the Wyoming Valley. Later, in 1867, the Lehigh and Susquehanna was extended to Easton. Its rail system was leased by the LC&N to the Central Railroad of New Jersey, and for this reason it became known locally as "the Jersey Central," or just "the Central."

The Lehigh and New England Railroad was organized by the LC&N in 1895, when the company picked up the pieces of several failed attempts that had started in 1872 to build a railroad connecting Pennsylvania with Boston. It was the most consistently profitable component of the LC&N until the late 1950s. By 1904 it had replaced the Lehigh and Hudson Railroad for transporting coal to New England and upstate New York. Around 1912 the Lehigh and New England built an extension through the Lizard Creek valley of East Penn Township to Tamaqua. There it connected with a line that reached from Hauto to Tamaqua, joining all the LC&N collieries in the Panther Valley. Its trackage linked the coalfields of the Panther Valley with the cement manufacturing centers of the Lehigh Valley, and stretched from Tamaqua in the west to Allentown in the south and Maybrook, New York, in the north and east.

The Lehigh Valley Railroad and the New Jersey Central were important carriers of passengers, as well as of coal and other freight. In fact, as we shall see, the LVRR played a key role in helping to develop early, rail-based tourism in the Carbon County region, as well as along its entire system. Even the Lehigh and New England and the tiny Chestnut Ridge Railway that ran from Palmerton to Kunkletown carried a certain number of passengers, although these were for the most part employees respectively of the Lehigh Coal and Navigation Company and of the New Jersey Zinc Company.

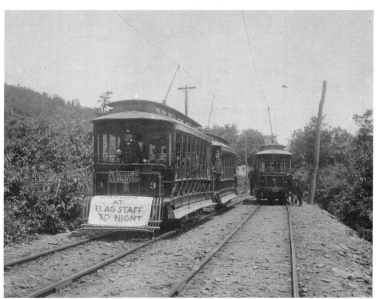

Trolleys on the Flagstaff-Lehighton line. Courtesy, Raymond E. Holland Collection.

All in all, trains represented a very important means of moving around the county, especially prior to the coming of the automobile. But they were not the only means; there also were trolleys, or electric railways. The first of these was run by the Carbon Transit Company, incorporated in 1892 and later known as the Carbon Street Railway Company. Its original line ran between Mauch Chunk and East Mauch Chunk. Later it ran a line over the Flagstaff Mountain to Lehighton. Flagstaff Park, with its famous "ballroom in the clouds," had opened in 1901. The easiest way to visit the park, which became a mecca for Big Band music, was by trolley.

Other trolley lines led from Lansford to other pleasure spots — Lakeside Ballroom, Lakewood Park, and Manila Grove in nearby Schuylkill County, for example. Hard as it now is to imagine, the Panther Valley area of Carbon County in particular once was criss-crossed by trains and trolley tracks, many of them offering mobility for the price of a few coins.

This situation continued well into the automobile age; but it was doomed in part by the illusion of even greater freedom offered by automobiles. Cars and trucks could go where even trolleys and trains could not. The hidden costs of this convenience — to the consumer's

The Lansford Depot in the Panther Valley, near the Hauto Tunnel, with a trolley on the trestle. Could that be ... an outhouse perched over the edge of the creek?

wallet and physical well-being, as well as to the environment — could not, in those early days, be foreseen.

As the mining and use of anthracite declined, the railroads of the region lost their main freight. As the use of the automobile spread, both they and the trolleys lost their passengers. Thus, perhaps inevitably, the county lost two things it has never really regained — an efficient means of moving heavy freight, and an efficient public transportation system.

The loss, of course, was not merely local. The pattern was repeated across the country in the period from about 1930 to about 1960. The results have been massive, but still gridlocked, superhighways; a new type of pollution known as smog; and a state of affairs in which large segments of the populace are far less able to get around than were their ancestors in the heyday of railroads and trolleys.

Construction of the trolley line to Flagstaff Park. This group photograph was taken at Flagstaff.
Courtesy, Raymond E. Holland Collection.

Death at Mud Run

October 10, 1888, was a festive day in Hazleton, Pennsylvania; on that day the town played host to some twenty thousand visitors. Under the auspices of the Catholic Diocese of Scranton, they had gathered to celebrate the birthday of the Rev. Theobald Matthew, a Catholic priest known in his time as the Apostle of Temperance. "Father Matthew's Day," as it was called, was a very big annual event in the diocese, as elsewhere. It provided an occasion for righteous exuberance and sober good times. But this particular celebration was to prove a prologue to tragedy. Before the day was over, sixty-six lives would be lost in the worst train disaster in Carbon County annals, and one of the worst in the history of American railroading.

The Lehigh Valley Railroad had allocated more than half of its passenger cars to carrying the excursionists to and from Hazleton. There were seventy-eight cars divided into eight sections, and each section was pulled by two giant eight-wheeled locomotives.

For the return trip, Section 5 was headed by the locomotive *Maine*, with engineer Thomas Major of Mauch Chunk at the controls. Harry E. Cook, engineer, and Hugh Gallagher, fireman, both of Wilkes-Barre, led the sixth section in the new locomotive No. 452, *Millcreek*.

At about 8 p.m., near the mouth of Mud Run between Penn Haven Junction and White Haven, Cook and Gallagher spotted Major's section ahead of them. They were then traveling at about twelve miles per hour, and the railroad signals indicated it was safe to proceed.

But suddenly Cook spotted a man waving a white signal with desperate energy from the station platform. He hit the brakes at once; but the weight of the two ponderous locomotives meant that the train could not possibly stop in time to avoid a crash.

The only passengers on Major's section who had a fair chance for survival were those few on the platform of the rear car. Seeing a collision impending, a number of them dived for safety, and lived.

Cook's lead locomotive sliced into the rear car of the section ahead of him, and carnage followed. The cars were made of wood; they telescoped into each other, crushing many of their occupants. Fire broke out in the rubble, so that some who had avoided being crushed were burned to death. In all, sixty-four people were killed outright, and two died later. There were numerous injuries as well, many of them permanently disabling. The dead included thirty-six members of a boys' drill corps from Avoca, a town whose total population at the time came to only about three hundred families.

Six months after the disaster the two locomotive engineers, Harry Cook and Thomas Major, were placed on trial for criminal negligence. It is said that in the interval, Major — a young man in his mid-thirties — had aged to the point where his hair was white, and he walked like an old man. The two were acquitted of the charges against them, and it is hard to see how it could have been otherwise. They were proceeding as the railroad signals had directed them; and Cook had reacted at once to the emergency signal from the station platform. In terms of the mass he had to control, it was simply too late for effective action. The tragedy haunted him for the rest of his days; he talked about it often, and always maintained his innocence of wrongdoing as if he himself could not quite believe in it. That, too, was to be expected. A jury acquittal, however justified by the evidence, does not guarantee an acquittal by one's soul.

(Above) The Lehigh Valley Railroad's inspection train, which inspected the rails to forestall problems that might result in loss of time or life.

(Right) A steam-powered wreck car on the LVRR, one of the pieces of equipment that would have been sent to the site of a wreck to recover derailed cars or locomotives. Lewis P. Peters of East Mauch Chunk was the photographer who took this stereographic view. *Courtesy, Raymond E. Holland Collection.*

(Below) A derailment on the Lehigh Valley at the coal dock at Black Creek Junction in October 1928. *Courtesy, Raymond E. Holland Collection.*

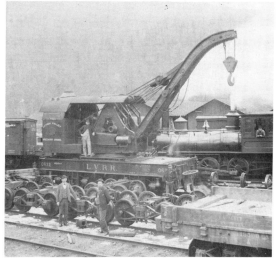

Carbon's Grand Old Highway:
The Lehigh and Susquehanna Turnpike

In the twentieth century, mammoth eighteen-wheel tractor trailers pause on Route 93 to downshift in preparation for the treacherous ride down Broad Mountain into the Nesquehoning Valley. Not quite two hundred years ago, four-wheel stagecoaches prepared for the same descent by hitching logs to the rear by chain and rope. Dragging heavy trees down the steep mountainside helped manage the speed of these early brakeless vehicles.

Although Pennsylvania roads can sometimes seem rugged, today's macadam and concrete highways are a far cry from the first trails laid through present-day Carbon County by the Indians. As irregular as they may have seemed to the white settlers who discovered them, these trails were not haphazard paths leading through the countryside, but rather well defined and well known to the various tribes that used them.

One of the most famous of these trails was the Nescopeck or Warrior's Path, which once crossed the Nesquehoning Valley before heading over the Broad Mountain toward Berwick on the Susquehanna River.

When white men set about to make roads through Pennsylvania's wilderness, they used these trails to the greatest extent possible. This was true of the Lehigh and Susquehanna Turnpike, which followed a substantial part of the Nescopeck Path, from Lausanne at the mouth of the Nesquehoning Creek through Luzerne County to present-day Berwick.

The Lehigh and Susquehanna Turnpike, sometimes incorrectly called the Easton and Berwick Pike, was a true turnpike, with special preparation of the roadbed and tollgates placed at intervals along its length. Although stage lines operated along the entire route between Berwick and Easton, between Lausanne and Easton there were no tollgates, except for a small private section near Parryville operated by John Dieter Bowman. And although the Lehigh and Susquehanna Turnpike did not run through Mauch Chunk, Susquehanna Street in that town was named after the pike.

The Lehigh and Susquehanna Turnpike was not the first highway to run along this well-defined route. Two earlier state roads terminated at Lausanne. The first, a road laid from Berwick to the Union Saw Mill at the mouth of the Nesquehoning Creek was constructed by Evan Owen, who later selected the site and established the village of Berwick. This road cost the young government of Pennsylvania one hundred and fifty pounds.

Another road, leading from the Lehigh Water Gap to the mouth of the Nesquehoning Creek, was laid out by Nicholas Kern, Jr., of Slatington for two hundred pounds.

The Evan Owen road appears to have been laid entirely over the Nescopeck path, except for a small section along the Nesquehoning Creek. The Nicholas Kern road used parts of the Moravian Road, constructed in the 1740s, which also used sections of the Nescopeck Path. Nicholas Kern, Jr., was awarded the contract to construct his road on July 26, 1792. By November 9, 1804, he had completed his work. Even while Kern's road was under construction, Governor Thomas McKean was considering legislation to incorporate the Lehigh and Susquehanna Turnpike Company. The act permitting the incorporation was signed on March 19, 1804.

The president of the corporation was Anthony Morris of Philadelphia. Some of the managers included William Turnbull, Godfrey Haga, Nathan Beach, Benjamin R. Morgan and Thomas C. James. Morris and James jointly owned land at Lausanne, at the mouth of the Nesquehoning Creek. Godfrey Haga was involved with the Lehigh Coal Mine Company and William Turnbull was responsible for sending down the Lehigh one of the first ark loads of coal from Lausanne.

When completed, the turnpike was thirty miles long. It boasted a capital stock subscription of $22,000 ($100 per share), $10,000 of which was subscribed by the State of Pennsylvania. The road was twenty feet wide and sixteen inches deep. The roadbed consisted of a base of earth covered by a layer of larger rocks, topped with gravel.

In December of 1805, upon receiving a report from the officers of the turnpike company, the governor of Pennsylvania appointed three commissioners to "view" the road and report upon its successful completion. Philip Ginder, the man who had discovered coal on Sharp Mountain in 1791, was one of these viewers. The other men were Thomas Chalkely James and Samuel Webb, Jr.

On December 20, 1805, after the viewers delivered a favorable report, the Lehigh and Susquehanna Turnpike Company was authorized to erect gates and collect tolls. The first tollgate was put up at the proposed village of Lausanne at the mouth of the Nesquehoning Creek. The final tollhouse was at Nescopeck, opposite Berwick. Other tollhouses were located at the base of the Broad Mountain in the Quakake Valley, on the summit of Spring Mountain, on the southern approach to Hazleton, on the ridge prior to the descent into the Conyngham Valley and on the Nescopeck Mountain.

Records indicate that the road was expensive to maintain. Tolls received during the years 1819 to 1821 averaged fifteen hundred dollars per year. Annual payout to the gatekeepers along the road was two hundred dollars. Annual repairs for the road ran from four hundred twenty-five dollars for 1820 to highs of nine hundred dollars and one thousand dollars in 1819 and 1821.

Turnpike roads turned out to be poor investments for the many who chose to invest in them. They were soon in competition with canals and railroads for passenger traffic. But before becoming obsolete, the Lehigh and Susquehanna Turnpike was important for helping to settle the lower parts of Luzerne County. Produce and other goods traveled south on the road while settlers from the lower part of the state, including Northampton County Germans, headed north over the road, helping to settle Luzerne and other upper counties.

One of the prime purposes of the turnpike was to divert farm goods away from Baltimore and toward Philadelphia. The turnpike was especially popular during the winter months, when sleds were used for hauling over the rough road.

As a result of the popularity of the turnpike, taverns sprang up along the route. These were generally warm and cheerful places where weary wayfarers could obtain a hearty meal and a good night's rest. One of the most popular was the Landing Tavern at Lausanne, which was a famous stopover on the Easton-Berwick stage route.

In spite of the many taverns along the way, sections of the route were dangerous. Along these stretches travelers could be waylaid by bandits and murderers. This included the seven-mile stretch over the Broad Mountain, which was particularly treacherous on dark nights and during the winter months.

In March of 1869 the state legislature authorized abandonment of the section of the Lehigh and Susquehanna Turnpike located between Lausanne and Beaver Meadow. Maintenance of this section of the road was turned over to the townships through which it passed; after 1885 the section was completely deserted. As a result, the Broad Mountain stretch became especially dangerous.

The remaining portions of the turnpike continued to be used. As late as November 20, 1875, a meeting of the Lehigh and Susquehanna Turnpike Company was held in Audenried to elect officers.

The route of the turnpike over the Broad Mountain was reopened in the twentieth century, but not as a tollroad. As the automobile became popular motorists formed auto clubs, which lobbied the state government for the improvement of various roads.

Today's Route 93 between the Nesquehoning Valley and Berwick, the original Route 309, was laid substantially over the whole of the Lehigh and Susquehanna Turnpike. Improvement of the roadbed began during the Great Depression, continuing a process that began in the dawn of Carbon County's past.

Wings Over Carbon County

Carbon County has never been a major aviation center; the place simply has too small a population base for that. Nevertheless, its involvement with flying is a long and interesting one, going back to the decade following Wilbur and Orville Wright's successful flight at Kitty Hawk, North Carolina. Dr. Joseph Humphries, Sr., a wealthy Lehighton dentist, is believed to have been the first county resident to own a plane. That was in the days when flight was synonymous with romance and excitement. Certainly it was exciting to the young boy who, one day in 1916, watched a biplane touch down in a pasture in Franklin Township. The pilot could have been "Dr. Joe," although there is no proof of this. The boy, though, was Jacob M. "Jake" Arner, considered the pioneering figure in Carbon County aviation.

The sight of the plane taxiing to a stop in the pasture was a life-changing experience, but it was not something Arner could act on at once. For a boy growing up in the county in those days, aspiring to a career in aviation simply was not realistic. When he was old enough, he went to work for the New Jersey Zinc Company in Palmerton.

Meanwhile, the aviation field was growing prodigiously, creating both heroes and victims in the process. Lindbergh conquered the Atlantic in 1927. In 1928 another aviator, once also famous but now almost forgotten, decided to come to Lehighton. Martin Jensen had been one of twelve pilots involved in the horrific Dole Pineapple Air Race, from Oakland, California, to Honolulu, Hawaii. Of the twelve, no fewer than ten had crashed on takeoff or been lost at sea. Jensen did not win the race, but his achievement in placing second — not to mention in merely surviving — gave him a certain notoriety. Now he wanted to manufacture aircraft, and to do it in a place close to moneyed New York, but far from New York's high labor costs.

The original airfield at Lehighton was the grassy center of the race track on

Workmen assembling a Jensen airplane inside the hangar at the Lehighton Airport. Courtesy, Byron Arner.

Pioneer Carbon County flyer Jake Arner, right, leading passengers from a plane following a flight. The airfield represented the latest in modernity at the time. Courtesy, Byron Arner.

the fairgrounds at the west end of town. When that grew too small, as it soon did, a nearby field was purchased — one that sloped away to a line of trees and a steep drop-off to the Mahoning Creek on the western end. Nervous passengers sometimes wondered whether, when they reached the end of the field, they would be airborne or creekborne. Next to this field, Jensen built a hangar, which became the main exhibit building of the Carbon County Fair and was converted in the early 1990s into school district offices. He opened a flight school, and laid plans for the manufacture of Jensen Aircraft. Young "Jake" Arner spent as much time as he could at the place, becoming a licensed aircraft mechanic and earning a pilot's license. Only two Jensen planes were ever manufactured. The Crash of 1929 intervened, and suddenly no one was buying aircraft. Martin Jensen left town under something of a cloud; some Lehightonians had lost money in his venture.

Famed aviator Martin Jensen, left, with Maurice Solt, Lehighton aviation enthusiast, who once wrote an aviation column for the Lehighton Evening Leader. Photo taken in California in the 1970s, shortly before Jensen's death.
Courtesy, Byron Arner.

Jake Arner kept the Lehighton airport going, and kept trying to fly. He barnstormed, landing at places like Deer Trail Park in the Poconos above Mauch Chunk, and taking passengers for rides. "At that time," recalled his son Byron Arner, "they used to take them up for a penny a pound."

During World War II, the hangar at Lehighton was used as a classroom for aircraft mechanics; around that time, Arner was in partnership with a man named Fred Getz.

(Above) An autogiro in the snow at Lehighton Airport in February, 1936. The pilot, William McCormick, had experience flying in the Antarctic. *Courtesy, Byron Arner.*

(Left) Recent view of the Jake Arner Memorial Airport, a county-run facility located in Mahoning Township west of Lehighton. It was opened in 1964. The Arner Flying Service is headquartered here. *Courtesy, Byron Arner.*

Air shows and plane rides were a cherished part of Carbon County Fair Week until the 1960s, when the fairgrounds field was closed and its activities were transferred to the county airport a few miles away. It may never be known how many thousands of people nervously paid a few dollars during Fair Week to have their first personal experience of flight, careening down the field toward the looming line of trees and the drop to the creek beyond.

Jake Arner sired a flying family, including some professionals. His son Byron, for example, served as a military pilot, and then flew for Eastern Airlines for thirty years. He later became the owner of Arner Flying Service, situated at the county airport in Mahoning Township named in memory of his father. Byron's son Jake also was a pilot for Air Products & Chemicals, Inc., People Express, and Eastern Airlines. Jake went on to own Flagstaff Park.

Living in the Land of Coal

In the earliest days of the coal industry in the Carbon County region, the men who worked at mining were of Pennsylvania German ("Pennsylvania Dutch") stock, in from nearby farms. They soon were joined by Welsh and English newcomers, experts on mining. In the years before the American Civil War (1861–1865), large numbers of Irish workers arrived in the region, driven by famine and oppression in their homeland. Being Catholic, largely uneducated, and unskilled in mining coal, these newcomers soon learned that oppression was still with them; their economic and social lot in the coalfields was not a happy one.

Beginning about 1880, the ethnic character of the coalfields started to change. These were the years of the "Ellis Island generations," the great influx of peoples who came to the United States through that famous gateway.

They came from Poland, Slovakia, Slovenia, Bosnia, Croatia, Italy, Russia, and other nations of southern, central, and eastern Europe. Their goals were to escape poverty and hunger, and in some cases political and religious persecution as well. Most of them spoke no English. In the coal regions they formed a new bottom rung on the social and economic ladder, beneath the Irish. Generally, no matter where they came from, they were called "Slavs" or "Hunkies."

Their coming was abetted by mine owners, who wanted the cheapest labor possible. It was resented by the Irish and other older residents, who saw the newcomers as threats to their jobs. It took time before common bonds developed between the new immigrants and those who had come before them.

Many of these ties were formed underground. The dangerous work of coal mining bred both individualism and strong camaraderie among the men who shared the perils. When disaster occurred in the mines, as it often did, the men were expected to come to each others' aid, to volunteer for dangerous rescue missions, and not to stop until the last possible man had been brought out alive, or the last body had been carried to the surface.

Working lives began early in the coalfields. At the age of nine or thereabouts — sometimes as young as six — boys would be sent to become slate pickers, or "breaker boys," at a colliery. Their job was to pick out the slate from the tons of coal that came cascading down chutes toward them all day long. It was difficult, painful work that often left them with "red top," or bleeding fingers. As mechanization increased, it could be dangerous, too; sometimes boys were mangled to death in the machinery.

Boys were not the only slate pickers. Sometimes miners who were incapacitated by black lung, or who had been injured in underground accidents and could not return to the mines, were given this job.

Dark, noisy, and dirty, coal breakers dominated the landscape, looming over patch towns all over the coal region until recent years. (Above) The patch town of Andrewsville, east of Lansford, in the early 1920s. At the end of the row of miners' houses is the breaker of colliery No. 6. (Below) LC&N's breaker No. 10 in 1904.

Breaker boys at an unidentified colliery. Courtesy, Raymond E. Holland Collection.

From breaker boy, a young man sooner or later graduated to employment underground. There he could work as a "nipper," or door tender, controlling the great wooden doors that directed air within the mines. Or he could have the dangerous job of runner, whose duty was to control the speed of coal cars moving through the mine tunnel. Or perhaps he was employed to care for the mules, who spent even more of their lives underground than he did. Once the mules were replaced by electric locomotives, called "trolleys," there were jobs for motor runners and brakemen.

After some years, a young man could aspire to become a miner's helper; still later, a miner. For most of the men in the mines, this was the loftiest goal life offered them.

Existence for their sisters was, if anything, even more circumscribed, although at least it was lived in the daylight. Girls helped with household chores, or perhaps went to work very young as maids in the house of one boss or another. They tended to marry at age thirteen or fourteen, and to become mothers shortly afterward. By the time they were twenty they often looked twice their age.

The household duties of women were burdensome, and they were very much subservient to their men. Sometimes they had boarders in their cramped mine patch houses — usually just two rooms downstairs and two upstairs — and in that case they had to cook the boarders' meals and do their laundry as well as performing similar chores for husbands and sons.

Street scene in Lansford, where mining companies erected rows and rows of two-up, two-down double houses.

English, Italian, Hungarian, Polish and Slovak warnings on a sign in a coal mine, photographed by George Bretz in the 1890s.

Mining was a high-risk occupation not only in physical terms, but in economic ones as well. Long layoffs could reduce families to illegal scavenging on culm banks for burnable lumps of coal, and to eating roots and berries.

When silk mills and, later, garment factories began moving into the region, these new industries provided jobs for women, offering many families a much-needed second income, and also getting many women out of a domestic setting for the first time in their lives. It was not much of an opening into the world; but it was one of the forerunners of the present state of affairs, in which women are found in every area of the work force.

The newcomers from central, southern, and eastern Europe were subjected to the same sort of discrimination the Irish had faced before them, compounded by the fact that many of them did not know English. Indeed, it was often the Irish who took the lead in discrimination. They were responding partly to economic fears — for the security of their own jobs — but partly also to what appears to be an inborn human fear of the unknown, and of the outsider.

In the face of harsh mistreatment, the new immigrants, no matter where they originally came from, learned to band together, to develop a sense of solidarity they had never known before. It was this solidarity that enabled them to spearhead the final, successful effort to unionize coal mining under the United Mine Workers of America — an effort in which some of them gave their lives.

It also was this sense of common interest with their fellows that enabled them to survive to see their children or their grandchildren inherit at least part of the American dream. Many of the descendants of the "Ellis Island generation" are among today's doctors, lawyers, office holders, and teachers in Lansford, Summit Hill, Nesquehoning — in fact, all over Pennsylvania's coal regions, and far beyond.

Ethnic diversity was a feature of life in the coal regions. This Croatian string sextet, or tamburitzan group, was photographed in Andrew Krexton's studio on West Ridge Street in Lansford. Left to right: Alec Repinec, Louis Vugrin, Charles Repinec, Joseph J. Geusic, group leader Victor Yanuga, and John (Yanks) Geusic. The band included descendants of the Geusics, a Croatian family who arrived in the Panther Valley in 1906 and settled in a patch near the No. 9 mine. In 1927 this group broadcast from radio stations WEEU in Reading and WAZL in Hazleton. A Christmas tradition was to travel around Lansford, Summit Hill, and Coaldale between Christmas and New Year's Day, stopping to play at the homes of Croatian families. Courtesy, Joseph J. Geusic.

(Above) Workers at the Baer Silk Mill in Lehighton. *Courtesy, Raymond E. Holland Collection.*
(Below) Band at Beaver Meadow, a major coalmining center. *Courtesy, Raymond E. Holland Collection.*

The Jews of Carbon County

For the historian, buildings are signposts. A church, a lodge or union hall, a factory, all indicate that certain groups of people were in a place at a certain time, or that certain types of activities went on there. If there are no buildings, or if the buildings do not survive, some digging may be necessary, either literally or figuratively, to reveal the patterns of life of a community. From the later nineteenth century, there were Jews in Carbon County. It was some decades, though, before they put the seal on their presence with a building; and so it is not surprising that they were overlooked by Fred Brenckman, the county's early twentieth century historian.

The Jews who came here originated in central and eastern Europe — Hungary, Russia, the Baltic states — with a few Germans as well. They were merchants and peddlers; names like Oberson, Cohen and Silver were very well known. What attracted them during the heyday of coal, zinc, the railroads and the canal was that prime necessity of any merchant — a good market for their wares. As time went on, there were also Jewish professional people such as doctors and lawyers. Some families, notably the Barsons and the Bishops, became entrepreneurs in the textile and garment industries.

At its peak, the Carbon County Jewish community had enough members to support two congregations — Congregation Sons of Israel of Lansford, and Temple Israel of Lehighton. The Lansford congregation also served the Jews of Coaldale, Mauch Chunk, Summit Hill, and Nesquehoning. It spent its existence in rented quarters, and disbanded around the mid-1950s.

Senator James Davis was the guest speaker at the groundbreaking for Temple Israel of Lehighton. The building is located on Bankway, and is the only synagogue ever built by Carbon County's Jewish population. Courtesy, Congregation Temple Israel of Lehighton.

The Lehighton congregation, which served the Jews of Weissport, Parryville, Palmerton and Slatington as well, also began its life in rented quarters. It met in Weissport's Patriotic Sons of America Hall and Culley's Hall, as well as in the Saengerbund in Lehighton. But in 1924 it built and dedicated a small synagogue, Temple Israel of Lehighton, on Bankway. High Holiday services have been held in the building yearly ever since, although the era when the congregation was served by rabbis and had weekly services is long past.

From 1939, and continuing for about twenty years, men from both the

Lansford and Lehighton congregations belonged to the Blue Mountain Lodge of B'nai B'rith, the national Jewish fraternal organization. The lodge, like the Lansford congregation, has ceased to exist. George Bloom, a prominent member of Temple Israel of Lehighton, estimated in 1993 that Carbon County had lost about 85 percent of what was once its Jewish population. Reasons for this are not difficult to seek: the economic decline of the area's former chief industries, coal, zinc, the railroads and the canal; and the changing nature of merchandizing, which has bypassed "mom-and-pop" stores in favor of malls and supermarkets.

Finally, like many young people from other groups, young Jews often left the county for educational and career reasons. Like their counterparts, they seldom came back.

The Italians of New Columbus

In the early days, newcomers to Carbon County's coal regions generally lived, or were forced to live, with others of their own kind — Welsh with Welsh, Irish with Irish, and so on. As time wore on and tolerance increased, families simply took the next available house. Slovaks, Poles and members of many other groups became neighbors, and gradually came to know and respect each other. Neighborhood ethnic divisions faded.

One of the few places in Carbon County that still retains a strong ethnic character is the Italian settlement of New Columbus, part of the town of Nesquehoning. The neighborhood's strong cultural identity does not mean that it is isolated; the newcomers took an interest in the wider life of the community, and soon earned a respected place in it.

The original Italian settlers in Nesquehoning arrived in July, 1884. They all came from the same town in Italy — Avigliano in the province of Potenza. This may have helped to assure the cultural cohesion of the group, although new elements moved in later. Their original settlement was called Little Italy, and its acknowledged first settler was a man named Angelo Vito Bochicchio.

Little Italy was situated southwest of Nesquehoning, and the Italians originally traveled to Sacred Heart Church to attend mass. In 1904 an Italian priest, the Rev. Paolo Gentile, began to travel to Little Italy to say mass; and in 1905 the groundwork for the future Our Lady of Mount Carmel parish was laid. For some time the Italian church was a mission of St. Joseph's Church, Pottsville; in 1915 it was raised to the rank of parish.

Mining operations made it necessary to abandon Little Italy in 1918. The Italian settlement was relocated to its present site on the east of Nesquehoning, and renamed New Columbus. The church was rebuilt and rededicated, and many of the houses also were moved.

The most famous pastor of Our Lady of Mount Carmel was the Rev. (later the Very Rev. Msgr.) Agnello J. Angelini, who served

The Rt. Rev. Msgr. Agnello Angelini was pastor of Our Lady of Mount Carmel Church in New Columbus (Nesquehoning) for 55 years. Monsignor Angelini was noted as the founder of the Shower of Roses Festival and the annual Blessing of Cars. During World War II he became known as "the hitchhiking priest" because, although he had no automobile, he managed to travel to the county seat at Mauch Chunk to see every Carbon County serviceman and servicewoman off to war.

the parish from 1932 to 1987. During World War II, Father Angelini achieved local renown by arising early every morning and traveling to the county seat at Mauch Chunk. There he spoke to every young man and woman about to leave for the service, and gave each a religious medal. Since he managed to do this without a car of his own, he became known as "the hitchhiking priest."

Fr. Angelini became known nationally for his annual blessing of cars and their occupants, and above all for his initiation of an annual festival in honor of St. Thérèse of Lisieux. Called the Shower of Roses, it has been held every year since 1932 on the first Sunday of October. Thérèse of Lisieux was a young French Carmelite nun of the late nineteenth century, widely popular among Catholics of many nationalities. As she lay dying, she is said to have prophesied that after her death a "shower of roses," meaning blessings, would fall. The literal annual enactment of this, with masses, a procession, and real roses dropped from a helicopter, is a religious and ethnic event that continues to draw visitors from many parts of the Northeast. There is much competition for the falling roses; those who catch them are said to be assured of good luck in the year that follows.

Outside Our Lady of Mount Carmel Church, the statue of St. Thérèse of Lisieux waits on a float for the start of New Columbus's annual Shower of Roses parade. Photo by Joan Campion.

The Shower of Roses festivity first originated in the old, wooden Our Lady of Mount Carmel Church. In the 1950s this was replaced by a new brick building. Near it can be found a rustic shrine of Our Lady of Fatima, constructed by a pious parishioner.

New Columbus and Our Lady of Mount Carmel also are known regionally for their St. Joseph's Table observance, held annually on the Sunday nearest the Feast of St. Joseph. Originally the commemoration was held on March 19, the actual feast day. It could, and presumably still can, involve as much as a week of cooking and baking in advance.

All comers are welcome at St. Joseph's Table, which is shared in gratitude for favors believed to have been received through this saint. Among the special foods prepared are *pignolatte,* tree-shaped cookies covered with sprinkles. The dough from which the *pignolatte* are made is rolled, cut, fried, and then fried again in honey. Since the parish began the St. Joseph's Table observance in 1949, at the instigation of its Sicilian members, *pignolatte* have become a sought-after delicacy in the coal region of Carbon County around St. Joseph's Day.

The Continuing Mystery
of the Molly Maguires

Were the coalfields of Carbon and Schuylkill counties bedeviled in the 1870s by the activities of a secret Irish terrorist organization called the Molly Maguires? The generally accepted answer once was an unqualified "yes." Now, historians are not so sure.

From 1877 to 1879, though, some twenty men lost their lives on the gallows, on the supposition that such an organization existed, and that they had committed murders and other crimes in its name. While some of the executed doubtless were linked to acts of violence, others were almost as certainly innocent. Yet all were convicted and sent to their deaths by a process of justice that might well be characterized, to put it mildly, as flawed.

Many books have been written on this episode in regional history, and all have been more or less controversial. These few pages will be a useful introduction.

At the core of the Molly Maguires tragedy lay the situation of Irish Catholic newcomers to the coalfields. Driven out of their native country by famine, disease and oppression, these proud, intelligent people were to find life in America not appreciably better than the existence they had left behind.

Some of the problems Irish Catholics faced in Carbon County and the surrounding region have been discussed in preceding chapters. They were the first Roman Catholics in the region, and they were despised for their religion, their nationality, and their hard drinking and other alleged moral failings by the Germans (or "Pennsylvania Dutch"), English and Welsh who came before them. Normally there was no love lost among these three groups; but in the Irish newcomers they found that most powerful of bonds, a common enemy.

Their relative lack of education held the Irish immigrants back, and effectively sentenced many of them to a life in the mines. The hopelessness of their situation certainly contributed to whatever group drinking problem they had, as it would create problems in any group similarly bereft. The coalfields were a hard-drinking region; the work and the grim grind of daily life guaranteed the attractions of alcohol.

In the mines, the Irish usually were assigned the worst jobs. They began underground as miners' helpers, as a rule; and it took them a long time to advance to miner. Even then, they were given the most dangerous and least desirable assignments.

They and their families also received the worst housing, and often they were segregated in separate mine patches. It is hardly surprising that they sometimes developed violent grudges against particularly unfair Welsh and English supervisors.

As will be seen in "Carbon County in America's Wars," there was much restiveness among the region's Irish Catholics as early as the Civil War; many of them were disinclined to fight for freedoms they felt they themselves were denied. The majority went to fight, of course, if only because they were conscripted or could not afford to pay the $300 required to remain out of uniform. Their record in combat, once they went, was resplendent; but it was a record built out of sheer necessity rather than glowing patriotic fervor.

Several additional things set Irish Catholics apart from other ethnic groups in Carbon County in the period before 1880. One was their attraction to trade unionism in the face of what they regarded, not unjustly, as oppression. Another was their noteworthy skill in politics. A third was the influence among them of a benevolent organization called the Ancient Order of Hibernians, or AOH.

Several attempts to establish a union for miners had failed before John B. Siney of Schuylkill County achieved a measure of success with the Workmen's Benevolent Association. In the course of time the WBA grew to have around thirty thousand members, distributed in some thirty locals. But Siney had difficulty in getting the men to act together; and in 1875 the union was effectively smashed as a result of what became known as the Long Strike. This five-month work stoppage was forced not by the unions, but by the mine owners. It was heavily punctuated by violence, in which both miners and mine bosses were killed by vigilante action.

The instigator and orchestrator of this strike was Franklin B. Gowen, president of the Philadelphia and Reading Company. Often referred to simply as the Reading Company, this was one of several railroads with large interests in the coal regions.

To prepare for the strike, Gowen reinforced the Coal and Iron Police, the only region-wide law enforcement agency. These police, however, respected no law except the will of the owners; and the owners had resolved to crush labor unrest in the coalfields at whatever cost. In the unfolding tragedy, Franklin B. Gowen was to continue to play a leading role.

Some Irishmen did manage to escape from life in the mines, through tavern-keeping or politics, or both. Alexander Campbell, for example, was able to buy a small hotel in Tamaqua, and later one in Lansford; and he seems to have had considerable influence among his fellow Irish. Jack Kehoe, famous for spitting on an American flag at an 1862 Carbon County Fourth of July picnic at which mine superintendent Frank W. Landon was stoned to death, later became chief of police in Girardville. Both men would pay with their lives for their relative prominence.

The Irish associated themselves from the first with the Democratic Party. This was hardly surprising, because the Whigs, the other major party of their early years in America, were nativist and anti-Irish. They came to hold many offices, from constable to commissioner, and to carry considerable weight in statewide politics. This influence was deplored by those who wanted to "pacify" the coal regions.

The Ancient Order of Hibernians was another element that set the Irish apart from their neighbors. It was not that other ethnic groups did not have benevolent associations; they did. The Welsh and the Germans had a group called the Modocs, and practically no group that came later lacked its own organization.

But none had quite the reputation of the AOH. For one thing, it was bitterly fought by the Catholic clergy, who regarded it as a secret society. This put its members at odds with their own church. For another, the AOH and the Molly Maguires were reputed to be one and the same organization. The only membership list of the alleged Molly Maguires that ever existed appears to have been a list of 347 AOH leaders supplied by Pinkerton undercover agent James McParlan.

The truth of the situation may have been something like this: In the turmoil that existed in the Carbon-Schuylkill coalfields in the 1870s, certain AOH leaders took vigilante-like action against mine supervisors and others deemed especially hostile to Irish Catholics. When the killing of such a person was decided upon, those assigned to carry out the murder were residents of a different town than the intended victim, so they could not easily be identified. Sometimes the victim seems to have been sent a warning note, featuring a rude drawing of himself in a coffin, and signed "Molly," or "Molly Maguire." The name is said to have been that of the woman leader of an anti-British organization in Ireland.

These notes, however, do not prove there was an organization called the Molly Maguires. They only prove that, in certain circumstances, it was the practice of the Irish vigilantes, for want of a better term, to send such notes.

Benjamin Bannan, the Welsh-American editor of the nativist, pro-business paper *The Miners Journal* of Pottsville, appears to have been the first to refer to "the Molly Maguires" as an independent organization of Irish terrorists whose tools were industrial sabotage and random murder. But it was probably Franklin B. Gowen, the "Mollies'" nemesis, who gave the term its broad popular circulation. During the 1871 strike by members of John Siney's Workmen's Benevolent Association, Gowen charged that the WBA was really a front for the Molly Maguires. Siney, whose cause had nothing to gain by violence, nevertheless was unable to offer an effective rebuttal to these accusations.

Franklin B. Gowen was a lawyer by profession, well educated, the son of a wealthy Irish-American Protestant merchant from Philadelphia. In early adulthood he moved to Schuylkill County, where he tried his hand at business but failed. He then read for the law, and soon was admitted to the bar. At the age of twenty-six he was elected district attorney on the Democratic ticket. Since he needed Irish Catholic votes to win, whatever animosity he may have felt toward this ethnic group was carefully hidden before and during his term.

After he left office, he joined the legal department of the Philadelphia and Reading Company. At age thirty-three, as a reward for a major legal victory, Gowen became the railroad's president. He became the spearhead in an effort to end unrest in the coal fields; and to him and other representatives of the owners of coal mines and lands, that meant crushing not only the Workmen's Benevolent Association, but also the Ancient Order of Hibernians.

Gowen began by strengthening the Coal and Iron Police. He then paid Allan Pinkerton of the renowned Pinkerton Detective Agency $100,000 to infiltrate the Ancient Order of Hibernians and the so-called Molly Maguires. The job of the infiltrating agent or agents would be to gather evidence against Irish Catholic leaders, and to foment violence between miners and supervisors. For this job, Pinkerton chose James McParlan — the same McParlan who compiled the list of 347 alleged Molly Maguires.

Born in Northern Ireland, McParlan was almost a stereotypical Irishman — handsome, ruddy-faced, a gifted singer of ballads and dancer of jigs. He was Catholic, but with a difference: he had gone to Irish Protestant schools, and prided himself on being on good terms with Protestants.

McParlan's education, and much else about him, was discovered in the course of research by Patrick Campbell, author of *A Molly Maguire Story*. Campbell, the great-nephew of Alexander Campbell (one of the victims), was led to write his book through his continuing interest in his family's tragedy. He theorized that McParlan's education might have made him an "Orangeman" (Northern Irish Protestant) in all but name, so that he lacked sympathy for his fellow Catholics. The only proof of this theory is McParlan's conduct in the coalfields in the years between 1873 and 1876. That conduct does not suggest any regard for Irish Catholics.

When the detective came to the Carbon-Schuylkill area, he had no trouble in gaining acceptance in local Irish taverns, and among their owners and regular patrons. He said his name was James McKenna, and that he was "on the run" to escape a counterfeiting charge.

Soon he became a popular and familiar presence, widely accepted. He also gained membership in the AOH, and attended its meetings. McParlan-McKenna now was in a position not only to report on what went on among the Irish Catholic leadership, but to follow the second part of his instructions and instigate trouble as well. During the Long Strike of 1875 he was seen trying to foment violence at the colliery in West Shenandoah. The miners, fortunately, backed off; their weapons were little more than wooden staves.

McParlan was to claim that, although he knew about several impending murders, there was nothing he could do to stop them without revealing himself. This may be true, although Patrick Campbell also has discovered that two of the detective's brothers, Charles and Edward, were with him, going by the maiden name of their mother, Loughrin. Campbell has raised the question of whether one of these brothers might not have been sent to deliver warnings to those in danger. The larger, and essentially unanswerable, question is to what extent McParlan himself was an instigator of murder.

The trigger that sprang the trap on the Molly Maguires, so called, was the murder of mine foreman John P. Jones in Lansford. Jones' employer, the Lehigh and Wilkes-Barre Coal Company, had known he was in danger. So had the Pinkerton Detective Agency, the Coal and Iron Police, and James McParlan — everyone, it seems, but Jones himself.

It appears that Coal and Iron Police were set to guard him at times when it was known he was not in immediate peril. The murder was planned for, and carried out, early in the morning, when Jones was on his way to work. There was not a single guard or policeman around at that time.

James Kerrigan, the leader of the group sent to kill Jones, also was personally implicated in the death of Tamaqua policeman Benjamin Yost. Kerrigan saved himself by becoming an informer. But, as Patrick Campbell has noted, there is strong reason to believe Kerrigan had sold out even before the murders; he maneuvered in such a way that he and his companions were seen by as many people as possible in the days leading up to the murders, and were caught as speedily as possible afterward.

Among those arrested in the roundup following the Jones murder was Alexander Campbell, who was charged with being an accessory before the fact.

The trials that followed are among the more unsavory legal episodes of American history. Essentially they were private trials, run by powerful corporate interests for the purpose of eliminating persons those interests regarded as troublesome. Over the short term, they succeeded very well in their object.

The trials were held in Mauch Chunk (now Jim Thorpe), Pottsville, Northumberland, and Berwick. Franklin B. Gowen appeared, in full formal dress, as chief state prosecutor. Another member of the prosecuting team was General Charles Albright, who had commanded Federal troops stationed in Schuylkill County during the Civil War. Albright appeared in court in his uniform. He seems to have nourished a special grudge against Irish Catholics, in part because he had once had difficulty in suppressing a wartime anti-draft riot in Cass Township. Samuel Dreher sat as judge for the Carbon County trials. Dreher had a reputation as a "hanging judge," a reputation he fully justified on this occasion.

Even the defendants who are likeliest to have been guilty of some of the charges against them cannot be said to have received justice. Juries were packed with known enemies of Irish Catholics. Some were Germans who did not know a word of English, and thus could not follow the proceedings. Convictions were obtained on the basis of the testimony of a paid informer (McParlan) and a turncoat (James Kerrigan). In some cases, notably that of Alexander Campbell, defense counsel mysteriously overlooked gaping discrepancies in the testimony of prosecution witnesses.

The court for its part chose to overlook challenges to the idea that all of the defendants were guilty. During the trials in Schuylkill County, for example, an eye witness to the murder of mine superintendent Thomas Sanger was brought face to face with Thomas Munley, who was accused of Sanger's murder. "Why, this is not the man I recognize at all!" exclaimed the surprised witness. Munley was convicted and executed anyway.

Alexander Campbell seems to have been deemed influential enough to warrant special efforts to guarantee he did not escape. Following his conviction and death sentence as an accessory before the fact in the murder of John P. Jones, he was tried and sentenced to death again for the 1871 murder of mine supervisor Morgan Powell. Although this new trial failed to reveal any reason for Campbell to feel animosity toward Powell, or indeed any real evidence that he was actually involved in the Powell murder, he once again was convicted and sentenced to death.

Contemporary newspaper depiction of the murder of Morgan Powell. Courtesy, George Harvan.

The first Molly Maguires executions took place on June 21, 1877. Ten men were hanged that day, six in Pottsville and four in Mauch Chunk. The Mauch Chunk victims were Campbell, Edward Kelly, John "Yellow Jack" Donahue and Michael Doyle. Those executed in Pottsville included James Boyle, James Carroll, James Roarty, Thomas Munley, Hugh McGeehan, and Thomas Duffy.

Especially in Mauch Chunk, the hangings took place in a macabre circus atmosphere. Rumors had been put about that the hills were full of thousands of armed Molly Maguires who were poised to rescue their leaders. The streets swarmed with militia, with extra Coal and Iron Police, and with so-called "Gowen Guards." In any event, the rumored rescue attempt never took place, and it is hard to see how it could have succeeded; both the Mauch Chunk and Pottsville jails were fortress-like.

In Pottsville, minutes before the executions, the Rev. D.J. McDermott, a Catholic priest who was noted for his fierce opposition to the Ancient Order of Hibernians, gave as his opinion that James Carroll and Thomas Duffy were almost certainly innocent. As Patrick Campbell has noted, if Carroll was indeed innocent, then by implication so was Alexander Campbell, since he and Carroll had been accused of conspiring together to arrange the murders of Benjamin Yost and John P. Jones.

At any rate, as Patrick Campbell argues, it is unlikely that the evidence against his great-uncle would have been sufficient to win a conviction in any regularly constituted court of law.

Jack Kehoe was perhaps the most prominent victim of later Molly Maguires trials. Kehoe was belatedly tried, convicted, and hanged for the murder of Frank Landon, the mine superintendent killed in the course of the Carbon County July Fourth picnic in 1862.

At that event, Kehoe had made himself conspicuous by spitting on the flag; and he had also threatened Landon. But the manner of Landon's death — public stoning — is more than enough proof that the Irishman was not the only person present with a grudge against the mine superintendent. There seems to have been no reason, except Kehoe's later relative prominence, to tie him, more than anyone else, to the murder. Kehoe received a posthumous pardon from Governor Milton J. Shapp in 1979. It seems at least possible that, under the right circumstances, pardons might be won for some of the others who were executed.

There is yet one small matter to discuss: the hand print of Alexander Campbell, imprinted on the wall of his cell in the Carbon County jail. Legend says Campbell placed it there as he was led out to be hanged. "There it will remain forever," he promised, "to shame the county that is hanging an innocent man."

And there, in fact, it still remains, more than a century later. County employees have painted over it many times, but it never fails to reappear.

Can it really be that the wronged ghost of a blameless Alexander Campbell continues to haunt the spot where he waited for death? That is a question not within the province of history to answer. But in a real sense, the mystery and the tragedy of the Molly Maguires continue to haunt Carbon County to this day, causing pain and divisions that may take another century to heal.

The Molly Maguires: Myth and Supposition

Myth and supposition, where facts are obscure or forgotten, often take on the mantle of truth. This appears to have happened with the story of the Molly Maguires, which has fascinated historians, reporters, and novelists since the 1870s. In the popular mind, the Molly Maguires were either symbols of resistance to oppression, early martyrs of the American labor movement, or were ruthless Irish gangsters who terrorized portions of Pennsylvania's anthracite coal fields.

Although it is probably impossible to discern the truth about the Molly Maguires, certain facts, outlined by Joan Campion in the preceding section, are known: Between 1863 and 1875 there were a number of unsolved murders in the southern and eastern portions of Pennsylvania's anthracite coal fields, twenty men were tried and hanged for these crimes, and all of the men who were convicted and hanged were Irish immigrants.

With no person or persons standing forward to claim responsibility for eradicating the so-called Molly Maguires, who were believed to have been responsible for these murders, an

Franklin Gowen

assumption has become popular in recent years that Asa Packer played a major, but secret, role in the conviction and subsequent hanging of the men. Packer is said to have been responsible for hiring the prosecution team led by Franklin B. Gowen that successfully won conviction of the men tried in Carbon County.

No known documentary evidence links Packer with the trial. Other documents, however, provide a clear link to another man, one even more influential than Packer. Consider that Packer's personal papers, if they exist at all, remain undiscovered; and neither the papers of Robert H. Sayre, the chief engineer and general superintendent of the Lehigh Valley Railroad, nor the LVRR's Board of Managers Minutes and letter books contain any documentation of Asa Packer's involvement in any way with the Molly Maguire trials.

Packer had a well-known intense personal dislike for Gowen, who was a major business rival. A strict laissez-faire capitalist, he was philosophically opposed to the anthracite coal marketing pools that were a cornerstone of Gowen's policies during the 1870s. Packer was continually attempting to find ways of building branch rail lines to tap the Reading's coal trade, while Gowen eventually retaliated by seizing control of the North Penn Railroad, the Lehigh Valley Railroad's primary link to Philadelphia. By 1877 relations between Gowen and Packer were so bad that they could not stand to be in the same room together.

All the Molly Maguire trials attracted great attention, and the press fed the public's appetite for gory detail. Opposite is the drawing published in the second edition of the Mauch Chunk Democrat on Friday, March 29, 1878, of the execution and last breath of Tom Fisher, found guilty of involvement in the murder of Morgan Powell. With the drawing was a lengthy account of the last hours, minutes, and seconds of the convicted man and his statement of innocence.
Inset No. 1 is Morgan Powell "the murdered man, for whose death Fisher was responsible." Inset No. 2 is Thomas P. Fisher "through whose instrumentality Powell was assassinated."

Certainly Packer, the founder of the Lehigh Valley Railroad, was an influential business-man in Carbon County. But he was probably not the dominant economic force in the county at the time of the Molly Maguire trials. The bulk of the anthracite tonnage carried by Packer's railroad came from areas that were not hotbeds of supposed Molly Maguire activities. In fact, the Lehigh Valley Railroad owned very little coal land in Carbon County. The only coal lands that Packer controlled within the boundaries of Carbon County were 1,094 acres of land at Beaver Meadows, which had been purchased along with the Beaver Meadow Railroad by the Lehigh Valley Railroad in 1864. Most of the anthracite shipped on the LVRR during the period of the Molly Maguire trials came from mines in the Hazleton area and other parts of Luzerne County, which were not areas of known Molly Maguire activities. It seems unlikely that Packer would perceive his economic interests to be directly threatened by Molly Maguire activities and, in particular, by Molly Maguire activities in Carbon County.

If Asa Packer's economic interests were not directly threatened, abundant evidence exists that a man who possessed greater wealth than Packer — and had a far larger stake in Carbon County's anthracite mining industry — did feel threatened by the Molly Maguires, and he took definite actions to counter what he perceived to be a danger. This was Edward W. Clark. For more than a decade Clark cast a long shadow over Carbon County, a region which, ironically, he probably never visited.

Unlike Asa Packer, Clark was not a man who founded his fortune in Pennsylvania's anthracite coal region. Instead, he was a New York- and Philadelphia-based capitalist who was looking for good investments to diversify his stock portfolio and who thought that he had found such an investment in Carbon and Schuylkill counties. He was part of a developing trend that by 1900 would witness the almost complete shift of control of the anthracite coal industry into the hands of outside owners, culminating in what historian Eliot Jones called "the anthracite coal combination."

Clark was born in 1811 in upstate New York near the village of Cooperstown. By 1851 he had become a successful lawyer and Wall Street investor with offices at New York and Philadelphia. In that year he formed a partnership with a struggling Yankee mechanic and would-be actor named Isaac Singer, who had developed the most practical of the many sewing machines that were beginning to enter the American market. A hedonist of the highest order who would eventually move to Europe to devote his enormous energies to gluttony, siring many children both legitimate and illegitimate, and producing operas, Singer readily ceded control of his invention to Clark.

Immediately, Clark displayed his organizational and entrepreneurial genius and ruthless-ness. Within a decade the Singer Sewing Machine Company had gained a virtual monopoly of the American market. Clark became one of the wealthiest men in America, and began to look for new places to invest his ever-increasing profits. One of the concerns that attracted his attention was the Central Railroad of New Jersey. The CNJ transported more anthracite by far across New Jersey to New York harbor than any other carrier, and had become one of the most profitable lines in America. By 1868 Clark had invested heavily in this railroad, thus becoming involved in the events that would almost completely reorder and consolidate Pennsylvania's anthracite coal industry.

The Lehigh Coal and Navigation Company fell under Clark's control due to the tremen-dous expenses associated with the extension of its Lehigh and Susquehanna Railroad from White Haven to Easton. This line would allow LC&N to move coal from its Wyoming and Carbon County coal fields to New York, using a connection at Easton with the CNJ. James Sitgreaves Cox, the son-in-law of Erskine Hazard, was president of LC&N at the time. It was his decision to extend and rebuild the Lehigh and Susquehanna using the most modern materials, making it the first American line to employ extensively imported steel rails. These rails lasted six times longer than conventional wrought-iron rails and would enable the Lehigh and Susquehanna to run heavier and faster trains than its rival Lehigh Valley Railroad.

Asa Packer and the other managers of the Lehigh Valley Railroad, fearing the competition of the Lehigh and Susquehanna, attempted unsuccessfully to reach an accommodation that would divert the Lehigh and Susquehanna's traffic to the LVRR at Mauch Chunk and make unnecessary the expensive extension of the Lehigh and Susquehanna to Easton. The Lehigh Valley chose to protect its interests by extending its own line northward to reach the Wyoming coal fields at Wilkes-Barre. Both the Lehigh and Susquehanna's line to Easton and the Lehigh Valley's line to Wilkes-Barre were completed in 1867.

Although the Lehigh and Susquehanna proved to be a technical success, its parent was soon facing financial difficulties. In order to finance the railroad extension and to build it with steel rails, LC&N had borrowed large amounts of money in short-term notes, in anticipation of a $5,000,000 bank loan in England. When a legal opinion (later overruled) negated the loan the management of LC&N was faced with the maturation of the short-term notes with no money to repay them. Cox resigned as president in order to make way for a prominent financier who would be able to provide the funds the company desperately needed to pay off the notes. The prominent financier who gained control of the company in 1868 was Edward W. Clark.

Clark purchased control of LC&N in order to protect his large investment in the Central Railroad of New Jersey, which was faced with the potential loss of its highly profitable anthracite shipments. On March 28, 1871, LC&N leased the Lehigh and Susquehanna Railroad, the Lehigh Navigation, its Wyoming Valley coal lands, and a portion of its Panther Valley coal deposits to the Central Railroad of New Jersey. This lease made Clark a very major player in the railroad and coalmining industry of northeast Pennsylvania: in particular he gained tremendous influence in Carbon County, where the majority of LC&N's anthracite mines were located. His power in the anthracite industry was further increased when the CNJ was forced into bankruptcy in 1876 and Clark was appointed trustee of its anthracite properties, which he reorganized as the Lehigh and Wilkes-Barre Coal Company. Coupled with his presidency of LC&N, this appointment gave him control over a far larger percentage of the anthracite mining industry than the holdings of the Lehigh Valley Railroad.

Edward White Clark

By the time of the Carbon County Molly Maguire trials of 1877, Clark was a prominent leader of the anthracite coal industry and a major economic power in Carbon County. He would have much to lose from a Molly Maguire conspiracy; and, as his past record had demonstrated, he could act decisively to protect his interests. The murders for which the Molly Maguires were tried in Carbon County occurred in Summit Hill and Lansford, towns dominated by the Lehigh Coal and Navigation Company — towns where Asa Packer's Lehigh Valley Railroad had little or no economic interest. The two murder victims, Morgan Powell and John P. Jones, were employees of the Lehigh and Wilkes-Barre Coal Company and LC&N respectively, both of which were controlled by Clark.

Clark clearly had a motive for seeking the elimination of the Molly Maguires. Documentary evidence supports his involvement. General Charles Albright, chief counsel of the Lehigh and Wilkes-Barre Coal Company, was the principal architect of the prosecution case against the Molly Maguires. Can it be a coincidence that the Lehigh and Wilkes-Barre Coal Company was controlled by Edward W. Clark during this period? Even more direct and unambiguous evidence of the link between Clark and Albright can be found in the Minute Books of the Lehigh Coal and Navigation Company. In the minutes of the April 24, 1877, meeting of the board of managers, the following entry is recorded:

> The President [Edward W. Clark] presented bills of attorneys Albright and Hughes for professional services in prosecuting the murderers of Morgan Powell amounting to $5,545, which on motion was referred to him for settlement with discretionary power.

Further evidence of Clark's involvement is contained in the minutes of the May 22, 1877, board meeting:

> The President [Edward W. Clark], to whom was referred the settlement of the bills of attorneys Albright and Hughes, reported that he had paid the bill of Mr. Hughes. He read his correspondence with General Albright in reference to his charges which he regarded as very high. Mr. Craig had reduced his charge from $1,250 to $450, and General Albright, in lieu of a reduction, proposed to make no further charge for pursuing the cases still undecided, unless when called away from home to argue before the Supreme Court.
>
> On motion, the president was authorized to make the settlement on condition that no further charges would be made.

Although the board of managers' minutes were never intended to be read by the public, Clark had no reluctance to publicize his involvement in the prosecution of the Molly Maguires. In 1878 the *American Railroad Journal* reported, under the heading "Lehigh Coal and Navigation Company," that "Mr. E.W. Clark made a short speech to show how the expenses had been increased among other items mentioned being one of $8,000 in securing the conviction of five Molly Maguires." The *American Railroad Journal* was the most popular and influential periodical devoted to the American railroad industry; it was read by prominent businessmen throughout America and Europe.

Clearly, Edward W. Clark and the management of the Lehigh Coal and Navigation Company felt that they had nothing to hide.

Entombed:
The Jeansville Mine Disaster

On February 4, 1891, twenty-five men went to work on the No. 1 slope of J.C. Haydon and Company's Spring Mountain Coal Company in Jeansville, a coal patch on the Carbon-Luzerne county border. Only twelve would survive the day — and, of these, four would return to the everyday world only after a long and nightmarish entombment. Two of the men, Charles Boyle and Patrick Coll, were assigned to remove the coal from a breast off the No. 10 gangway. What they did not know was that there was a grave error in the mine charts. The area in which they were working was not, as they supposed, a massive, solid pillar of coal, but a thin wall separating them from a flooded shaft that had been abandoned years before. Moreover, the abandoned shaft lay at a higher level than their work area.

When, around mid-morning, Boyle set off a powder charge in the coal face, the water from the neighboring shaft broke through in a powerful stream. Boyle kept watch on the evolving catastrophe as his companion went to warn the other workers. Coll quickly returned with another man, William Coyle. The three of them managed to squeeze through a tiny gap to a gangway on a higher level, and thus avoid the rolling waters. They were found by fellow miner John Mitchell, who led them from the mine.

Four of their co-workers were already on the surface: Harry Gibbons, John Nelms, John Martin, and John E. Watkins. Instead of being washed to their deaths by the subterranean deluge Boyle's charge had accidentally unleashed, which was the fate of many of their comrades, these four had been borne up the slope toward the mine entrance on the crest of the flood. This left seventeen men unaccounted for. Search-and-rescue operations began at once. The company even brought in a deep-sea diver from New York; but the diver was unable to locate the victims.

By February 23 the mine had been drained and thirteen bodies recovered. The toll included Edward Gallagher, James Ward, Bernard McCloskey, Harry Ball and Lawrence Reed, miners; Michael Smith, James Balock, Patrick Kelly, Samuel Porter, Michael Polish, Joseph Orsock and Thomas Goke, laborers; and James Griffith, bottom man.

It did not seem possible that the four men still missing could be found alive; yet the rescuers were determined to at least bring out all the bodies. At this juncture a search party led by foreman Joseph Kelshaw discovered what appeared to be fresh footprints in the mud that covered the floor of the mine. Startled, the foreman called out, "Hello! Who's there?" To the astonishment of everyone, back came the answer, "Me. Joe Matuskowitz." So the last survivors of the catastrophe were found — not only Matuskowitz, but his companions John Tomasuzcsci, Wassil Finko, and John Barno. All were so weak and emaciated that they had to be given medical treatment underground before they could be brought to the surface.

When the waters descended upon them, these four men had managed to retreat to a higher pocket in the mine tunnel. The air was good at first, though later it deteriorated; and they carefully shared and rationed their food. There was fresh water in a nearby working, but after the food ran out only Matuskowitz was strong enough to go for it. During the two days before rescue even he had been too weak to make the trip.

Having no clocks or watches, the four had lost all conception of time. They had been buried alive, at the time of their rescue, for between nineteen and twenty days. "Big Joe," as Matuskowitz was called, was the only one of the four men to refuse to return to work in the mines. Instead, he became a carpenter and saloon keeper, and prospered in his new trades. He turned down offers to appear in vaudeville with the comment, "God saved me for some other purpose."

This 1891 accident set Carbon County anthracite industry records for the number of fatalities, the number of men rescued alive, and the length of time the survivors had been trapped.

After a catastrophe of such magnitude, it would seem that little Jeansville had had more than enough. But on February 17, 1938, flood waters trapped eight miners working under the same town. This time, fortunately, the proportionate toll was not so great: one man died, but the others were rescued the following day.

Encounter at Lattimer

Not much could be done to alleviate the danger and drudgery of anthracite mining; these elements were built into the work. But the actions of individual mine bosses and the companies they worked for could do much to render the already difficult lives of the miners and their families close to impossible.

Under the influence of the Quaker Josiah White, the Lehigh Navigation Coal Company appears to have been a relatively benevolent employer; for example, it encouraged its employees in the building and owning of homes. But the LNC was not the only company with operations in the anthracite fields, even in Carbon County. And the knot of coal baron families centered in Hazleton, Luzerne County — the Pardees, Coxes, Markles, Van Wickles, and Fells — were entrepreneurs of a different stripe, hard-driving and unyielding.

Unheated, unplumbed shacks from which they could be evicted at a moment's notice were more often than not the living quarters of the miners and their families. Perpetual bondage to the company store typified their economic circumstances. After their store bills were deducted from their pay on pay days, many miners found themselves with little or nothing to take home. Small wonder that perhaps the most famous piece of folk literature from Pennsylvania's anthracite fields is a miner's epitaph from St. Gabriel's Cemetery, Hazleton. It reads:

> Fourty years I worked with pick & drill
> Down in the mines against my will,
> The Coal Kings slave, but now it's passed;
> Thanks be to God I am free at last.

(From George Korson's *Black Rock*)

The companies' policies, or at least their indifference to the welfare of their workers, often were reflected in the conduct of their supervisors and mine bosses. In "The Continuing Mystery of the Molly Maguires," we have seen how the frequent petty tyranny and capriciousness of these men helped spark labor unrest, as well as the wave of assassinations that were attributed to "the Mollies."

That conduct also led to several attempts on the part of the men to unionize. But, as has been seen, all these attempts came to nothing. In the wake of the Molly Maguire executions the miners were left still restive, but as far from effective organization as ever.

This state of affairs gratified the mine owners. To assure its continuance, they relied on an influx of new immigrants — Poles, Slovaks, Italians, and others from central, eastern, and southern Europe. It was believed that these men would be much more docile and controllable than their Irish co-workers. The Irish for their part saw the newcomers as threats to their jobs, and felt an intense antagonism toward them.

That was to begin to change, as the result of a bloody, brief encounter between labor and capital that took place at the patch town of Lattimer in Luzerne County in the late summer of 1897. It was what is now popularly called a "defining moment," after which nothing would be quite the same — not the roles of capital and labor, and certainly not the way in which the new immigrant mine workers were perceived. For it was they who took the lead in confronting the mine owners — although on an entirely peaceful basis — and it was they who paid the price.

The incident at Lattimer took place after nearly a month of labor unrest involving the operations of the Lehigh and Wilkes-Barre Coal Company, which had some operations in Carbon County. The unrest began at the Honey Brook colliery near McAdoo, Schuylkill County, because of the actions of the company's district superintendent, Gomer James.

On August 14, James succeeded in provoking the company's mule drivers to strike when he announced new procedures that would have meant extra hours of unpaid work for them. The next day he approached a group of the strikers and attacked a young boy named John Bodan with a crowbar. The workers retaliated by attacking James, and only the intervention of a foreman kept the superintendent from being beaten to death.

Bodan filed charges, and James was arrested. While he awaited trial the workers set out to close down all Lehigh and Wilkes-Barre Company operations.

For some weeks the stoppages continued and spread. The coal barons at length decided they could tolerate no more strikes and closings of mines and collieries, and ordered their hand-picked Luzerne County sheriff, James L. Martin, to restore order. To do this, Martin had to declare a state of public disorder. At that point the center of strike activity was in McAdoo, so he had to persuade the sheriff of Schuylkill County to back him up. This was not a difficult task; the sheriff of Carbon County also joined in the declaration. Martin then assembled his posse. It included such well-known names as Calvin Pardee, Jr., and Ario Pardee Platt.

The coal companies also assembled a large additional force of deputies and company guards, plus three hundred Pinkerton detectives. By this time there were some ten thousand strikers, spread out over several square miles. But it was Sheriff Martin and his posse who would encounter the contingent sent to close down the mines at Lattimer. The collision came on September 10.

Warned by John Fahy, a local organizer of the new United Mine Workers, which many of the men had joined, the strikers were resolved to avoid violence. They went without weapons, and they marched behind men carrying American flags. They had an early encounter with the sheriff's posse, during which Ario Pardee Platt tore the flag from one of the bearers and ripped it to pieces. At that point, the police chief of Hazleton intervened, insisting that the men had a right to march as long as they went around Hazleton rather than through it.

The march continued peacefully, going around the city. The posse hastily took trolleys for Lattimer.

As the strikers approached the mine patch town, Slovak miner Steve Jurich marched in front, bearing the remaining American flag. Jurich and many others soon would be dead.

Sheriff Martin confronted the strikers at the head of some one hundred fifty men, many of whom lined both sides of the road down which the miners were advancing. The sheriff drew his pistol and ordered the marchers to disperse. Most of them could not hear him, and continued to press forward.

A scuffle ensued, and Martin pulled the trigger of his pistol. It did not go off. Then someone — a witness said it was Martin — shouted "Fire!" and carnage followed.

According to one witness, at least one hundred fifty shots were fired. Men were shot down where they stood, or as they ran. When it was over, at least nineteen men were dead, and another thirty-two wounded.

In the aftermath of the massacre, the state sent in its Third National Guard Brigade under General John Gobin. The general had to contend at that point with a revolt by the wives of miners, who refused to let their men return to work. Led by a boarding house keeper, "Big Mary" Septak, about one hundred fifty women, called "amazons" by the press, raided collieries and disrupted work.

"I thought we had come to Hazleton to fight men," said a disconcerted General Gobin.

The activities of "Big Mary" and her followers were something of a rearguard action. By September 28 the miners were back at work.

The trial of posse members that followed the Lattimer Massacre was rigged in favor of the defendants, and all were acquitted. But things would never again be as they had been before. The "docile" new immigrants were docile no longer.

The strikers buried their dead in anguish and resolve. Thousands of miners hastened to join the United Mine Workers to express their solidarity with the victims. Through the tragedy, ethnic barriers began to crumble. The UMW, which, ironically, had once opposed the "new immigrants," was set on its way to becoming the single, powerful union representing virtually all anthracite miners.

The union's eventual triumph, after many previous organizing efforts had failed, was bought and paid for in large part by the sacrifice of the European immigrant miners who died at Lattimer.

Miner with his Wolfe safety lamp, used to test for mine gases, before the beginning of his shift at the No. 6 Colliery, Lansford. *George Harvan, 1951.*

George Harvan
Photographer of the Coal Fields

One picture is not always worth a thousand words: but there are exceptions, and the brilliant photographs of George Harvan are among them. In his photographic record of coalmining and the structures, artifacts, and above all people associated with it, Harvan provides us with an imaginative link to a world and a way of life that have virtually disappeared, at least from Carbon County. Presented here is a selection of his images from the Panther Valley.

"At the Breast." Miners working at the breast in the sixth level of No. 8 Colliery, Coaldale. 1949.

(Above) Mike Sabron, Joseph Mariotti, and Paul Petrash place a timber (or collar) in a notch in the gangway at Lanscoal No. 9 mine. 1969.

(Right) Ice formations had to be broken before the men could enter No. 9 mine during the winter months. 1969.

(Below) Paul Paslawsky of Coaldale walks in the water level, or ground level gangway of No. 9 mine. At this level, the water drained without having to be pumped. 1972.

Smokestacks and Black Diamonds

(Left) Two miners enter the breast from a manway at the 6th level of No. 8 Colliery. The coal here is part of the Mammoth Vein, which measures forty feet thick under the Panther Valley. 1952.

(Below) Paul Petrash of Summit Hill guides a jackhammer steel while his buddy drills a hole in a rock that is blocking a chute in Lanscoal No. 9, prior to blasting. 1969.

(Below left) Two important objects in the work of an anthracite miner were his canteen and his safety lamp. 1970.

Mike Lukas of Lansford uses a pick to drive lagging into place, while Joe Mariotti waits nearby with a sledge hammer. 1969.

(Above) Michael "Tarzan" Lukas opening the gate to allow coal to run down the chute into mine cars in the main gangway. Lanscoal, 1969.

(Top left) Mike Lukas attaching wire to dynamite in the coal seam. Lanscoal, 1969.

(Left center) This facility was neither private nor antiseptic, but it was a long way to the top. The chalk markings on the wall, or rib, were made by mine inspectors. 1970.

(Left) Stanley Stanek at the rear of a recently loaded mine car. Lanscoal, 1970.

Second from the left, above, is Sister Methodia of St. Michael's Church, Lansford, who originated the idea of making a shrine for the miners of Lanscoal. 1969.

The Holy Shrine in the water level of the No. 9 mine, below, was dedicated by the Sisters of St. Michael's Church. 1972.

(Above) Miners wait for a ride to the top in the shanty at the fourth level of No. 6 Colliery, Lansford, after their shift. Direct current heaters provided some warmth during the wait. 1953.

(Right) Clothes hang in the rafters of the wash shanty at Lehigh Coal and Navigation Company's No. 8 Colliery. A chain and pulley system hoisted the clothes to the roof beams, where they would dry overnight. 1953.

(Opposite, above) Miners eating lunch at an underground shanty at the No. 6 Colliery. 1952.

(Opposite, below) John "Cooney" Lazar. Chewing tobacco was popular with miners because smoking was prohibited under-ground. It tasted good, kept the mouth moist, and helped trap coal dust. 1969.

(Above) Miners loading a mine car with cement and brick to be used to build a barrier to hold back a mine fire in the sixth level of No. 8 Colliery. Things didn't look too good for the future of mining in the Panther Valley in 1953.

(Left) Miners at No. 8 Colliery, Coaldale, are entertained by a fashion show staged by Hess's department store of Allentown. 1952.

(Opposite) John L. Lewis, second from right, surrounded by officers of The United Mine Workers of America during a meeting held at the Altamount Hotel in Hazleton. Left to right: Marty Brennan, Tom Kennedy, Lewis, and David Stevens. 1949.

Mine cars sit empty and abandoned at the No. 8 Colliery after mining ended in the Panther Valley. The Lehigh and New England Railroad tracks and the borough of Coaldale are in the background. 1962.

Head frames, No. 8 Colliery. 1958.

Men pick up their mining gear in the wash house of No. 8 Colliery after being notified that the Lehigh Navigation Coal Company operations were being closed out. 1954.

Joseph "Mexie" Mariotti enjoys a cold beer after a hard shift at the No. 9 mine, Lanscoal. 1969.

(Above) Paul Paslawsky trudges through the snow to the wash shanty on a winter afternoon. 1967.

(Left) Mike Lukas carries a lump of coal for the stove used to heat the wash shanty. 1967.

(Opposite, above) "Long" John Matika gets a taste of fresh air as he leaves the No. 9 mine, Lanscoal, 1969.

(Opposite, below) Number 9 mine after it closed in March of 1972, and the entrance was blocked. 1973.

"Breaker Boys"
George Harvan was a publicity photographer for Paramount Pictures' film "The Molly Maguires," which was shot in Carbon and Luzerne counties. This photo was made between takes on a hot August day during filming at Eckley. 1967.

Not By Coal Alone

Anthracite coal was beyond question the prime reason for the initial development of the Carbon County region. Without the discovery of "black diamonds" on the upper reaches of the Lehigh, it is difficult if not impossible to envision the building of the Lehigh Navigation or the early pushing through of the railroads. Transportation systems seek out locations where both markets and materials for transport are plentiful. In this case, it was coal that drew thousands to the region, thus providing a market for goods shipped in; coal was the main commodity to be transported out.

Under these circumstances, it is easy to forget how numerous and how diverse were the other early industries of the region. Some of them grew up to serve the coal industry, either wholly or in part. Others were more or less independent. All affected the environment and the quality of life of the people who worked in them, lived near them, bought their goods, or drew dividends from them.

The influence of these industries was in one important way beneficial: they provided a living for thousands of families. In other ways, the influence could be less than constructive. Like coal, the mining of which involved the literal turning inside out of mountains, at great risk to the life and health of the miners, some of the county's other economic activities left lasting scars on the land.

Forest Industries

In the beginning were virgin woods. They did not long survive the coming of people of European stock to the upper Lehigh. Wood had a myriad of uses in those early days, many more than it normally has today. It was used to build houses and other buildings, and to heat them. It was needed to build arks to carry coal to Philadelphia in the earliest days; on arrival in that city, the arks were broken up and sold as timber.

Later, wood also was used to build canal boats for multiple uses — thirteen miles' length of boats in 1831, according to Carbon County's early twentieth-century historian Fred Brenckman. (Brenckman gives no source for this, nor, for that matter, any other information.)

By the early 1830s, the fledgling town of Mauch Chunk sang with the rasp of sawmills, and was an important center for boat building. Farther down the river, in 1832, Lewis Weiss started a boatyard along the Lehigh Navigation System Canal at Weissport; there he manufactured boats for the Lehigh Coal and Navigation Company, and also for the Morris Canal and Banking Company of New Jersey. Weiss was the grandson of Colonel Jacob Weiss, whose important role in the early history of the Carbon County region has already been discussed. Other prominent boat builders were Andrew Graver, who came from Lehighton but who set up business across the river in Weissport in 1836 and worked until he retired in 1847, and Nathan Snyder, another Weissport builder, whose business was active between 1846 and 1872.

In addition to the uses previously mentioned, wood was used for shoring up coal mine shafts, for railroad ties, and, in the beginning, for fueling locomotives.

Lumbering began very early in the Carbon County region — almost as soon as freedom from fear of Indian attacks made it feasible for white people to move back to the area following the American Revolution; and, for a few individuals, even earlier. One of the improvements the Quaker Benjamin Gilbert erected on the shores of the Mahoning Creek before being carried away with his family to captivity in Canada was a sawmill. As has been seen, Col. Jacob Weiss was drawn to the region by the opportunities in the timber industry. Before 1800, George Walk had a lumbering operation along Sawmill Creek in what is now Franklin Township.

When, in 1824, the Moravians of Bethlehem sold a tract of timber land near Rockport to the Lehigh Coal and Navigation Company, the company immediately established a lumbering settlement called Lowrytown. Within a few years, timber in the Laurytown Valley was seriously depleted.

(Above) Photo by famed nineteenth-century photographer William Rau of typical lumbering activities.

(Below) Way bill for a carload of lumber shipped from Carbon County to Hellertown in Northampton County.

From the northernmost part of the future county to the southernmost, lumbering or some aspect of it seemed a natural business for people to get into. There were, after all, so many trees — at least in the beginning. John Wetzel came to Packer Township (then part of Lausanne) in 1812, and set up a sawmill. Among his counterparts at the southern end were Jacob and Nicholas Snyder, who built a sawmill on the Aquashicola Creek near Lehigh Gap shortly after the American Revolution. The Snyder mill was to endure for many decades. A sawmill begun by Lewis Zimmerman in the 1850s in the Mahoning Valley survived into the twentieth century.

It was in the northern townships, among them Kidder and Penn Forest, that lumbering was most clearly the dominant industry. In Penn Forest, logging began perhaps around 1835; by the 1860s the most valuable timber was gone from the township.

In Kidder, the industry may be dated from the 1840s. As with coal operations, many of the entrepreneurs were outsiders — Israel D. Saylor and Samuel Saylor of Easton, Isaac and Samuel Gould, Mahlon K. Taylor of Bucks County. Villages naturally grew up around each company's operations. Among them were Bridgeport, dating from 1856 and resulting from the operations of Keck, Childs and Company; Saylorsville on Hickory Run, named after Samuel Saylor; and the village of Hickory Run itself, which owed its start to the Gould operations.

The town of Weatherly, originally called Black Creek, also had lumbering antecedents. In 1825 John Romig erected a sawmill along the creek at the town site. Ten years later John Smith, an agent of Asa Packer, established another such mill.

Some of the timber from the north end of the county traveled far before being sawed into saleable lumber. One town in central Carbon County, Parryville, owes its modern existence to the timber industry. Organized in 1836, the Penn Forest Lumber Company owned timber land in what is now the area of northern Carbon and southern Luzerne counties. Its sawmills, however, were at the mouth of the Pohopoco Creek, south of Lehighton; and a settlement grew up there — though the first European-stock settlers in the place had come decades earlier. The settlement around the mills on the Pohopoco was called Parrysville (later Parryville) after Daniel Parry, the president of the Penn Forest Lumber Company.

Because of its need for forest products, specifically hemlock bark, tanning may be included in this discussion of forest industries. Before 1830 a man named Meckle established what was perhaps the first tannery in the county, at Millport (now Aquashicola), Lower Towamensing Township. Reuben Miller later owned this operation, which was destroyed by fire three times before its final abandonment in 1874.

The scope of the Meckle-Miller tanning operation was small compared to that built by Thomas Smull and Company in Kidder Township in the late 1850s. It was enlarged in 1860, after which its capacity of eighty thousand hides a year made it for a time the largest tannery in the country. The village of Lehigh Tannery grew up around it, having its own post office and other amenities. The tanning vats still are visible along the upper Lehigh.

The tannery had several owners in its day, the last of which was I.M. Holcomb and Company. When it was burned in the Great Fire of 1875, discussed below, it was not rebuilt; the available hemlock bark had been exhausted, and the hemlock trees never grew back.

The fate of Lehigh Tannery was paradigmatic. Forest operations at the time were carried out without a thought for conservation — the cutting of every available tree was the rule and not the exception. Even timber not suited to any other purpose often could be used to shore up mine shafts; and Samuel W. Hudson, the most prominent early settler of Hudsondale, for one, made mine timber a very important part of his business interests.

Fires were allowed to burn out of control in the woods, although sometimes "allowing" did not enter into it. Such was the case with the Great Fire, which began near the mouth of Mud Run on May 14, 1875. After burning slowly for eight days, a period of time during which it presumably could have been brought under control, it was whipped into a fiery tempest by high winds. Before the fire had run its course it had destroyed not only Lehigh Tannery, but also houses, lumber camps, and the remaining vestiges of the timber industry in Kidder and Penn Forest townships. It also burned into Monroe County, where it did similar if not quite as extensive damage.

But the Great Fire of 1875 was only the end of a long story — a story in which, by the thoughtless squandering of resources, people progressively robbed themselves of their own livelihoods. Fred Brenckman, a Hudsondale man (and certainly no social critic), recounts that in his time nothing grew on the Broad Mountain except huckleberries, due to then-current

A lumber-related industry closely tied to the transportation of coal was the Lehigh Coal and Navigation Company's boatyard at Weissport. From 1828 to 1923 this was the company's major facility for building and repairing its boats. Company boats were stored at Weissport during winters, so they could be maintained and repaired. Boats that were well maintained lasted at least twenty years.

logging practices that left no tree standing and the habit of permitting fires to burn themselves out. Those who think of the upper part of the county as heavily forested today are, of course, right — but they should reflect that this is new-growth forest, and ponder upon the regional loss of such a fine species as the hemlock. Nature is forgiving — to a point.

Following the fire disaster of 1875, Kidder and Penn Forest townships shared a trait with the Broad Mountain; little but huckleberries grew there. The people of the townships made the best of the situation, and turned the huckleberries into a reasonably lucrative cash crop. Some economically significant distilling of wintergreen and birch oil also went on. Samuel Donner of Penn Forest Township appears to have been the first in the region to distill wintergreen oil. His operation began in 1861, and thus antedated the Great Fire by more than a decade.

The population of the townships, never very large, dropped off precipitately after 1875. Kidder Township fell from 1,207 in 1880 to 427 in 1910. From 653 in 1880, Penn Forest Township's population sank to a mere 417 in 1910.

Like the coal patch towns of the region, Carbon County's lumber towns came and went — and in most cases left even less trace, destroyed as they were by fire, or permitted to decompose back into the surrounding landscape. A coal patch town's former presence at a site is at least often signaled by abandoned mine shafts and culm piles; where the lumber camps stood there is likely to be only silence in the new-growth forest.

Think of the term "ghost town," and the imagination turns to the American West and Southwest. Yet Carbon County too is rich in ghost towns, in the form of these lost coal patch and lumber settlements. Unlike many of the western towns, they left not even a complete skeleton of a house as a reminder of their former existence.

This small graveyard in Hickory Run State Park is all that remains of a mid-nineteenth-century lumber camp.

Today, most of them are not even memories in the minds of the county's oldest inhabitants. The only traces of their existence are names in old books, or inscribed upon old maps.

Iron

It is hard, today, to imagine Carbon County as the site of an important iron industry; and yet, for a long period in the nineteenth century, the landscape was dotted with furnaces where iron ore was smelted into pig iron; forges, where it was hammered into tools and implements; foundries, where molten iron ore was fashioned into products; and rolling mills, where manufacture was by a combined process of forging and rolling.

Considering that the county has no iron ore of its own except for some pockets of paint ore or ocher, the existence of an iron industry may be hard to fathom. But what the region had to offer the iron-making process was fuel.

In the beginning, when the potential of anthracite as a fuel had not been fully understood or exploited, that fuel was wood, which was made into charcoal. Like those industries referred to as forest industries, charcoal iron-making operations consumed thousands of acres of trees; one furnace might consume an acre of forest a day. Later, when it was better understood how to make use of the abundant local hard coal, anthracite-fired furnaces were built close to the canal. Most, though not all, were gone by the beginning of the twentieth century. They fell victim to the economic depressions that occurred periodically during the latter part of the nineteenth century, and they were unable to compete with the advanced technology and economies of scale of firms like the Bethlehem Iron Company, later the Bethlehem Steel Corporation.

Iron-making and iron-working in the Carbon County region began before 1830, in what became the southern end of the county. Ore for smelting was brought in from iron deposits along the Lehigh Canal at Whitehall, while pig iron to be forged came in from Berks County. Limestone also was needed for iron-making, and much of it came from quarries in Lehigh County near the canal.

Carbon County's iron pioneers were David Heimbach, Sr., and his sons, David, Jr., and John. When he came to what was to become Carbon County, David Heimbach, Sr., was already a leader in the iron industry of his native Lehigh County; there, in Upper Milford Township, he had built Hampton Furnace in 1809.

Around 1819 he and his son David built a forge on the Aquashicola Creek, just northeast of Lehigh Gap. David, Jr., was put in charge of this forge, and in 1827 the younger Heimbach added to it the Clarissa Furnace, named after his wife. The Heimbach forge at Aquashicola is said to have provided the ironwork for the famous chain bridge which spanned the Lehigh just below Lehigh Gap for over a century, beginning in 1826. The bridge's wooden portions burned in 1926, but it was in use for some time after that. When it was razed at last, its charcoal-iron links were remarkably free of corrosion; six of them, mounted in cast-iron columns, are on display in Palmerton as a monument erected by the Board of Trade in 1936.

David Heimbach, Sr., meanwhile, had not been idle after establishing the forge at Aquashicola. In 1827 he built the New Hampton Forge in Franklin Township, near the later settlement of Harrity on the Pohopoco Creek. His son John was put in charge of the operation. David Heimbach, Sr., then returned to Lehigh County, where he died in 1834. Returning from his funeral, David, Jr., and John contracted typhoid fever, and died within twenty-four hours of each other.

After two years, William Miller acquired the New Hampton Forge and renamed it the Maria Forge after his own wife. It operated under various owners until January 1, 1859.

Other early iron entrepreneurs in the Franklin Township area included James and Daniel Laury. They seem not to have been as successful as the Heimbachs; their forge, erected in 1849 on Pine Run near the Pohopoco Creek, lasted just a few years.

In Lower Towamensing Township, the death of David Heimbach, Jr., meant that the forge and the Clarissa Furnace on the Aquashicola would pass to new owners. They were acquired by Joseph J. Albright and some of his associates. Albright was a great admirer of American statesman Senator Henry Clay of Kentucky, and renamed the complex the Ashland Iron Works in honor of his political idol's plantation home.

After the firm was flooded out by the freshet of 1841, the furnace was never rebuilt. A new, enlarged forge was constructed, only to be severely damaged by a fire soon afterward. In 1851 the property changed hands again, and in 1860 it was abandoned.

East Penn Township also was a site associated with the making of charcoal iron. In 1828 Stephen Balliet and Samuel Helfrich established Penn Forge and Furnace near what was then called Pennsville, but later became known as Ashfield.

After Helfrich died in 1830, Balliet became sole owner of the firm. He built another furnace near the original in 1837. Following Balliet's own death in 1854, the enterprise was run in succession by Solomon Boyer, Charles H. Nimson, and Balliet's son, John. It remained a charcoal furnace. Nimson, born in 1834 in East Penn Township, moved to Lehigh County in 1860, where he became superintendent of Allentown's Roberts Iron Company in 1863. He remained general superintendent when the company was acquired by the Allentown Rolling Mill Company in 1871, managing the only integrated iron company in Lehigh County during the anthracite-iron era.

Leaders in the scientific, business, and political communities were well aware of the potential impact if anthracite could be used as a fuel to smelt iron. In 1825 the Franklin Institute offered a gold medal to anyone who produced at least twenty tons of iron using mineral fuel. Nicholas Biddle, president of the Bank of the United States, and some of his business associates offered $5,000 in prize money to the first person who kept a furnace in blast for at least ninety days using anthracite alone. Legislative initiatives promoted the use of anthracite, and the pages of the *Journal of the Franklin Institute* were filled with accounts of experiments and discussions of theories and practices for using anthracite in blast furnaces. Early (1826) experiments in Mauch Chunk by Josiah White and Erskine Hazard were not too successful. They were followed by the attempts of Henry High, Joseph Baughman, F.C. Lathrop, and Julius Guiteau, begun in 1837 at White and Hazard's old site. They were a greater technological success, but not a financial one.

It was at the Crane Iron Company of Catasauqua, Lehigh County, that both the technological and financial problems were solved at last in 1840. Within ten years, ten furnaces had been constructed along the Lehigh River in Lehigh and Northampton counties — all of them dependent on anthracite from Carbon County. By 1880 there were fifty furnaces in the "Lehigh District."

But that did not mean an end to iron-related industries in Carbon County. Around 1830 the Lehigh Coal and Navigation Company sold a foundry it had built on Broadway in Mauch Chunk, near its original furnace, to John Fatzinger. Fatzinger and his partner Jacob Salkeld ran the business successfully for many years. The machinery for the Mount Pisgah planes was made by Fatzinger & Salkeld. In 1845 Edward Lippincott and Elias Miner founded the Mauch Chunk Iron Works, which continued into the twentieth century.

From 1848 to 1852, the Lehigh Coal and Navigation Company manufactured wire rope in the town. Located in the old abandoned grist mill in the center of Mauch Chunk at the foot of Race Street, this was the first indoor wire-rope factory in the country. The machinery for making long lengths of wire rope was designed by company engineers Edwin A. Douglas and George Washington Salkeld, based on an idea suggested by Erskine Hazard to adapt the concept of a French bobbin machine for twisting the strands of wire. The wire mill was leased in 1852 to Erskine's son, Fisher Hazard, who operated it in partnership with Douglas until it was transferred to a larger facility in Wilkes-Barre as part of the Hazard Manufacturing Company in 1870. In 1927 the wire rope mill became part of the American Chain and Cable Company. After several reorganizations the company continues to manufacture wire rope in the Wyoming Valley.

N.R. Penrose, a member of the famous Pennsylvania family that produced the powerful U.S. Senator Boies Penrose, opened a foundry in Beaver Meadow (then part of Banks Township) in 1848. After some years it was moved to Jeansville as the Jeansville Iron Works. Later it was relocated yet again, to Hazleton in Luzerne County. This firm supplied much of the iron for the Mahanoy Division of the Lehigh Valley Railroad.

In 1851 Merritt Abbot and Alexander Lockhart established a foundry in Summit Hill. When, after some twenty years, the building housing the venture burned down, it was not replaced.

The Parryville Furnace (above), viewed from the north. This was not the only furnace to dump its slag directly into the Lehigh River.

(Below) The town of Parryville

Lewis Weiss started a rolling mill in Weissport in 1855. That same year the brothers Dennis, Henry, John and David Bowman (or Baumann) set up the Poho Poco Iron Works, an anthracite blast furnace at Parryville. Soon the Carbon Iron Company was formed, with Dennis Bowman as its president. The company added two new furnaces in the 1860s, but found survival difficult in the 1870s. This was due both to the technological revolution in iron making, which was fast making small operations obsolete, and to the decade's prevailing atmosphere of economic depression.

The Carbon Iron and Pipe Company's furnace at Parryville, modernized by 1894 with the three regenerative stoves seen above. The Northeast Extension of the Pennsylvania Turnpike crosses directly over the furnace site.

In 1876 the firm was taken over by the Carbon Iron and Pipe Company, and pipe manufacturing became one of its offerings. Later still it was operated by the Carbon Iron and Steel Company, headed by Mahlon S. Kemmerer of Mauch Chunk. Around the beginning of the twentieth century this company had the only iron furnace in the Lehigh Valley that was still operating north of the Blue Mountain.

In Weissport, William and C.D. Miner established the Fort Allen Foundry in 1874. Like many such ventures — ultimately, like nearly all those in Carbon County — it failed to thrive over the long haul, and closed around the turn of the century.

The Weatherly Foundry and Machine Company was organized in December of 1899, eleven months after the closing of the Lehigh Valley Railroad's foundry in Weatherly. At its height it employed several hundred men. Located along the Lehigh Valley Railroad tracks, on the site of a former bicycle works, within a short time it was turning out large orders of castings for the Lehigh Valley Railroad. The foundry's other major customers in its early years included the Baldwin Locomotive Works in Philadelphia and the United States Government.

The big foundry bay of the Weatherly Casting and Machine Company. On the left are flasks, core making is on the right. *Courtesy, Mike Leib*

(Above and left) Grinding and inspecting the casting for a 3000 horsepower dredge pump for Long Island Sound. 1950s. *Courtesy, Mike Leib*

Its original directors were Fred Bertolette, president; W.H. Koons, vice president; James F. Kressley, secretary; Elmer Warner, treasurer; and J. Walter Lovatt, J.R. Cassler and J.G. Eadie.

By 1911, Weatherly Foundry and Machine Company had become the largest foundry within fifty miles, except for the giant works of Bethlehem Steel. It was acquired in 1920 by financiers from Hazleton and New York, and its name was changed to Weatherly Foundry and Manufacturing Company. In 1925 it merged with the old Hazleton Iron Works Company. Pump manufacturer Barrett-Haentjens and Company of Hazleton acquired a majority interest in the firm in 1982 and operated it as an independent unit until 1989, when Michael J. Leib, formerly the foundry superintendent, purchased the firm and changed its name to Weatherly Casting and Machine Company. The firm remains a major employer in Carbon County; it now produces a broad range of sophisticated alloy castings for specialty markets.

The Carbon Iron Works Company was established in Lehighton in 1911 by W.S. Koch. Its subsequent history is unknown. Originally founded in Palmerton, Blue Ridge Pressure Castings, Inc., operates in Lehighton today.

Other Mineral Industries

Carbon County possessed some valuable non-coal mineral deposits of its own, which permitted other mineral industries to grow up locally. In some cases these industries still survive, though they are not perhaps as vigorous as they once were.

While these mineral deposits are located in various parts of the county, special mention should be made of the Stony Ridge, or Devil's Wall. This is a ridge of craggy, resistant sandstone that begins on the East Penn Township side of the Lehigh and runs for about ten miles behind the town of Palmerton, roughly parallel to the Blue Mountain. (Sometimes the Stony Ridge outcropping on the East Penn side of the river is referred to as the Devil's Pulpit, a term which also is applied to a stony outcropping on the western wall of the Lehigh Gap.)

Except of course for coal, just about any mineral that was found in any other part of the county was found here as well, making the Palmerton-Bowmanstown area a center for mineral industries.

One thing was found in the Palmerton area that was found nowhere else north of the Blue Mountain; that was a deposit of slate. This heavy, blue-black stone was once very widely used for roofing, sidewalks, burial vaults, billiard table tops, sinks and counter tops, and school chalk boards (then called, appropriately, "blackboards.") Pennsylvania's so-called "slate belt" is a narrow area just south of the Blue Mountain. The industry still operates there on a limited basis, and it is the only place in the United States that still produces billiard-quality slate.

About 1864, Stephen Lentz discovered an anomalous slate bed on the Carbon County side of the mountain, just east of Millport, now Aquashicola. It was developed and exploited first by the Millport Slate Company, then by the Brilliant Black Slate Company, and it continued to be worked into the twentieth century.

Sometime in the 1860s, Jacob Scherer began developing sand deposits on the Bowmanstown end of the Stony Ridge. By about 1910, this industry employed some seventy-five men in the Bowmanstown area. Other sand quarries were located at Little Gap on the Blue Mountain, in East Penn Township, in Penn Forest Township, and on the east side of Weatherly.

Ocher, or paint ore, was discovered in a number of locations around the county, from the productive Stony Ridge to the northern reaches. Around 1855 Henry Bowman began using the ore from the Stony Ridge to manufacture dry metallic brown paint at Bowmanstown. His company, the Poco-Metallic Paint Company, was succeeded by the Carbon Metallic Paint Company, which was still in existence in the early years of the twentieth century.

In Millport (Aquashicola), a Mr. Lawrence established a paint factory which he later sold to A.C. Prince. This factory burned in 1881.

In 1858, Robert Prince set up the Iron-Ore Metallic Paint Company at Lehigh Gap. Moved to Bowmanstown in 1879, it was renamed the Prince Manufacturing Company, and was headed by A.C. Prince. The Prince firm also operated the Carbon Metallic Paint Company mills. During the late nineteenth century it ran an ocher mill at Walcksville, Franklin Township, as well; but this operation was relatively short-lived.

Ocher also was found in Penn Forest Township, and in a rich vein about two miles west of Hudsondale. In 1887, the Hudsondale Ocher Works was established. The firm's founder, Marshall L. Smith, took over the buildings which once had housed the foundry and machine shop of Samuel W. Hudson, Hudsondale's namesake.

The paint ore (or ocher) industry continues to exist today, but on a much smaller scale. It is virtually gone from Carbon County.

Building Stone

A certain amount of quarrying for building stone went on in the early days of Carbon County. As might be expected, the Stony Ridge was one source for such stone, producing a kind of gray granite. Rockport, formerly Lowrytown, produced a very different kind of stone, a rich brownstone. The stone for the county's current (1894) courthouse was quarried here; and a glance around Jim Thorpe's historic district suggests that more than one other building also may contain stone from this small village on the upper Lehigh.

Travel, Tourism, Recreation

Tourism and recreation are often thought of as "new" Carbon County industries; and certainly many of their late-twentieth-century expressions are new. Not too long ago there were no such things as Mauch Chunk and Beltzville lakes, the Blue Mountain Ski Resort, Jack Frost Mountain and Big Boulder, or whitewater rafting on the Lehigh. Not too long ago George Hart's complex of train cars and locomotives at the Central Railroad Station in Jim Thorpe were not museum pieces, but were everyday means of transportation. Even in those days, and long before, people visited Carbon County for sightseeing, rest, and recreation.

Perhaps the first visitors whose purpose can be classified as "recreational" were those who came to visit the mineral spring discovered by the Moravians near Gnadenhuetten; its exact location was on the western edge of what is now the Lehighton Community Grove, and it survived into the twentieth century, when it became the water source for the town's first public swimming pool. Unfortunately, it grew so polluted by drainage from the septic systems of nearby houses that at last it was condemned by the state and covered over with earth.

Here was the embryo of what is today called a spa, although it never actually became one; and in 1748 the Moravians petitioned the Bucks County commissioners to build a road so that people could come and benefit from the springs. (At the time, Carbon County was still part of Bucks County.)

Visitors did come to the spring in the eighteenth century, though the road was long and dangerous. But the place was never commercialized, nor were bath houses ever built.

A few decades after the discovery of the Gnadenhuetten springs, more mineral springs were found in the vicinity of present-day Palmerton. For years, these springs were believed to have been along the Aquashicola Creek, based on an early map of eastern Pennsylvania by Nicholas Scull.

Palmerton area researcher John Connelly, however, theorized that the springs actually were near the present-day Blue Ridge Country Club. His view was based on his own replotting of the old Moravian road that ran through the area, as well as on the facts that there still are mineral springs in the country club area, and that a well-worn Indian path once led to them.

Wherever they may have been, their waters were analyzed and certified as healthful in 1806 by Dr. Thomas C. James of the University of Pennsylvania. Bath houses were built, and a small stream of health-seeking visitors began; but it did not last long. The location may simply have been too difficult for people to reach easily.

The big influx of early visitors to the county really began only with the coming of the Lehigh Navigation and, even more, of the railroads — the Lehigh Valley Railroad, and, later, the Lehigh Coal and Navigation Company's Lehigh and Susquehanna, which as we have seen soon became a leased part of the New Jersey Central system. In an effort to increase passenger travel on its system, the Lehigh Valley Railroad even hired photographers, the most famous of whom were M.A. Kleckner and William Rau, who made hundreds of poetic photos of scenes along the LVRR track system.

Lewis P. Peters of East Mauch Chunk, one of the photographers who made stereoscopic views for the tourist trade. Courtesy, Raymond E. Holland Collection

Soon Mauch Chunk in particular, also known as "the Switzerland of America," was awash with tourists. From the late nineteenth century, traffic on the Switchback Railway was tourist traffic; this continued until 1933, when the effects of the Great Depression closed the Switchback.

In its heyday, the likes of the great inventor Thomas Edison came by to take a ride. It is said, too, that the Switchback inspired the invention of that paragon of amusement park rides, the roller coaster; this claim is accepted by the Smithsonian Institution.

One of the sights the Switchback riders gaped at was the famous Burning Mine,

Tourist car at "Five Mile Tree Bridge" on the Switchback.

Outing to the dam at Lehigh Gap. Courtesy, Raymond E. Holland Collection.

which was discovered burning on February 15, 1859. Despite the best efforts of the LC&N to extinguish the blaze — which might, with bad luck, have turned the local coalfields into an earlier version of the Centralia mine disaster — the mine burned for over a century, long after the last visitor had glided by on the last Switchback passenger car.

In the early years of the twentieth century and beyond, a trolley led up over Flagstaff Mountain and down into Lehighton. The Flagstaff view was already popular with visitors, as it still remains. A pavilion that was built on the top of the ridge in 1901 drew lovers of Big Band music for many decades. It remains in use as a venue for rock music concerts.

At the peak of the early period of tourism, visitors also swarmed over picturesque Glen Onoko in Lehigh Township near East Mauch Chunk. Once known as Moore's Ravine, the place was reinvented by Lehigh Valley Railroad publicists, who equipped it with a legend of an Indian maiden who leaped to her death after her white lover was killed. In the renamed glen the railroad installed a station, stairs, picnic pavilions, and trails, to enable tourists to enjoy the imposing cliffs and waterfalls in safety and comfort. From 1885 there also was the picturesque Wahnetah Hotel, but that was destroyed in 1911 when sparks from a forest fire set it ablaze.

A certain number of the visitors and local people also trekked up the escarpment of the Pocono Plateau to Lake Harmony in Kidder Township, where they would camp. Soon rows of cottages and bungalows belonging to regular summer residents began to grow up around the lake. It was decades before overbuilding would lead, as it did in large parts of the Poconos, to the destruction of the pristine qualities for which people had originally sought out the place.

Such, in broad outline, was Carbon County's early tourism era. What was left of it was, for the most part, wiped out by the effects of the Great Depression of the 1930s, just as the Switchback attraction had been. But tourism and recreation as industries were destined to return within a few decades, modernized, appealing to new types of visitors, and ready to play as important a role in the county's future as in its past — if not more so.

The Glen and Its Legends

It sometimes seems as if there is hardly a scenic crag or bluff in the United States that does not come equipped with a legend about an Indian maiden who hurled herself to death from its heights. In the case of Glen Onoko, there is more than one version of the legend, and that is probably true in other locations as well. In one version of the local tale, a chief's daughter named Onoko fell in love with a white man. Her lover was captured by her fellow Indians, was sentenced to death, and was executed by being thrown over the glen's second waterfall.

Onoko herself had observed the white man's trial and execution from a nearby hiding place. Mad with grief, she, too, leaped from the falls, and joined him in death.

This is substantially the form of the story that appeared in the *Mauch Chunk Gazette* on June 29, 1888. In a variant, Onoko's lover was an Indian hunter named Opachee, who lived in the Nesquehoning Valley. But when Onoko's parents rejected Opachee's suit for Onoko's hand, the young woman committed suicide by hurling herself over the falls.

It is possible to recognize, in stories such as this, the imagination of local "boosters." For the people of the nineteenth century, in particular, a tragic story often heightened the effect of a scenic vista; so it was good policy to have such a story with which to regale visitors.

Psychohistorians, those who study history from a purely psychological point of view, no doubt have a very good time with the facts that the victims of these stories are almost always women, and almost always members of a despised, "inferior" race. It would not be surprising to find that at least one doctoral dissertation has been turned out on this subject. But our ancestors doubtless meant no conscious harm in inventing such fictions.

In the case of Glen Onoko, the legends that belong to it were not imagined by local businessmen promoting the beauties of their home area. Instead, they were conceived in the

Pavilion at the park at Glen Onoko. Fred Bauer, winter caretaker of the grounds at Hotel Wahnetah, is holding a broom. *Courtesy, Raymond E. Holland Collection.*

Tourists admiring the top falls at Glen Onoko. From the stereoscopic collection "Scenery of the Lehigh Valley R.R." published for Schneur's Switch-Back Bazaar at the Mansion House hotel in Mauch Chunk. This was one of the series entitled "Switch-Back R.R., Mauch Chunk and Glen Onoko."
Courtesy, Raymond E. Holland Collection.

Stereoscopic view by G.F. Gates of Watkins, New York, of Terrace Falls at Glen Onoko.
Courtesy, Raymond E. Holland Collection.

The Hotel Wahnetah, built for tourists visiting Glen Onoko in "the Switzerland of America." It had no access by road, only by train on the Lehigh Valley Railroad. *Courtesy, Clarence Hendricks.*

fertile minds of publicists for the Lehigh Valley Railroad. In the early 1870s, someone from the LVRR noted the charms of what was then known as Moore's Ravine, a place of multiple waterfalls and wild vistas. A decision was made to place a station there to make the place accessible to travelers on the railroad, and to local residents as well. From 1870 to 1872, a walking trail to the falls was constructed; and in 1885 the railroad built the Hotel Wahnetah near the site, with a footbridge across the Lehigh River for access from Mauch Chunk. The imposing four-story hotel featured thirty-six rooms, an eighty-foot bar, and a spacious dining room.

Together with these tangible improvements, the railroad invented for the location a new, mellifluous name, and a new historical legend. The name and legend stuck; they have endured longer than the glen has lasted as a visitors' attraction.

The story of its decline is briefly told. Floods in 1901 and 1902 washed out the footbridge across the Lehigh. In 1903, an East Mauch Chunk entrepreneur named Pius von Schweibinz, owner of the Eagle Brewery, bought the Hotel Wahnetah. He restored the

The walkways and bridges that made it possible for nineteenth-century tourists, the women in long dresses, to walk to the falls at the top of Glen Onoko have few traces today. The glen is reverting to nature and has become dangerous in its upper sections. *Courtesy, Raymond E. Holland Collection.*

footbridge and improved the hotel; but it burned in 1911 and was never rebuilt. Within a few years, the number of visitors to the glen had fallen off sharply. The trail through the glen decayed over the decades, until today it can be visited only by experienced hikers.

In its current state, Glen Onoko possibly may serve as a warning against depending entirely on tourism, or on any other single industry, as an economic base. But it also offers an outstanding opportunity for redevelopment. Perhaps the day will come when visitors once again will follow restored trails into the wildness and the beauty of the glen.

Other Industries

As we have seen, a technology for the use of anthracite coal had to be developed before this fuel could be used to its full advantage. This was true not only for industries such as iron making, and for transportation, but also for the home.

Mauch Chunk's John Wilson ("John Wulson, the tinker") is credited with making an early workable anthracite home heater — and very likely the first anthracite cooking stove as well. The noted merchant and engineer Asa Lansford Foster experimented with improving the design of such stoves; and John Mears, another Mauch Chunk stove maker, adopted many of Foster's ideas.

Later, two firms made Lehighton famous for the quality of its stoves. They were the Lehigh Stove and Manufacturing Company, founded in 1867 with Asa Packer's son-in-law Dr. Garrett B. Linderman as its president and most prominent stockholder; and the Crescent Stove and Manufacturing Company, founded in 1904 with Edward E. Walters as its president.

A gang of men setting props in a coal mine. Timber was used for props in coal mines, for railroad ties above and below ground, and for ancillary buildings such as breakers. Courtesy, Clarence Hendricks.

The existence of the coal mines meant that other businesses, in addition to the transportation systems, grew up to serve the needs of the coal industry. This has already been observed in part in the section on forest industries: much timber went to shore up mine shafts and to other mining needs, including the transportation of the coal to market once it was mined.

This is just one example of an industry that directly or indirectly served the needs of coal, at least in part. In what is now Mahoning Township, for example, Henry Arner manufactured miners' shoes beginning around 1820; the shoe business was continued by Henry Bretney until 1855. The location was a good one, since many of Summit Hill's miners came from Mahoning Township, lured over the mountain by the promise of a steadier income than they could get by working their farms.

Arner and a partner, Abraham Hanline, also tried from 1832 to 1854 to supply the mines with another need — blasting powder. By the time they abandoned their plans, two explosions at their plant had cost two lives.

In 1842 John Erb founded another powder plant in Mahoning Township. This, too, claimed several lives during its history.

The Hoover Brothers, with Elijah Hoover as firm president, established a blasting powder plant in the western part of Packer Township in the late 1860s. In 1873 they sold out to the Laflin Powder Manufacturing Company, and in 1878 the business was moved to Wapwallopen. Like the Mahoning Township ventures, this one was plagued by its share of explosive accidents.

In early Banks Township at least two powder mills manufactured black powder for railroad construction and mining: one, built by N.R. Penrose in 1855, was blown up and abandoned in 1866; the other was built about the same time by William Cool. It, too, was blown up and abandoned.

In Packer Township powder was manufactured at the Quakake Mills for about ten years until the works blew up in about 1878. The company, purchased by the Laflin Powder Manufacturing Company in 1873, moved to Laflin, near Wilkes-Barre. Also in Packer Township, several sizeable powder magazines were established, two of them as early as 1836 by the DuPont Powder Company.

There were other industries, some of them surprising today. In early Carbon County history, Weatherly was the site of a short-lived lock manufacturing company. The town got better economic mileage out of the Allen Candy Manufacturing Company, which moved there from Allentown in 1899 and remained in business for decades thereafter. This company was substantially the brainchild of Andrew W. Horlacher, a German immigrant who for twenty-three years ran a bakery in Weatherly.

Maintenance on the canal and the railroads was a major industry. Here, repairs are underway at the Lehigh Gap dam in 1886. Dams were constructed of wooden cribbing filled with stone, and were sheathed with wooden boards. They needed frequent repairs.

(Above) D.B. DeLong's delivery wagon on Ridge Street, Lansford. DeLong had a butcher shop on Ridge Street, and a slaughter house near the Panther Creek about a quarter mile west of the Lehigh and New England Railroad station.

(Below) In the days before mechanized refrigeration, ice houses were to be found in almost every community and on every farm. This is the large commercial ice house at Lehigh Gap. Both photos, courtesy, Raymond E. Holland Collection.

Another German immigrant, Joseph Obert, did very well in Lehighton as a meat packer. The Joseph Obert Company, which he established in 1865, prospered well into the twentieth century.

Bricks were another product of Carbon County. They were, for example, manufactured in Franklin Township prior to 1864 by Joseph Wintermuth. In 1906 Ira Seidle and Dallas Bowman established the Lehighton Brick Company.

Beginning in the 1890s two firms, one started by Stephen Ziegenfuss and another by H.R. Kreidler, built wagons and carriages in East Weissport, Franklin Township. Around the same time, Landon B. Wagner was manufacturing fencing in nearby Phifer's Corner. Wagner also had once manufactured stoneware and pottery, but gave up those products.

For some twenty-six years, beginning in 1874, William Lilly's Lehigh Valley Emery Wheel Company made emery wheels in Weissport. J.W. Heller's Eureka Manufacturing Company made furniture there, too, until well into the twentieth century.

Carbon County had several fish hatcheries, each an employer of at least a few county residents. The first, the hatchery of the Penn Forest Brook Trout Company, was located in Penn Forest Township, and was established in 1895 at the junction of Hell and Wild creeks by Mauch Chunk businessman W.A. Leisenring and Henry A. Butler. It became known as the largest hatchery of its kind in the world.

In 1899 Charles Wolters, Sr., of Philadelphia established another hatchery, at Harrity on the Pohopoco Creek in Franklin Township. A few years later, in 1903, the Hayes Creek Trout Company was set up in Kidder Township. It contained eight hundred eighty acres, including about fifty acres of ponds.

During the nineteenth and twentieth centuries, tuberculosis was the dreaded "white death," a disease which carried off millions. In many ways it was more frightening than AIDS is perceived during the 1990s because nobody could delude themselves that they could not catch it.

From this horror, Carbon County drew some economic benefit; for the clean, fresh air of the Pocono Plateau was believed to be helpful to tuberculosis victims. Two institutions for them — the public Free Sanatorium for Poor Consumptives at White Haven, Luzerne County, and the Sunnyrest Sanatorium, the first private tuberculosis hospital in Pennsylvania, at East Side Borough — were established in 1901.

The atmosphere, even at Sunnyrest, must have been far removed from that of a spa, which had strong social aspects, and more like the claustrophobic desperation of Thomas Mann's novel *The Magic Mountain*. In such institutions, every patient fought for his or her life every moment of every day. Many lost the battle.

As is the case with every medical institution, these two sanatoria contributed to the economy by providing jobs for local residents. They were an important part of the health care industry of the early twentieth century.

This chapter does not try to be an exhaustive summary of every type of industry and business to be found in Carbon County in the earlier stages of its history. It does, however, establish that, in economic terms, there was much more to the county than coal, even in the days when coal was said to be king.

John Shigo, banker and agent, had an office in the Scott Building on West Ridge Street in Lansford. The Citizens' National Bank later used the same offices. The sign in Slovak on the door means "Banking and Shipping Exchange." Shigo was a banker, steamship agent, and foreign exchange provider, offering financial help and other services for many immigrants from Czechoslovakia. In one typical transaction he sent $16 (about 8000 Czech crowns) for Ignatius Orsulak to his wife, Helen, in Biksard, Czechoslovakia. *Courtesy, Raymond E. Holland Collection.*

Early Financial Institutions

To develop a raw region, such as Carbon County once was, requires a great deal of money as investment capital. The patterns followed in raising the necessary funds are much the same everywhere: first the investment decisions are made by banks and investors in distant cities. As the population grows, banks and other financial institutions grow up in the region itself and local people take some measure of control over their own financial destinies.

This pattern was followed in Carbon County. The distant cities where the original financial decisions were made were Philadelphia and New York; but the county soon began to develop banks of its own. Perhaps the first of these was a private institution, Rockwood, Hazard and Company, which operated in Mauch Chunk from 1852 to 1857. It was owned by Charles Rockwood and Fisher Hazard, third son of Erskine Hazard. The young Hazard (he was only 23 in 1852) operated a wire mill in Mauch Chunk during these years.

Private banks remained fairly constant for many years, and not only as the preserve of the relatively prosperous. Often immigrants would entrust their funds to merchants belonging to their own ethnic group; thus, these merchants became private bankers. Regionally, perhaps one of the best examples of these private ethnic banks was the Gosztonyi Bank of South Bethlehem. It failed during the Crash of 1929.

There were, of course, private ethnic banks in Carbon County as well, such as John Shigo's in Lansford. But none of the ethnic bankers here seems to have cut quite the swath John Gosztonyi and his wife Rose cut in South Bethlehem. Banking's future was with more public institutions, under greater public control. In 1855 the Mauch Chunk State Bank opened its doors; in 1863 it became the First National Bank. The following year the Second National Bank entered the banking field in the county seat.

In 1867, another well-funded private bank opened its doors. This was G.B. Linderman and Company, and its principal was Asa Packer's son-in-law, Dr. Garrett B. Linderman. In 1882 this was chartered as the Linderman National Bank, and in 1903 it merged with the First National Bank to form Mauch Chunk National Bank.

The charter of Mauch Chunk's Second National Bank expired in 1902. Its institutional successor was the Mauch Chunk Trust Company.

Meanwhile, other communities also were developing banking institutions. The First National Bank opened in 1875 in Lehighton; in 1902 the Citizens' National Bank commenced operations in the same town.

In 1873 the Miners' Bank was organized in Summit Hill. It moved to Lansford in 1880, and failed three years later. Other banks soon opened their doors in Lansford, among them the First National Bank in 1899, and the Citizens' National Bank in 1903.

The year 1902 was marked by the opening of the First National Bank in Weatherly; and in 1907 the new town of Palmerton opened its own First National Bank. Two other Palmerton institutions, the Citizens' Bank and the Palmerton State Bank (Palmerton Savings and Trust Company), merged late in 1928 into the Citizens' Bank and Trust Company.

Founded in 1921, the Citizens' Bank of Bowmanstown became, first, the Bowmanstown Bank, then the Tri-County State Bank. It later became part of Meridian Bancorp.

In 1912 Weissport welcomed a bank of its own, named, not illogically, the Weissport Bank.

A more specialized type of financial institution was the building and loan association. An early regional example was the Fidelity Building and Loan Association of Summit Hill. Around 1875 the first such institution was established in Lehighton. It had two offspring, the Lehighton Building and Loan Association and the Lehighton Building and Loan Association No. 2, both of which failed.

In 1893 the Homestead Building and Loan Association of Summit Hill was chartered, and in 1903 Workmen's Building and Loan opened its doors in the same town. The Panther Valley Building and Loan Association commenced operations in 1903.

To follow the further course of the development of banking and other financial institutions in Carbon County would require a book in itself — a book which would chronicle the rise and decline, mergers and acquisitions over the better part of a century.

Perhaps only a specialist would be interested in such a book. But there is one thread in the story of banking in the county which just about everyone who has a bank account is aware of, and that is the end of locally owned banks as we have known them. Since about the beginning of the 1980s, local residents, in common with other Americans, have seen their hometown banks become part of large, regional banks, and even of interstate bank holding companies. The town banker, once a key figure in any community, is now for the most part just an employee of a giant corporation. At this time there are very few independent banks in the county. Among them are the Citizens' Bank and Trust Company and the First National Bank, both of Palmerton, and the Mauch Chunk Trust Company and Jim Thorpe National Bank in Jim Thorpe.

And so, it can be argued, things have come full circle. Once again financial decisions about Carbon County are being made in distant cities, such as Philadelphia and New York.

part two

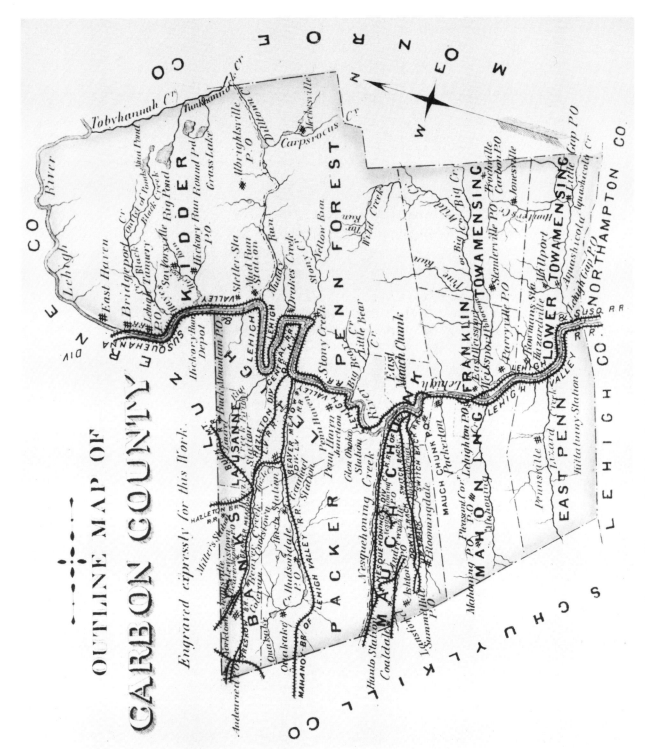

OUTLINE MAP OF

CARBON COUNTY

Engraved expressly for this Work.

From the 1884 history of Lehigh and Carbon Counties by Mathews and Hungerford.

The Founding of the County

Cannon Blasts, "Illuminations" and Flaming Tar Barrels: The Anthracite County is Born

In 1993 residents of Carbon County celebrated the sesquicentennial anniversary of their separation from Northampton and Monroe counties. One hundred and fifty years earlier, in 1843, Carbon County was carved out of these two counties, forming a new county of approximately 390 square miles.

One year before the anniversary celebration, in 1992, issues resurfaced that had been prominent at the time of the founding of the new county. These issues were plans for a new county jail, and the limited space within the county seat, leading to the proposal for a parking deck in downtown Jim Thorpe.

From 1843 until as late as 1889, the issues of space limitation within Mauch Chunk and the condition of the county buildings, including the jail, were used by those people calling for the establishment of Lehighton as the seat of the county of Carbon.

Efforts to establish Lehighton as the county seat of a desired new county can be traced as far back as 1810, in a petition to the state legislature found within the Jacob Weiss papers at the Historical Society of Pennsylvania in Philadelphia.

After demarking the desired limits of the county the petition went on to propose "Leheiton," at the confluence of the Mahoning Creek and the Lehigh River, for the county seat north of the Blue Mountain.

> From its advantageous Situation it bids fair to become a thriving Place on account of the Trade and Intercourse with the Susquehanna Settlements by means of the Lehigh and Susquehanna Turnpike... The at present practicable Boat & Raft navigation of the Lehigh from thence — the increasing Improvements of the adjacent country — and above all its almost central Situation of the proposed Division — with the many other advantages such as Lumber &c for building — which can be procured much cheaper than south of the Mountain makes it appear the most eligible, and prompts us to recommend it as suitable for the aforesaid purpose.

According to other sources, it was as early as 1803 that the inhabitants of the wilderness north of the Blue Mountain were petitioning the legislature for the formation of a new county.

Another early written record was penned into the daily journal of Isaac Abel Chapman, while he lived at the Lausanne Landing on the Lehigh River. Chapman was employed by a group of Wilkes-Barre investors who had taken a lease of the Sharp Mountain Quarry from the Lehigh Coal Mine Company.

Among Chapman's accomplishments were the opening of some of the earliest mines at Room Run, in 1816 and 1817, and, in 1826, the surveying of the original route of the Mauch Chunk and Summit Hill Gravity Railroad, more commonly known as the Switchback.

On January 24, 1816 Chapman recorded in his diary: "In the afternoon rode to Lehighton to attend a meeting for considering a new county."

Chapman was heavily involved in the development of the Lehigh coal trade, but did not live long enough to see its greatest successes. After surveying the route of the Mauch Chunk gravity railroad, Chapman caught a cold while supervising the digging of the Hacklebernie Tunnel. He died on December 8, 1827, and was buried in the cemetery in Upper Mauch Chunk, directly above the old railroad.

Over the years prior to 1829 many petitions were presented to the state legislature for the formation of Carbon County, although few have survived to this day. It was not until 1829, and the publication of Mauch Chunk's first newspaper, the *Lehigh Pioneer and Mauch Chunk Courier*, that any details of the process were recorded.

The Battle of Words

Early editions of the *Mauch Chunk Courier* served as a battlefield for wars waged between letter writers using strange pen names. The first battle that was fought in the *Courier* was over the "division" of Northampton County, and the opening shots were fired by "Many" and "Economy."

On August 27 of that year the following notice appeared in the newspaper:

NOTICE

Is hereby given to the inhabitants of East Penn Township in Northampton County, that a public meeting will be held on Saturday the 12th September next, at 2 o'clock P. M. at the house of John Hagenbuch in Lehighton, for the purpose of taking into consideration the propriety of petitioning the Legislature for a division of the County aforesaid. As this is a subject of importance, punctual attendance is expected.

John Hagenbuch was landlord of a hotel in Lehighton that was later the site of the Exchange Hotel. He was succeeded as landlord by his son Reuben, who a decade later would also become involved in the proposed division.

The newspaper also reported that "agitations" for the division of Northampton County into a new county had been going on for many years, but had been unsuccessful, due to lack of interest as well as opposition from citizens of Easton and other parts of Northampton County. It is not known when it was decided, or who it was who suggested, that the new county would be named Carbon after the predominant mineral found in the area.

A group of men, hiding behind a pseudonym, signed the notice as "MANY." At that time it was the policy of newspaper editors to allow the use of a "pen" name, provided the signature of the author was on the original letter sent to the editor; the author's real name would not appear in the newspaper.

The principal argument of "Many" for the "Division" of the county was that the county town, Easton, was anywhere but "where it ought to be." They argued that reason dictated that the county town should be in the center of a county, rather than at one corner, as Easton was situated.

Although the same trip today would take about an hour, early residents of the part of Northampton County "over the mountain" were greatly inconvenienced by having to travel thirty to fifty miles, often in bad weather, over terrible roads. They complained that this resulted in a waste of time and a neglect of personal business, just so they could attend to the details of court and "serve Justice." As an example, when a man living in Mauch Chunk or Lehighton was called to jury duty, he had to leave two days early, just to be sure of arriving on time. If court was to be held on a Monday or a Tuesday, that meant traveling on the Sabbath, which "Many" considered immoral.

The group also accused the government of Northampton County of mismanagement and urged every citizen living "over the mountain" to sign the petition for division that was then being circulated:

> These circumstances, when duly weighed, must render it apparent to every unbiased individual, that a Division is highly necessary. We therefore trust, that every public spirited citizen, who has the welfare of his fellow citizens at heart, and who wishes to see them relieved from an unnecessary oppressive grievance, will, when called upon, make the same evident, by signing his name to the Petition for said Division.

This August 1829 notice touched off a storm of controversy that was to last for several months. The notice by "Many" attracted a written rebuttal from "Economy" who claimed citizenship near the Blue Mountain, but on the northern side. "Economy" claimed:

> ... I have been a supporter of the expenses of the county for many years; have attended the courts at Easton pretty regularly, and through them have so far been able to get my business transacted without difficulty, and I believe at the ordinary expense of court business.

He therefore was against the division of the county, as conducting personal business at Easton would become "an individual tax." "Economy" also claimed that creating a new county would be very expensive:

> The expenses of erecting a court house, a jail, &c. connected with the support of a Prothonotary, Sheriff, Recorder, Commissioners, Auditors, a dozen lazy lawyers, and other contingent expenses, would involve us in a public debt that we should neither be willing or able to pay. I hope therefore, that the project of a new county may for the present, at least, be abandoned.

On October 17, 1829, a meeting was held in Mauch Chunk at the home of E.W. Kimball (second landlord of Mauch Chunk's Mansion House Hotel) for the purpose of opposing the proposed division of the county. This meeting and the resolutions passed there only increased the fury of the storm.

In a reactive letter to the *Courier*, "A Friend to the Intended Division" dismissed "Economy's" letter as "the dying groan, the final effort of a desperate and selfish opposition." He also charged that the citizens of Mauch Chunk opposed to the division were

> ... composed principally of individuals resident there and dependent upon the Company [the Lehigh Coal and Navigation Company] for their livelihood, and who may be considered as mere fugitives, birds of passage, here to day and Goodness knows where to-morrow.

"Friend's" most ironic charge was that the citizens of Mauch Chunk would be ready for division when their private plots of land in and around Mauch Chunk were properly cleared off for the receipt of the county town.

"Vindex" jumped into the fray with a letter fired off to the editor of the *Courier*. He responded by claiming that the "Friend" was none other than John Leisenring (Senior). "Vindex" also hurled the charge that the proposed division of the county was being advanced by Lehighton property owners, gambling on an increase in the value of their land:

> ... the most powerful argument that these epithet dealers can advance, is, that Lehighton is a delightful site for a county town, such capital lots for building and gardens. Give us but a division, and our fortunes are made.

According to "Vindex," who turned out to be an employee of the Lehigh Coal and Navigation Company, the choice was clear:

> Town Lot speculation, and individual aggrandizement, vs No division, moderate taxes and the interest of the community at large.

"Vindex" wrote a wordy letter that could have been summarized in just a few short paragraphs. The following is an example of one of his more verbose sentences:

> I have known instances of the success of a peaceable and harmless man in giving his fellow what he would call a sound drubbing through the momentary excitement of his anger for some trifling difference of opinion acquire for him the reputation of a real bully, nay, of even establishing him in the belief that he was, in fact, a man of most uncommon powers, a valiant fellow; and in order that nothing might detract from his fair fame, so nobly acquired, has ever after, been ready and willing to seek an engagement with any person whom he might think a fit subject for the exercise of his bullyism.

Lehighton residents Leisenring and Charles H. Williams responded to "Vindex" by denying authorship of any articles printed in the *Courier*, claiming that they only forwarded the article to the editor, as requested by the author, who was a friend of theirs and who resided not in Lehighton, but in Easton.

"Vindex" was not the only person to respond to the "Friend to the Intended Division." "A Friend to the Public" also wrote a letter in opposition to the division:

> The liberal minded gentleman I think has had his pericranium a little overheated at the time of his writing, and his reasoning faculties have in consequence refused to do their office. If he had studied the interest of community as well as he has his own, he would certainly have known that a division of the county at this time would not meet the approbation of a majority of our citizens, setting aside the 'fugitives, or birds of passage' as he is pleased to term us.

The controversy was covered in the *Mauch Chunk Courier* until early 1830, when it completely degenerated into a pure attack of personality against personality. Finally, all correspondence between opponents disappeared from the Mauch Chunk newspaper and the battle for division was replaced by a new battle. This was the controversy of railroad versus canal, in which Josiah White took a stand, giving voice to his greatest mistake in favoring canals over railroads.

In the meantime, John Leisenring, Sr., moved with his family to Mauch Chunk, replacing Josiah White as postmaster in 1831 after White relinquished the job and returned to his family in Philadelphia. Leisenring also succeeded Kimball as landlord of the Mansion House.

One of his sons, John Leisenring, Jr., later became involved in construction of the Panther Creek Railroad and the working of coal mines in the Panther Creek Valley. He eventually went to work for the Lehigh Coal and Navigation Company as superintendent and engineer in 1859, after the death of Edwin A. Douglas. Leisenring Senior's daughter, Caroline, married Daniel Bertsch, who was an LC&N contractor in the Panther Valley.

It appears that no more "agitations" for a division occurred until near the end of 1836, when a group of citizens, this time from Mauch Chunk, called a public meeting for the purpose of "deciding on the propriety of petitioning the Legislature for the erection of a new county." Isaac Salkeld, Sr., was called to the chair and B. Needham was appointed secretary.

Salkeld, one of Mauch Chunk's earliest residents, had arrived there in 1823 with his family. Among his accomplishments were superintending the construction of the Mansion House Hotel, the Stone Grist Mill, and the Room Run Railroad.

John Leisenring, Jr., in later years

Other people in attendance at the meeting, held on November 30, 1836, were John G. Martin, John Fatzinger, Asa Lansford Foster, Jacob S. Wallace, and Dr. Benjamin Rush McConnell, the LC&N's paid physician and the first practicing doctor at the Summit Hill, Panther Valley and Nesquehoning mines.

At the meeting the same complaints as had been voiced over the years were again repeated, and a petition drawn up to present to the state legislature. On February 13, 1837, the *Mauch Chunk Courier* reported that George Shantz of the House of Representatives had presented a bill for a new county out of parts of Northampton and Schuylkill to be called Carbon. This petition, as previous petitions, was voted down in the state legislature.

Only two years later, on February 11, 1839, another petition was presented to the state legislature by Robert E. James, Esq. Again the petition was voted down.

The issue was revived by the Lehighton committee in late 1839 and early 1840 when a meeting, chaired by John Leisenring, Sr., was held at Reuben Hagenbuch's in Lehighton. This was a very important meeting, since one of the persons in attendance was Asa Packer. Packer would be elected to the state legislature for the 1841–1842 and for the 1842–1843 sessions. He would play no small role in the final success in the division of the county.

Other people in attendance at the December 21, 1839, meeting in Lehighton were Reuben Hagenbuch, John Dieter Bauman (Bowman), Joseph H. Chapman, Joseph Butler and Cornelius Connor.

This meeting, as previous meetings held in Lehighton, produced opposition, but this time the opposition did not come from the Mauch Chunk citizens, who were now on the side of the Lehighton petitioners.

The Lehighton meeting drew opposition from the citizens of Beaver Meadow, who were preparing their own petition for separation from Northampton County, and who desired that several townships from Luzerne County be included in the new county. These townships were Sugar Loaf, Nescopeck, and parts of East Hanover and Newport.

So began another newspaper war, with "Beaver" and "Veritas" writing to the *Mauch Chunk Courier* to "vent [their] spleen at us in a style of unprecedented learning." The opposition from Beaver Meadow charged that the citizens of Mauch Chunk collared all strangers passing through the town, slapped quills into their hands, and forced them to sign their petition. They also claimed that the Lehigh Coal and Navigation Company promoted this action and were also sending agents into Luzerne County to pass pamphlets supporting the petitions from Mauch Chunk and Lehighton. In his closing remarks "Veritas" showed his true colors by admitting "that the people of Beaver Meadow acknowledge that they would like to see their borough the county seat of a new county."

It appears as if the Mauch Chunk/Lehighton petition was the one that made it before the state legislature in February of 1840, where it was supported by Abraham Shortz and opposed by a Mr. Kingsbury. The petition was defeated by a vote of 21 against the division and 9 in favor. But this would not be the end of the effort.

Success At Last — Carbon Becomes a New County

The process of the separation of a new county from existing counties was a highly political process, and that may explain the lack of success in getting Carbon County started. While new counties around Carbon were being formed, "agitation" for the separation of Carbon County from Northampton had no success. It took someone with much political power and interest to get the job done. Although there is little documentation of how it was accomplished, the newspaper of the day credited Asa Packer with this achievement.

Packer, elected to the state legislature in 1841, had much to gain from the formation of a new county, especially if Mauch Chunk became the seat of justice. Using profits earned from building canal boats on the Lehigh and Schuylkill canals, as well as from contracting work on sections of the upper division of the Lehigh Navigation, Packer had bought lots in the town of Mauch Chunk. Appreciation of the value of these lots would bring him great wealth.

Asa Lansford Foster

But Packer was not the only entrepreneur to make money in Mauch Chunk, and many other individuals cashed in on Mauch Chunk's rise to prominence. Whether any of these individuals influenced the issue of division is unknown.

The fact that it was at all possible to purchase lots in Mauch Chunk was due to Josiah White, one of the founders of the Lehigh Coal and Navigation Company. White was a devout Quaker and a compassionate human being. He realized that true prosperity would come to the Lehigh Valley only through a free system, where others besides the company could make money. Taking a course of action vastly different from other coal companies to follow, White abolished the company store and, in 1831, surveyed plots and made lots available to individuals in the towns of Nesquehoning, Mauch Chunk and South Easton. Company laborers could opt to rent company houses or buy their own land and build houses. The company store was turned over to Asa Lansford Foster, who eventually bought it outright, making it a famous trading center.

Although the governor signed the act forming Carbon County on March 13, 1843, the news of the passage of the bill did not reach Mauch Chunk until the evening of March 14. A cannon blast from the top of Chute Hill, the unloading depot for coal trains on the gravity railroad, reverberated throughout the narrow ravine, shaking the residents of Mauch Chunk out of their beds.

With the dying echoes of the cannon blast bouncing off the hills, the residents of Upper Mauch Chunk rushed into the streets. News of the formation of the new county traveled fast, and a celebration was soon under way.

J.H. Siewers and O.H. Wheeler, publishers of the *Mauch Chunk Courier* who had recently purchased the press from its founder, Asa Lansford Foster, celebrated the occasion by changing the name of the newspaper to the *Carbon County Transit*. The first issue of *The Transit* hit the streets of Mauch Chunk on March 21, 1843 with news of the success of the latest Division petition.

Birth-night Celebration

Gentlemen:

Allow us to introduce you to Carbon County!

"To be or not to be? that is the question"

"For twice ten tedious years" this has been the burden of our aspirations and now the question has been triumphantly answered. Old Northampton literally notwith-standing, and we have once and for all made our "Transit" over the disk of the Political State Orb, to revolve about its central influence, we certainly may be allowed to felicitate ourselves upon the result. But to sit down passively would be to do injustice to the importance as well as the good humor inspired by the event, and accordingly the news of the Division, circulating rapidly produced a general disposition to testify our joy.

The Harrisburg celebration for the formation of Carbon County began on March 16, the same day that the House was meeting to consider the formation of Blair County. The measure soon passed, and another celebration began. The parties were held so close to each other that some individuals, attending both celebrations, became confused and raised toasts to the wrong county at the wrong meeting. Whether it was truly confusion or the politicians were just drunk is anybody's guess.

The Mauch Chunk celebration, held in the dark of night on snow-covered ground, was much more romantic and less drunken, although a Stroudsburg newspaper claimed other-wise. A blazing fire was lit on the back of a sled, which was drawn from Upper Mauch Chunk to the lower village, accompanied by the Mauch Chunk band. A "merry mass of townsmen" followed the sled in "picturesque disorder." Bonfires, fireworks and flaming tar barrels lit up the town. The editor of the *Carbon County Transit* followed the celebration, and

as we gazed upon the scene, the feeling was irresistible, and we mingled with the joyous train and listened alternatively to the music, the jest, and the cannon peal, which in midnight thunder announced the birth-night of our County.

Selection of the County Seat

With the realization of the dreams of many people, the real work of establishing the new county began. An immediate task would be to locate the county seat. This process was sure to revive some of the old animosities. Then would come the task of building and paying for a court house, a jail and other public buildings.

Mauch Chunk's cramped location between mountains and lack of space for expansion is evident in this view from Flagstaff made by William Rau later in the nineteenth century.

David Rittenhouse Porter, the governor of Pennsylvania who signed the Act establishing Carbon County, was directed by the Act to appoint three distinct and impartial persons <u>not</u> resident in Northampton, Luzerne, Lehigh, Columbia or Carbon County, to decide upon the best and most central site for the location of the county seat. The men selected were J.H. Brodhead of Pike County, W.J.B. Andrews of Clearfield County and Charles W. Hegins of Northumberland County.

On April 1, 1843, residents of the lower part of the new county called a meeting at the public house of Lewis Van Horn, in Parryville. John Dieter Bowman (Bauman) was selected chairman of the meeting while Charles Snyder was appointed secretary. The purpose of the meeting was supposed to be to "get the sense of each of the legal voters of each of the respective townships and the name of the place he wishes to designate as his choice for the county seat..." However, at the meeting resolutions were adopted expressing the views of the committee that Mauch Chunk was entirely unsuitable for a county seat due to its cramped position in the narrow ravine surrounded by rugged mountains, "totally unfit for improvements and increase of population." On the other hand, Lehighton was "pleasantly situated" at one end of the Mahoning Valley, on a plot that had been laid out with plenty of space for public buildings and plenty of room for expansion.

The citizens of Mauch Chunk were not to be caught with their guard down. Although it seemed that the Lehighton committee made a valid point concerning space limitations in Mauch Chunk, a meeting was called on May 13, 1843, at the house of Alexander Stedman in Mauch Chunk. Stedman (or Steadman) was the landlord of the Mansion House Inn at the time. The meeting was organized by John Fatzinger, chairman, and Samuel Wolf, secretary.

Postcard view of Lehighton from 1906, showing the difference in its location and layout from that of Mauch Chunk. The town may have had wider streets, open spaces, and room for expansion, but it had inadequate political muscle. *Courtesy, Vince Hydro.*

Fatzinger was a prominent Mauch Chunker who operated an iron foundry in partnership with Jacob Salkeld. This team constructed the steam engines and machinery for the Mount Pisgah and Mount Jefferson inclined planes on the Switchback railroad.

The Mauch Chunk meeting was held in order "to receive offers of donations for the purpose of erecting the Public Buildings in the County of Carbon," but was most likely held to counter any tactics used by the Lehighton Committee, and push Mauch Chunk as the seat of justice. An important aspect of the Act establishing Carbon County was that persons who donated money toward the construction of the county buildings could make their donation contingent upon their desired site being selected. The race was on to see which team could raise the most money and get the most votes.

One Mauch Chunk "business man" was asked, "When you get your own county, and have the seat of justice located at Mauch Chunk, where will you build the addition to your village which the natural growth will require?" The man had an immediate response, "Oh, we'll dig down *one* story and build up *two*."

The governor's committee began their examinations on June 16, 1843, first visiting Lehighton, where petitions for the establishment of Lehighton as the county seat were thrust upon the men by Stephen Balliet, Thomas Weiss and John D. Bowman. The residents of Lehighton pledged to the committee that should Lehighton be selected as the county town, they would construct county buildings at least equal to those found in Monroe County.

Next in line was a visit to Mauch Chunk. The Mauch Chunk committee proposed to purchase the Lehigh Coal and Navigation Company's "Old Store" on the corner of Broadway and Susquehanna, together with a connecting lot in the rear, refurbish the building, and construct a jail and all other necessary buildings "free of all expense to the citizens of the

Susquehanna Street in Mauch Chunk in the 1870s, as it would have appeared to a traveler coming by train from Weissport.

county." At that time over $4,000 in donations had been pledged by people wanting Mauch Chunk selected as the county seat, more money than the public buildings of Monroe County had cost only a few years earlier (1836).

On June 19, 1843, at 1:00 P.M. the governor's committee finished its deliberations, assembled in Mauch Chunk, and made a report. Much to the surprise of many citizens, especially those in the lower part of the county, the committee selected Mauch Chunk over Lehighton as the new county seat.

The committee announced that "[we] do unanimously fix upon the said town of Mauch Chunk, as 'a proper and convenient site, as near the centre of said county as is practicable,' for the erection of a Court House, Prison and County Offices ..."

It appears as if the committee's decision was swayed by the Lehigh Coal and Navigation Company's offer to make a gift of the "Old Store" to the county. It was an impressive gift, although within a few years there would be rethinking concerning the title to the property. The residents of Lehighton would use this in an attempt to force a rethink of the Mauch Chunk decision.

The announcement of the selection of Mauch Chunk as the new county town was followed by another cannon blast from Chute Hill, and a "regale" provided by Cornelius Connor, proprietor of Mauch Chunk's Golden Swan Hotel. The men of the governor's committee paid a "flying visit" to the celebration, and even some of the Lehighton losers, John D. Bowman and Thomas Weiss, heartily joined in the festivities.

The *Monroe Democrat* reported that the announcement of Mauch Chunk's selection was followed by "drinking, carousing, &c., &c." The editor of the *Carbon Transit* replied to this charge as follows:

> Wrongly informed, gentlemen of the Democrat. We had no "drinking, carousing,
> &c, &c." which signifies a general drunken scrape — and we would inform you
> that the good citizens of Mauch Chunk indulge in no such luxuries at any time ...
> We did not see one drunken man during the whole day and evening. "Drinking,
> carousing, *&c. &c.*" indeed, sirs, you astonish us!

By August of 1843 the building committee in charge of the county buildings had made contracts with Isaac T. Dodson for the carpentry and joinery work of the court house, and with Jesse K. Pryor for the masonry and carpentry work of the jail. Richard Blay was given the plastering contract and Justus Gould the iron work.

Representatives of the county accepted the buildings before the end of the year. The LC&N's "Old Store" was no longer recognizable. The first floor had been converted into office space for the county officers; the court room was on the second floor. The attic, lit by sky lights, housed the jury rooms. Above the roof towered a cupola with a unique vane on top, designed by John Mears in a manner appropriate to the coal-mining region. The vane pictured a train of coal cars with a locomotive and engineer, below a pick crossed with a shovel.

The new county jail was not so well constructed, and it was only accepted by the grand jury after lengthy deliberation. The editor of the *Transit* described it as "safe as need be, and as comfortable as it ought to be for the violator of law and order."

Agitations for Removal of the County Seat to Lehighton

Mauch Chunk's easy slide into position as the county seat of the new county of Carbon would not be so easily accepted by the residents of the neighboring town of Lehighton.

While Mauch Chunk went about doing what a town does after it has just been selected a seat of justice, the citizens of Lehighton attempted to undo the selection. Less than a year after the formation of Carbon County, a petition was presented to the state legislature for the removal of the county seat from Mauch Chunk to Lehighton. Lehighton had originally been laid out with the object of one day becoming a county seat. Its streets were wide with spacious lots, and there was plenty of room for the expansion that would naturally come in the future.

The petition remained on the books without a vote being taken until the year 1846. In February of that year an attempt was made to quietly withdraw the petition, and put to rest the issue of removal of the seat of justice. This spurred some people into action and on February 13, one Mr. Samuels read before the state legislature a bill entitled "An Act Relating to the removal of the seat of Justice in Carbon County." The bill was referred to a "select" committee consisting of representatives from Lehigh, Carbon, Northampton and Monroe counties.

On February 14 a Mr. Strauss presented the 1844 petition containing the signatures of 730 Carbon citizens who favored removal. The petition, along with numerous signatures opposing the measure, was presented to the same committee.

The bill and petition were resurrected in 1846 because the Lehighton advocates had discovered a difficulty with the title to the property donated by the LC&N for the county buildings three years earlier.

In 1843, soon after Carbon County was separated from Northampton and Monroe, the governor's committee had selected Mauch Chunk when the Lehigh Coal and Navigation Company donated its old store along with an adjoining lot for the much-needed jail.

What was not given to the county at the time was title to the property.

With money pledged by the citizens of Mauch Chunk, the county had remodeled the donated building into a court house and county offices and constructed a jail in the lot to the rear of the court house. Within a few years these structures needed repairs. Because of the question of the title, there was some hesitation about repairing the property. The Lehighton advocates seized upon the apparent title defect as a prime motive for the consideration of removal of the seat of justice.

On February 13 of 1846 the Act for Removal was proposed, authorizing "qualified" voters in Carbon County, who could claim at least six months residence before the October election, as eligible to vote for or against the removal of the seat of justice from Mauch Chunk to Lehighton. The bill contained several "howevers," which would take effect should enough people vote in favor of removal.

St. Mark's Church stands tall above the jumble of buildings in crowded Mauch Chunk. *Courtesy, Raymond E. Holland Collection.*

First, the residents of Lehighton would be required to erect the necessary structures to support the bureaucracy of a county government. This was no problem. The citizens of Lehighton had been prepared for this all along, and certainly had enough empty space in the town to support the buildings.

In addition, the LC&N had until August 1, 1846, to provide the county with a clear title to the property and buildings or indemnify the county. If the LC&N did this, the proposed bill would be null and void.

The fact that there was some difficulty in regard to the title should have come as no surprise to the county officers.

In March of 1845, an inquest by the Grand Jury of Carbon County "urged the importance of speedily securing a perfect title," and suggested that should this not be possible, suitable buildings be procured elsewhere.

In January of 1846, apparently trying to head off the title problem, Milo M. Dimmick, Esq., directed a letter to the Lehigh Coal and Navigation Company, asking: "what has been done, or what can be done to secure the title to the County?"

James Cox, president of the Lehigh Coal and Navigation Company, assured Dimmick that the managers of LC&N company intended,

> at the earliest period practicable, to convey to the County for a consideration merely nominal, and free from incumbrance, the property now occupied, with the sanction of this Company, as first stated, for County purposes.

At first glance the issue of the title problem appears to have been a direct result of the January, 1841, flood of the Lehigh River. The flood, also known as the Great Ice Freshet, was the worst that any resident of the valley could remember, at that time. (The flood of 1862 would be much worse.) In January of 1841 the Lehigh River, swollen by melting ice and snow and falling rain, washed away every bridge that crossed the river.

The deluge destroyed the LC&N's prime source of income, tolls from canal boats operating on the Lehigh Navigation. The company's mines had not been damaged, and could still produce coal, but there was no way to get the coal to market and no money to repair the damaged canal. To make matters worse, the company had several large loans coming due. "Impatient" loanholders and other creditors filed judgements and clamored for satisfaction, racing to see who could get payment of their loans first, at the expense of the remaining creditors and, indeed, the security and future of the company itself.

The Lehigh Coal and Navigation Company frantically attempted to solicit unsecured loans in order to obtain money for repairs. Some funds were collected, but were quickly spent in making the most pressing repairs and satisfying the most demanding of creditors. Much more money was needed to complete the repairs and put the navigation back in service. But to obtain any more money would require more than simply the company's "pledge of faith."

There was only one solution to the problem of survival: a large secured loan. In March of 1842 the company mortgaged all its property to the tune of one million dollars, conveying the property to assigned trustees Josiah White, Caleb Cope, and James Cox. This tactic averted the sale of the company's property to satisfy the creditors, which would have ruined the Lehigh Coal and Navigation Company.

It was this mortgage of March, 1842, that seemed to hold the key to the title problem that kept the "Removal" wolves howling at the door of the Carbon County Courthouse. Indeed, in response to the letter of Milo Dimmick, James Cox had also written:

> But at once to relieve the property from the Mortgage referred to ... is not within the competency of the Board of Managers. That the title to the property, free from all incumbrance, will be ultimately vested in the County, I see no reason whatever to doubt ... It is not, however, within our ability to relieve it, nor will it be in our power to do so before the maturity of the loan for the payment of which it is pledged.

By this response, the president of the LC&N seemed to confirm the idea that the LC&N could *not* convey a clear title to the county property, since it was encumbered by the mortgage loan made in March of 1842 to repair the flood damage of January 1841.

There was only one problem with this theory. The minutes of the LC&N's board of managers meetings include many transfers of property from the LC&N to various individuals, these sales and transfers taking place after March of 1842. Was the company merely transferring the use of these properties, but *not* clear title?

The deed of trust by which the LC&N transferred property following March, 1842, contained the following wording:

> The Board of Managers of the Lehigh Coal and Navigation Company ... do hereby grant and convey in fee simple ... [the said property] ... free and clear of the lien and incumbrance of the said mortgage ...

That being the case, why the hesitation and why the excuse made by the LC&N concerning the granting of clear title to the county buildings? Indeed, it appears that Cox's claim that the company could not give clear title was an outright lie.

The Lehigh Coal and Navigation Company was never called to task about the possible lie. The president of the LC&N, spurred by the impending county vote on the removal issue, called a special meeting of the board of managers on July 1, 1846. In attendance at the Philadelphia meeting were President James Cox and managers Erskine Hazard, Josiah White, Joseph Fisher, George Abbott, Henry J. Boller, John Brock, and Otis Ammidon.

The meeting was for the purpose:

> to sell and convey in fee simple to the County of Carbon, in the State of Pennsylvania, for the purpose of suitable accommodations for the holding and continuance of the Seat of Justice of the said County at Mauch Chunk, and for no other purpose, free and clear of the lien and incumbrance of the said Mortgage ... the buildings and property previously donated to the county.

However, the transfer was subject to one condition: should the seat of justice of Carbon County ever be moved from its Mauch Chunk location, the indenture would be null and void and possession would revert to the Lehigh Coal and Navigation Company.

The "nominal" consideration for the transfer was two dollars.

Why the LC&N waited three years to convey clear title is not known. Possibly the company never intended to relinquish control of the land.

Why the company finally handed over clear title in 1846 is simple. The petition pressed by the citizens of Lehighton raised the distinct possibility that the seat of justice could be moved. Since the LC&N owned most of the property in and around Mauch Chunk, removal of the county seat would cause a drastic decline in the value of their holdings.

The possibility that Mauch Chunk could lose its prize position as seat of justice of Carbon County over the title question had been foreseen as early as June 19, 1843, when a committee of "responsible parties" in Mauch Chunk signed a legal instrument, registered in the recorder's office, obligating themselves to "procure and convey to the county a good and sufficient title to the land on which the county buildings are erected." The document was signed by John Fatzinger, Asa Packer, Nathan Fegley, George Belford, Cornelius Connor, William H. Knowles, George Fegley, Ezekiel W. Harlan, Alexander Lockhart, John Mears, John Leisenring, John H. Salkeld, G.W. Smith and John Lentz.

In an attempt to revive the newspaper wars of the 1830s, a letter from "Anti-Removal" to the *Mauch Chunk Gazette* resurrected this document:

> Good men, are they not? You need not be alarmed about the title to the Land. Those who are liable for the land are able to buy it ten times over if necessary.
>
> Citizens of Mauch Chunk! Wake up; call a meeting, send a circular to every member of the Legislature, containing the statement published in the "Gazette," of the 19th ult; circulate remonstrances and let the Legislature hear both sides of the question; be up and doing before it is too late. You, particularly, who have subscribed for the County buildings, do you intend what you have paid shall be made a dear loss? if not, "stir about!" Let us hear from you.

"Anti-Removal" claimed that the new question of moving the county seat to Lehighton had been instituted

> through the petitions of a glorious minority of the voters of this county, residing in the lower townships, having a personal interest in removing the County seat to the ancient settlement which is known by the name of Lehighton, who are using every exertion first to get the act passed, and then to make use of the great

bug bear of the inability of the Lehigh Company to give a perfect title at this time, to the land occupied by the County buildings and the tremendous influence of that awful CORPORATION, the Lehigh Coal and Navigation Co., to influence the votes of our citizens in favor of removing the seat of Justice to Lehighton.

"Anti-Removal's" letter of exhortation was the last that was heard of the removal issue in the Mauch Chunk newspapers for several years. Most likely the issue never went to vote after the LC&N transferred clear title to the property. Other news also captured the headlines, including completion of the backtrack of the Mauch Chunk and Summit Hill Gravity Railroad, which was put into operation to eliminate the need for animal power in returning empty coal cars to the mines. The backtrack, although completed in November of 1845, was not placed in service until the opening of the boating season of 1846.

The backtrack utilized steam engines on the summit of Mt. Pisgah and Mt. Jefferson, constructed in Mauch Chunk itself by the firm of Fatzinger and Salkeld. Of great news in 1846 was that completion of the backtrack would allow passenger service to be resumed on the gravity railroad. This service had been discontinued in 1837 due to interference with coal-car traffic.

The issue of removal would be revived several times over the coming decades, but the greatest effort would be made following the great fire that swept through the business district of Mauch Chunk.

It happened on Sunday, July 15, 1849, at approximately 9:00 in the morning. The blaze broke out in a store house on Race Street and, fed by an intense northwest wind, spread so quickly that within a short period of time Asa Packer's store and dwelling houses were completely consumed along with those of John Leisenring. Other important structures in the Mauch Chunk business district also lay in the path of the fire. The *Carbon Democrat* and the *Carbon County Gazette* were put out of business by the blaze.

The county buildings were not spared. The court house and jail were completely destroyed, although not before the prisoners were set free. Also saved from the blaze were the county records. This was a minor miracle, and only resulted from the fact that the fire occurred during daylight hours. The fact that the county records were not stored in a place safe from fire had been pointed out many times, including the following report from the grand jury to the judges on March 26, 1845:

> We feel it our duty to call the attention of the court to the fact that as yet no provision has been made for the security from fire of the books and papers belonging to the county, and to express the hope that the commissioners will, at as early a period as practicable, take the necessary measures for providing the county with a fire-safe.

The destruction of the county buildings meant that Mauch Chunk remained the county seat in name only, giving perfect excuse for the residents of Lehighton to attempt again to force removal of the seat to their village.

The attempt was unsuccessful, but Carbon County's recovery from the fire would be a long and slow process.

Following the fire the county records were stored in a temporary location that was still insecure from the danger of destruction by fire. It wasn't until April 17, 1850, that the grand jury was able to report that the county papers were now in a safe place. By then the county offices and jail had been completely rebuilt. The court house would be a while longer.

Mauch Chunk became the county seat, and remained the predominant economic community in Carbon County. In this rare M.A. Kleckner stereo view from the 1860s, private and Morris Canal boats are waiting in the boat basin on the east side of the river to be loaded with Beaver Meadow anthracite, to be shipped to Newark, Philadelphia, or elsewhere. *Courtesy, Raymond E. Holland Collection.*

The contract for rebuilding the court house was awarded to Messrs. Root and Blay in February, 1850. By June the foundation of the court house had been completed. In October of 1850 the tin roof was installed. In May of 1851 work on the new court house had advanced to the point that the contractors were able to raise the cupola and add the finishing touch to the large columns standing in front of the building. This cupola would be minus the finishing touch of the old court house, the mining-car weather vane constructed by John Mears.

The officers of the county had not learned a lesson in 1849. In January of 1852 the grand jury reported that the public buildings were in "a very precarious situation," as they were not covered by fire insurance. It also appears that the new buildings were not being maintained very well.

The grand jury examined the jail in 1853 and reported that it was not secure. Indeed, although the county jail was never really up to par it was not until 1864 that building a new jail was proposed. The plan met intense opposition, and so was tabled. But in the sessions of June and October, 1868, and January, 1869, the grand jury recommended the erection of a new prison. On February 17, 1869, the county commissioners purchased lots 90, 92, 94, 96 and 98 from the Lehigh Coal and Navigation Company, this being the site of the present county jail, prior to construction of the new jail on Broad Mountain. The old jail was converted into more county offices.

The dissatisfaction of the jury with the jail spurred another removal vote. In January of 1869 "An Act authorizing an election to be held in the County of Carbon relative to a change of the County Seat of said county and the erection of new county buildings" was presented to the state legislature.

The act provided that all qualified voters in the county of Carbon were authorized to vote for or against removal of the county seat to Lehighton, at the next election which was to be held on October 12, 1869. Voters were to label a ticket "County Seat" on the outside and on the inside write either "For Removal" or "Against Removal." If "For Removal" was indicated, the voter was to indicate the desired location of the county seat.

If a majority of votes indicated that the citizens were in favor of removal, the act provided that certain commissioners were to select an appropriate location within the town chosen by

Late 1930s-early 1940s postcard view of Main Street in the "ancient settlement which is known by the name of Lehighton." The monument to Colonel Jacob Weiss is on the left, at the entrance to the town park. Courtesy, Vince Hydro

the voters. The men selected in the act were Dr. Garrett B. Linderman, who had married Asa Packer's daughter Lucy in 1856, Dennis Bowman, Thomas Coons, Peter Hartz, and John Balliett.

The act also provided that, should the county seat be removed from Mauch Chunk, the county commissioners were authorized to sell the county property to the "highest and best bidder" at a public sale, and apply the proceeds to the debts created by the process of removal. The initiators of this act were apparently unaware of the reversionary clause within the deed to the property, providing that should Mauch Chunk ever lose its position as the county seat of Carbon, title to the county property and buildings would revert to the Lehigh Coal and Navigation Company.

The 1869 vote did not go in favor of removal.

The jail was not the only county building to deteriorate over the years. The court house quickly decayed with time. By January of 1852, although fairly new, the roof leaked so badly that it damaged the plastering in the rooms below. But the county's second court house, constructed after the first one perished in the Great Fire of 1849, would have to serve the county for almost four decades before a new one would be considered.

In 1889 the grand jury formally recommended the construction of a new court house. Edward H. Rauch, the editor of the Lehighton newspaper, the *Carbon Advocate*, used the issue to rekindle interest in the old removal question, and call for the transfer of the county seat to Lehighton.

Although a new court house was badly needed, and would be constructed on the site of the two former buildings in 1893, the editor of the *Mauch Chunk Coal Gazette* referred to the report of the grand jury as "needless clamor," and called the Lehighton agitators a "hopeless minority."

Needless to say, the removal issue never was successful.

Today Lehighton remains the spacious town that it was designed to be and Mauch Chunk, now Jim Thorpe, continues to wrestle with the space problems it has inherited from those who have gone before.

The second Carbon County Courthouse, built in 1851-52. Courtesy, Raymond E. Holland Collection.

For generations, taverns were the principal public meeting places. Here, politics was discussed and voting took place. Above is the White Bear Hotel at the foot of Summit Hill, one of the most famous and popular inns in Carbon County. After the inn was razed, its name was preserved in the form of a small statue of a white bear in a neighbor's yard. NCM; Bill Richards Collection.

The best-known hotels in Mauch Chunk were the Mansion House, of which there are a number of photographs in this book, and the Broadway House.

Below is the Exchange Hotel in Lehighton. Courtesy, Vince Hydro.

EXCHANGE HOTEL AND ANNEX. LEHIGHTON. PA.

(Above) The Bowmanstown Hotel. Courtesy, Raymond E. Holland.

(Right) The Fort Allen House hotel in Weissport, which got its name because it was built on the site of Fort Allen, the most important of Benjamin Franklin's line of fortifications in old Northampton County. Courtesy, Vince Hydro.

(Below) The Weissport Hotel. A quiet town today, Weissport was a major center during the canal era. The Lehigh Coal and Navigation Company had its main boatyard here. Courtesy, Raymond E. Holland.

The Postmasters of Mauch Chunk

The post office in Jim Thorpe has a display of former postmasters, some of them very prominent — even founding — members of the community. With the coming of the railroads, communication by mail was rapid and reliable. A letter mailed in Mauch Chunk in the morning, for example, would arrive in Philadelphia in time to be delivered by the afternoon, and a reply could be sent and delivered in Mauch Chunk by the following morning.

Here, in order of service and with the dates of their appointment, are the postmasters of old Mauch Chunk from its foundation to the beginning of the twentieth century. These pictures were first posted on the wall of the post office in 1906, when the fourteenth postmaster, E.F. Luckenbach, collected them for display.

The first postmaster of the young settlement, Erskine Hazard, was the son of the first Postmaster General of the United States under the Constitution.

Erskine Hazard
11/23/1819 – 4/15/1826

Josiah White
4/15/1826 – 5/18/1832

John Leisenring, Sr.
5/18/1832 – 1/29/1842

Alexander Stedman
1/29/1842 – 4/11/1849

James Miller
4/11/1849 – 1/12/1850

Alexander Leisenring
1/12/1850 – 12/2/1852

Eliza Cooper
12/2/1852 – 3/22/1860

John Cooper
3/22/1860 – 7/14/1860

Jane Righter
7/14/1860 – 8/20/1880

Nathan Cortright, Jr.
8/20/1880 – 8/9/1889

Julius Remmel
8/9/1889 – 1/12/1894

Frank Sharkey
1/12/1894 – 1/21/1895

George Esser
1/21/1895 – 3/8/1899

Edwin Luckenbach
3/8/1899 – 3/4/1912

The Right to Know:
Schools and Newspapers

America is a nation whose survival hinges on a free and informed electorate. For this reason, schools and the press play a key role in our society. This chapter will examine education and the newspapers in Carbon County's past.

Before Public Education

Despite the acknowledged importance of learning, it took some time for the concept of free public education to take root in the young United States; and Pennsylvania was not among the leaders in the movement. As we shall see, not until the 1830s were provisions made for free public schooling in the state; and not until 1895 did such schooling become compulsory. There were schools available before the 1830s, of course; but they charged tuition, and attending them often required considerable sacrifice.

Of Carbon County's first schools, it may be stated with assurance that they did not teach English even as a second language. The first school was the Moravians' school for American Indian converts at Gnadenhuetten Mission, on the present site of Lehighton. The school was opened in 1746. Aside from religion, it taught agriculture and mechanical subjects, all in the Lenape language.

In addition, there were schools associated with churches — German churches, in the Carbon County region. These were often so-called union churches, built jointly by Lutheran and German Reformed Church congregations. (The German Reformed Church, later the Evangelical and Reformed Church, is now part of the United Church of Christ; but there are many places where union churches continue as Lutheran-United Church of Christ partnerships.)

Having their own culture and their own commitment to education, German churches naturally taught school in their own language. One example was the school of Ben Salem Church in what became East Penn Township, a union church (now United Church of Christ only) founded around 1790. Its German-language school was the first educational institution in the township.

St. John's Church, in what is now Lower Towamensing Township, was founded in 1798. It, too, organized the first school in its area; and here again the language most likely was German.

By about the 1820s a new type of tuition school began to evolve. As a rule, a group of trustees was selected to build a schoolhouse, generally in some waste area where the land was cheap. A would-be schoolteacher would then apply to the trustees for permission to use the building. If permission were granted, the teacher would charge a modest tuition — perhaps $1.25 or $1.50 per quarter — for each student.

Obviously, teaching under these circumstances, and at this rate of pay, was not a highroad to wealth for those involved. But the tuition, however minuscule, was sufficient to keep many young people out of school.

Schools along this plan were erected in various parts of the county. East Penn had one, with teaching in English, at Ashfield in 1817. There was one at Lehighton, on the approximate site of the old Gnadenhuetten Mission, by about 1820. This was run by the Moravians, and part of the building was used for church purposes. Teaching here still was conducted in German.

In 1820 a board of school trustees was selected at Summit Hill, but the three members could not raise the money for a building. At that point the Lehigh Coal and Navigation Company built and donated a school building, and George Adams became the schoolmaster.

The school in what was to become Nesquehoning began in 1830, with the Bible, *Murray's Introduction and English Reader*, and Conley's *Primer and Spelling Book* among its texts. Mauch Chunk already had a school at this point; and by 1829 it had attracted the legendary irish schoolmaster James Nowlin, a well-educated but eccentric man, and a strict disciplinarian. His leather "taws" struck terror into the hearts of his students, and cut like fire into their skins.

For all his disciplinary cruelties, Nowlin was regarded as so fine a teacher that he drew students from miles around.

By the early 1830s, Carbon County had about twenty-eight schools of the type over which "Jimmy" Nowlin presided. Such schools were better than nothing; but they had obvious disadvantages. Control over what was taught and how it was taught was close to nonexistent, since the highest school authorities were the local boards whose members erected the school buildings. Thus, no uniformity of learning could be assumed on the part of those who passed through the education experience.

An even greater flaw in the system was that it effectively denied education to the poor. The Pennsylvania legislature had enacted a law in 1809 that required each county to provide free education for all children between the ages of five and twelve whose parents were unable to pay for their schooling. It became known as "The Paupers Law" because parents had to declare themselves indigent in order to take advantage of it. Few were willing to do so. A visionary Pennsylvania governor was about to change all that, opening the door of educational opportunity to everyone.

Governor George Wolf was born in Northampton County, the son of German immigrants. Because of his efforts on behalf of free public education, he may well be the most influential leader Pennsylvania has ever had. His leadership literally touched the lives of all who came after him.

In 1834, under pressure from Wolf, the General Assembly enacted a law calling for the establishment of free public schools. Wolf was aided in his championship of this law by Thaddeus Stevens, who later became the firebrand Speaker of the House in the Civil War and Reconstruction eras.

The free schools law must have been unpopular with certain classes, most notably the property owners who would have to pay for it. In 1835 it was almost repealed; but Wolf and Stevens stood firm, and it survived. At first, adherence to it was voluntary. The people of each district in the state could accept or reject it, and many chose to reject it. Not until 1849 was free schooling made applicable statewide. An 1854 act took matters further, creating the office of County Superintendent of Schools and authorizing the levying and collection of school taxes.

Originally the administration of the free schools fell under the jurisdiction of the Secretary of the Commonwealth; but an 1857 law established the post of State Superintendent of Common Schools. That same year, a normal school law was passed, to provide for the training of teachers.

Until 1893 all students still had to pay for their textbooks; but in that year a Free Text Book law was passed, removing the last barrier the poor faced in their quest for at least elementary schooling. Finally, in 1895, the General Assembly passed an act that made elementary schooling compulsory.

By 1843, when Carbon County was established, all of the townships and municipalities of the new county had accepted the Free School Act of 1834. The social and economic status of the teachers in the new public common schools was not, probably, very much improved over that of their predecessors in the tuition schools; but there was one interesting change: women teachers began to appear, or at least to appear more frequently. They had not been totally absent even in tuition school days; when the Lehigh Coal and Navigation Company established a school in Mauch Chunk in 1823, its first teacher was Miss Margaret Sanders of New Jersey.

> "If an elective republic is to endure for any great length of time, every elector must have sufficient information, not only to accumulate wealth and take care of his pecuniary concerns, but to direct wisely the Legislature, the Ambassadors, and the Executive of the nation; for some part of all these things, some agency in approving or disapproving of them, falls to every freeman. If, then, the permanency of our government depends upon such knowledge, it is the duty of government to see that the means of information be diffused to every citizen. This is a sufficient answer to those who deem education a private and not a public duty — who argue that they are willing to educate their own children, but not their neighbors' children."
> Thaddeus Stevens to the Pennsylvania House of Representatives, 1835.

As the free public school era dawned, more and more women were to seek a career in teaching. One example was Miss Lydia Bidlack, the first free public school teacher in Beaver Meadow.

Miss Bidlack was truly a pioneer of her time and her profession; but she should not be thought of as "liberated." For many years, women teachers earned less than men. Moreover, well into the twentieth century their lives were bound by rules that were, to say the least, unconstitutional.

Here, for example, are some 1915 rules for women teachers, laid down by the Pennsylvania Teachers Organization:

- You will not marry during the term of your contract.

- You are not to keep company with men.

- You must be home between 8 p.m. and 6 a.m. unless attending school functions.

- You may not loiter downtown in ice cream stores.

- You may not smoke cigarettes.

- You may not dress in bright colors.

- You may not under no circumstances [sic] dye your hair.

- You must wear at least two petticoats.

- You must sweep the schoolroom at least once daily, scrub the floor once a week with hot soapy water, start the fire at 7 a.m. so the room will be warm at 8 a.m.

While there are those who argue that the situation of today's teachers, women and men, is if anything too comfortable, few would deny that some amelioration in the early status of women teachers was definitely in order.

The door to the Chapel in Normal Square was the gateway to learning for many Mahoning Township children.
Photo by Joan Campion

The townships and municipalities reacted in different ways to the necessity of providing educational facilities for their young people. Lower Towamensing Township, for example, built seven or eight sturdy stone buildings in various parts of the township. Mahoning Township, on the other hand, set up a series of ephemeral but four-square little white schoolhouses, scattered from Beaver Run in the northern part of the township to Nis Hollow in the south.

Once Mahoning Township's schools had outlived their usefulness for educational purposes, they were destroyed or converted to other uses — sometimes, in the case of conversion, moved to other sites. They became homes or Sunday Schools. Many of the schools that were moved or destroyed left no indication that a school had ever been on the site.

Miss Arlene M. Haupt, a veteran of forty years of teaching in Mahoning Township and Lehighton schools and an educational legend in her own right, offered an explanation for the placement of township schools. Originally they were far-flung, to be within walking distance of the children they served — though "walking distance" could be a matter of opinion. For several years the author made a daily round trip of three miles to Normal Square, either on foot or by bicycle, to catch a bus or to attend grades five through eight in the village.

After the township began to offer bus service the schools were placed along main roads, like routes 443 and 902 (now Blakeslee Boulevard and Mahoning Drive). For a time there were only two of them, Horn's School on Route 443, on the north side of the road just west of the present Carbon Plaza Mall, and Sendel's School at the intersection of the present Mahoning Drive and Sawmill Road.

Near-legendary teacher Miss Arlene Haupt with her pupils from the multi-grade Horn School in Mahoning Township.
Courtesy, Arlene Haupt

As was the common practice in many places, each of these schools was named after the landowner who made the site available, and each had multiple grades. Toward the end of its independent existence, the Mahoning Township School District reverted to a pattern of one grade per school, except that the old chapel at Normal Square housed grades six, seven and eight on two floors.

Asked whether the multiple-grades-per school pattern did not complicate educational progress, Miss Haupt denied it.

"It made things easy," she asserted. "The younger children picked up part of the material for the advanced classes just by overhearing it while they were studying other things, and the older children helped the younger ones."

The system — or at least this particular teacher — must have had some merits. One of Miss Haupt's students was Lee Gaumer; she taught him for all eight years of elementary school. He went on to become Lee Gaumer, Ph.D., the nation's acknowledged leading expert on rocket fuel.

Amenities in rural schools were few. Plumbing in almost all of them was nonexistent; there were outhouses situated on the grounds, and children were delegated to carry pails of drinking water from nearby farms.

There were no gym classes; but the children were ingenious at improvising games of baseball and rounders (the game from which baseball is derived) during recess. Or they might bring jump ropes from home, or sketch hopscotch boards on the ground, or start a game of Red Light, or Tag, or Hide and Seek.

There were no art teachers, but the grade teachers saw to it that the students had time to draw, cut, and paste. There were no music teachers, although for a time Mahoning schools had a local musician and bandleader named John Kresge visit the upper grades and attempt to teach band instruments to interested children. Kresge also founded Wos-Wit Foods, the subject of a later article.

Besides, as former Mahoning teacher Marian (Mrs. Paul) Kresge recalled, music was never lacking from school life. Each day began with opening exercises that included a Bible reading, a prayer, the Pledge of Allegiance, and the singing of old songs and hymns.

"I can still hear the voices of the children singing 'The Little Brown Church in the Vale,' " she remembered many years later.

A combination of teacherly devotion and the ingenuity of both teachers and students patched over much more than apparent deficiencies in curriculum. Even the lack of school lunches was made up for by the contents of rattling metal lunch pails, sometimes with creative modifications. Students of Florence (Mrs. Earl) Simmons in the sixth grade at Normal Square, Mahoning Township schools, used to provide themselves with a fine hot lunch by bringing potatoes to roast on the coals of the heater, and a sandwich (often lebanon bologna, or "summer sausage") to grill on a sort of communal griller, also held over the coals. A thermos of hot soup or hot chocolate, an apple or a cupcake, completed a satisfying meal.

Marian Kresge was among those who felt there was something special about teaching and learning in such a setting. "There was a real closeness about it," she commented. "Above all, there was a real feeling of community. The parents would back you up on anything."

In the late 1950s and early 1960s, such rural schools were to fall victim to the movement for consolidation. Perhaps much was gained by the change; but, without question, something also was lost.

Towns also had their public schools, of course. These were often relatively palatial multi-story buildings with plumbing, and sometimes with paved or asphalt-covered playgrounds. Nevertheless, they lacked cafeterias and many other items and offerings now regarded as standard.

Through special circumstances, the small town of Weatherly in the northern part of the county wound up with the most palatial public school of all, a three-story brick structure with an imposing central clock tower. It cost the then-princely sum of $75,000.

Emma Eurana Dinkey was the granddaughter of Jacob Dinkey, one of the most prominent early residents of Ashfield, East Penn Township. Jacob Dinkey was a key figure in early county politics; with Asa Packer, he was one of the county's first associate judges.

Her father was Reuben Dinkey, who during her girlhood was general manager of the Lehigh Valley Railroad shops in Weatherly; thus she grew up in the town. (Reuben Dinkey, incidentally, managed to more or less immortalize himself when he invented a small locomotive that became known as "the Dinkey model," or just "the Dinkey." Popular usage has transformed this into "dinky," meaning something small and insignificant.)

In the course of time, Eurana Dinkey married Charles M. Schwab, millionaire steel man, former head of the Carnegie Steel Company and U.S. Steel, and founder of the Bethlehem Steel Corporation. The consequences for Weatherly were to be anything but small and insignificant; they included not only the imposing Mrs. C.M. Schwab School, but also the town's Eurana Park.

Weatherly's Mrs. C.M. Schwab School. Courtesy, Clarence Hendricks.

September 19, 1903, must have been easily the most festive day in the history of Weatherly. Thousands turned out as Schwab arrived in his private railroad car to dedicate the new structure. Until 1935 it was used as an elementary, junior, and senior high school. In 1936 an annex was added. The Schwab school is empty now. It was put up for sale in 1991, and the townspeople keep it in good repair. Even in its decline, the old building still dominates and symbolizes the town in a way no other building can.

High Schools

High school attendance was not the norm until well into the twentieth century; an elementary education was considered sufficient to meet the needs of most people. The schools did exist — in Fred Brenckman's time there were thirteen of them, including eight borough high schools, three in various townships, and the schools run by the independent Franklin and Packerton school districts. But it was a challenge to attend them; to mention just one problem, transportation was not provided. Furthermore, jobs were readily available to non-high school graduates, so that it took a special commitment to learning — or special social inducements, such as Styles S. Butz and his classmates were to try to provide at their high school in the new community of Palmerton — to keep young people in school after the first eight grades.

The faculty of Lansford High School around 1900. From The Story of the Old Company, *published by the Lehigh Coal and Navigation Company in 1941.*

Today, following consolidation, there are five public high schools in the county — Weatherly, Panther Valley, Jim Thorpe, Lehighton, and Palmerton. With the mandatory school attendance age raised to sixteen, the percentage of adolescents attending high school has increased dramatically. Of course, some other problems have been solved as well, such as that of transportation. Where the wheels of the familiar yellow school bus will not take today's students, their own wheels will.

Parochial Schools

As the public schools burgeoned, another system of schools grew up alongside them. These were parochial schools, founded by and for people who wanted their children to receive religious instruction together with the basic educational staples of reading, writing, and arithmetic. When the majority of people think of the term "parochial schools," they think of Catholic schools — certainly the most familiar examples throughout much of the United States. But "parochial" merely means "of a parish." In a loose sense, any religious school offering a full range of academic subjects, whether it is Catholic, Protestant, Orthodox, Jewish, or some other faith, may be though of as "parochial," or at least "congregational." The early Protestant German-speaking church schools of the Carbon County area were more alike than different from the Catholic schools that began to appear in the county in the late nineteenth and early twentieth centuries, although of course they offered very different views of theology.

Episcopalians attempted to establish a parochial school in Mauch Chunk very early on, an effort that was unsuccessful. But the burgeoning number of immigrants from Catholic countries meant that students were available in sufficient numbers to make schools run by that faith viable. It appears that the first Catholic school in the county was Lehighton's Ss. Peter and Paul. Founded in 1869, this school survives today. In the decades that followed its establishment, many other Catholic parishes in the county set up their own schools. St. Nicholas parish in Weatherly had one for a time; and there were schools at St. Ann's and St. Michael's, Lansford, and St. Joseph's and St. Stanislaus, Summit Hill.

Palmerton had its Sacred Heart School. Nesquehoning had a school by the same name, as well as one at Immaculate Conception parish. The list is meant to be suggestive, not necessarily exhaustive.

Today, consolidation has become the rule in Catholic as well as in public education. Our Lady of the Valley School in Lansford serves St. Ann's in that town, as well as St. Joseph's and St. Stanislaus in Summit Hill and Sacred Heart, Immaculate Conception, and Our Lady of Mount Carmel, Nesquehoning. St. Michael's, Lansford, continues its independent existence at this writing.

Immaculate Conception parish in Jim Thorpe no longer has a school; it sends its students to St. Joseph's Regional Academy on the east side of town. St. Joseph's also serves the children of St. Peter the Fisherman, Lake Harmony.

St. John Neumann, with its lower school in Slatington, Lehigh County, and its upper school in Palmerton, serves Assumption parish in Slatington, Sacred Heart in Palmerton, and St. Nicholas in Berlinsville, Northampton County.

The same move toward consolidation has occurred in the Catholic high schools of the region. The modern Marian Catholic High School in Hometown, Schuylkill County, brought together the former Mauch Chunk Catholic High School, St. Mary's in Coaldale, St. Ann's in Lansford, and St. Jerome's in Tamaqua.

Higher Education

Higher education remains something for which most Carbon County residents must leave the area, at least if they want anything more advanced than an associate degree. All of the county's school districts support Lehigh Carbon Community College, which is headquartered in Schnecksville, Lehigh County. The college offers quality education at an affordable price, especially in a wide range of technical fields. A branch in Jim Thorpe opened in the mid-1990s to make its opportunities more accessible to Carbon County residents. The college does not offer the bachelor's, master's, or doctoral degrees, although it does provide an excellent foundation for transfer to institutions that do.

In the nineteenth century it seemed at least possible that the county would develop a full-fledged college or two. The potential for such a development lay in the establishment of several seminaries, academies, and institutes, none of which, unfortunately for home-based higher education, survived for very long. Park Seminary, Mauch Chunk, was the first of these; it was founded in 1832. Later there was a Fairview Academy in East Mauch Chunk. There was also the Carbon Academy and Normal School, founded in 1853 by R.F. Hofford, who later became county superintendent of schools. This institution was located at first in Weissport. When the cataclysmic flood of 1862 destroyed the Weissport building, Hofford rebuilt at once in Lehighton.

Following Hofford's appointment as county school superintendent in 1863, the academy was taken over by A.S. Christine. Christine died in 1868, and the place was closed forever.

The last of the county's abortive institutions of higher education was the Normal Institute, originally known as the Normal Select School. Its founder was Thomas

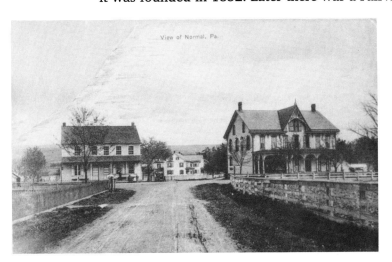

Postcard view of Normal (Normal Square), dating from the early twentieth century, several years after the heyday of Professor Thomas Balliet's Normal Institute. Courtesy, Ernest Eidam

M. Balliet of Mahoning Township, and it was located in the village of Center Square (now Normal Square) in the township. Balliet began the school around 1878, and it lasted into the 1890s. It was staffed during its existence primarily by students and teachers of Lancaster's Franklin and Marshall College.

Like R.F. Hofford of the Carbon Academy, Balliet became county superintendent of schools; in fact, he succeeded Hofford in that post in 1881. He went on to become superintendent of schools of Springfield, Massachusetts, and dean of the School of Pedagogy at New York University.

With the probable exception of the Park Seminary in Mauch Chunk, which was established before the free school law of 1834, the main goal of all these schools appears to have been the preparation of elementary teachers. That is betrayed in the titles of two of them, the Carbon Academy and Normal School and the Normal Institute. Until fairly recent times, a teacher training school was called a normal school.

Accepting that Carbon County residents were and are, on the average, as intelligent as people anywhere, it may be asked why no college ever did grow up here. Perhaps the answer lies in the hard, gritty conditions of life during most of the county's history.

A work schedule of fifty or sixty hours or more a week in mine or mill, or on the farm, did not provide much leisure to think of bettering oneself through education, even assuming one had the money to do so. Also, the sometimes long intervals between periods of work virtually guaranteed that the money would not be there for such a luxury. Periods of unemployment were struggles for survival that mortgaged the future.

Many of the immigrant mine and mill workers knew little if any English. Thus, they would have found it difficult, if not impossible, to function in an American classroom of the time. Even for their children, they hardly dared to dream of more than they had themselves.

They were good stock, the best there is — intelligent, hard-working, courageous, family- and community-oriented. But, for them, education was not destined to unlock the door to new worlds and opportunities.

School Days in Early Palmerton:
One School Boy Remembers

Palmerton was originally a subdivision of Lower Towamensing Township, and its schools fell at first under the jurisdiction of the Lower Towamensing Township School District. Prior to 1904, the township school board built a two-story red brick school for the burgeoning new village. It was set in marshy surroundings, with no road leading to it, and its amenities and comforts were few — specifically, a potbellied stove, a water bucket with a dipper, and an outhouse. Even taking an elevated pathway to what is now Fifth Street and Delaware Avenue, young Styles Butz had trouble keeping his feet dry on his way to and from school.

This building survived its original educational use to become a residence, 523-525 Franklin Avenue.

In the fall of 1909 the new Delaware School opened, and it must have seemed palatial by comparison to its predecessor. It was an eight-room building with heating and ventilating systems, a drinking fountain, restrooms, and a black-topped playground.

A high school was established in 1904, as a one-room, one-teacher school offering a two-year course, and located on the second floor of the New Jersey Zinc Company store building. In 1909 it was moved to the Delaware School; but it still occupied only one room and had only one teacher.

The Franklin Building opened in 1913, after the borough had been incorporated and had set up its own school board. In the new building, the high school was allocated three upstairs classrooms, a small library, and an office for the superintendent of schools, C.E. Cole. Cole was something of a universal man, educationally speaking; he also taught mathematics and served as high school principal.

When Styles Butz entered the high school in 1916, his class was instantly reduced from twenty-four to five, although it later picked up some recruits from rural schools. At that time, children were allowed to leave school at fourteen, and could almost certainly get a job if they did so. Palmerton High School offered a rigorous straight academic program and nothing else — English, Latin, mathematics, science, mechanical drawing, history and civics. There were no sports and no social events, nothing to compete with the immediate satisfaction of having money jingling in one's pockets. So, many students quit early.

Butz and his classmates (they graduated in 1920, since the high school program had been extended first to three years, then to four) decided things would be different. They would take a class trip to Washington following graduation. Meanwhile, they would do what they could to liven up the school and make it more appealing to the students.

They decided they would like to have a basketball team. This was a natural for Butz; he had played in the intramural program of the Junior Cooperative Association, and he had marked leadership abilities. The boy was delegated by his friends to go to Superintendent Cole and explore the prospects for a team.

Cole was not opposed to the idea, but said it would be necessary to petition the school board. Young Butz drew up a petition and collected the signatures of most of the students, and the superintendent presented the document to the school board.

The board approved, but there was one difficulty. There was no money in the budget to pay for such things; the school would have to raise the money itself. Once again Butz, only a freshman, was placed in charge. A Halloween social by the junior class netted around ninety dollars, with which he ordered the rudiments of uniforms.

The first Friday night after Thanksgiving, 1916, clad in its makeshift uniforms, the Palmerton High School basketball team won the first game it ever played, a hard-fought scramble against Northampton High School's junior varsity. Thus, seeking only relief from academic monotony, Styles Butz and his classmates laid the foundation for Palmerton's great high school basketball tradition.

There followed four years of what he called the "Free Enterprise System," during which the high school students raised the money for all extracurricular activities, and received no subsidy from the school board. "We probably had more fun doing it our way than we would have had by receiving funds from the school's budget," he wrote decades later.

In 1918, following World War I and the devastating flu epidemic of that year, Palmerton teachers went on strike for more money. They found scant support in the town, and the school board summarily fired them all and replaced them with substitutes.

Neither the "Free Enterprise System" of funding activities nor the school board's rigorous treatment of the striking teachers was to set a pattern for the future, in Palmerton or elsewhere.

Newspapers

In an era in which print journalism is on the decline, it is difficult to imagine the former importance of newspapers to Americans. Before radio and television, papers were the average family's only link to what was happening in the world and the nation. Small cities and towns often supported two or more vital papers. This situation prevailed even in not-very-populous Carbon County.

The county's newspaper tradition began in Mauch Chunk, with the *Lehigh Pioneer and Mauch Chunk Courier*. Founded in 1829 by Asa Lansford Foster, one of the area's most famous entrepreneurs, it was for a long time the only newspaper in the region. Its first editor and publisher was Amos Sisty.

In the course of time this paper had many names and many owners. It was known successively as the *Mauch Chunk Courier*, the *Carbon County Transit*, the *Mauch Chunk Gazette*, and the *Mauch Chunk Coal Gazette*. During the Civil War, an entrepreneur named Harry Vernon Morthimer printed a paper called *The Union Flag* in its offices.

Morthimer was to become one of the best-known names in Carbon County press circles. Harry Morthimer and J.P. Rowland founded the *Weatherly Herald*, first called the *Carbon Herald*, in 1880. After several changes of ownership, the paper was sold more than a century later to Mr. and Mrs. Jay E. Holder of White Haven. The Holders also owned the *White Haven Journal*; the combined paper that resulted was known as the *Journal-Herald*.

The senior Morthimer also founded the weekly *Carbon Advocate* in Lehighton in 1872. His son, George, attempted another paper, called *Truth*, which lasted only eighteen months before it was absorbed by the *Carbon Advocate*. In 1902 George started a longer-lasting publication, the Lehighton *Evening Leader*. This paper survived until the early 1970s, and remained in Morthimer family hands for all but the last few years of its existence. George Morthimer's only son, Guy Vernon Morthimer, succeeded his father in the paper's ownership. Its final owner was Richard G.W. Searles of Palmerton.

Boyle is, of course, another well-known name in county journalistic history. In 1872, O.M. Boyle launched yet another Lehighton paper, the *Weekly News*. It lasted only until the fall of 1873. O.M. Boyle seems not to have been related to a more successful publisher who shared his last name. James J. Boyle of Mauch Chunk helped to establish a journalistic tradition that endures today.

In 1883, O.B. Sigley had established the *Mauch Chunk Daily Times*. James Boyle bought Sigley's paper in 1908, and became its editor and publisher. Later it was called the *Mauch Chunk Times-News*. Boyle's son Joseph, or "Joe," was to become the dean of county newspapermen, and a leader in the effort to transform the economic life of the county; he is the subject of a separate article. The *Times-News*, now owned by Pencor Services and published in Lehighton, is a lineal descendant of the *Mauch Chunk Times-News*.

There were other papers in Mauch Chunk, among them the *Carbon Democrat*, started in 1847. In 1870 Joseph Lynn bought this publication and changed its name to the *Mauch Chunk Democrat*. Edward H. Rauch founded a rival paper, the *Carbon County Democrat*, in 1878. Eventually the two papers were merged under Rauch's ownership, and under the name of the *Mauch Chunk Democrat*.

In 1893 Edward H. Rauch's son Lawrence established the *Mauch Chunk Daily News*, which later was to merge with James Boyle's *Daily Times* as half of the *Mauch Chunk Times-News*. Lawrence Rauch also continued to publish the *Mauch Chunk Democrat* until 1911, when the paper suspended publication.

In Summit Hill, Daniel Eveland and Robert Harris founded the *Weekly Intelligencer* in 1873. Its lifespan was short — only about two years. J.W. Malloy, famous for his poisonous pen, established the *Summit Hill and Lansford Record* and in 1910 he sold the paper to William Gormley. Its independent existence continued, under various owners, until the 1960s.

A Republican-oriented weekly, the *Lansford Leader*, was founded in 1893 by Lincoln Davis. It continued to publish until 1933.

Palmerton, Carbon County's newest town, developed its own newspapers fairly early. The weekly *Palmerton News-Times* debuted in 1907. The *Palmerton Press* was published from 1912 until 1952, under the auspices of the Palmerton Printing Company. Joseph Nanovic's weekly *Palmerton Post* appeared from 1946 until 1985.

Today only one daily paper is published in Carbon County — the *Times-News*, owned by Pencor Services and with its main office in Lehighton. The paper is in part an amalgam of the Mauch Chunk *Times-News*, the Lansford *Evening Record*, and the Tamaqua *Courier*.

This successful consolidation represents, in itself, a triumph of technology. It also inevitably represents the loss of many other voices; that is its down side. The loss of newspapers is a trend all over the county, and it may be irreversible.

The *Times-News* has rivals within Carbon County — *The Morning Call* of Allentown, which has a Lehighton bureau, and the *Standard-Speaker* of Hazleton, which serves many families in the northern part of the county. Others take a Wilkes-Barre paper. These papers help provide a variety of journalistic viewpoints to readers.

Will there be newspapers, or even schools, when the next county history is produced — in, say, a century or so? Education in some form will be necessary as long as there is human society; but perhaps, in the future, the computer will be at the core of both educational and economic life — a learn/earn center that will make commuting to school or work unnecessary.

The same electronic circuitry may make it possible to perform such tasks as ordering the groceries — or the news, for that matter. It already shows promise of being far more sophisticated than newspapers, or television or radio news, delivering news and analysis of matters of interest to the system user.

The gadgetry in this admittedly optimistic scenario (for we might also destroy ourselves) can do much to set us free, and to preserve scarce resources. Whether it frees us to live larger, more interesting lives or smaller, narrower ones is something that will become apparent in the future.

Of schools and newspapers as we have known them, and as we are unlikely to know them in the years to come, two things may be said: they built communities, and they opened doors to wider worlds.

Palmerton and the
Coming of the Zinc Industry

"What Good Was Zinc?"

The term "smokestack industry" no doubt conjures up in the minds of most people the images of steel mills silhouetted against the sky, and of steel girders being hoisted into their places as part of the skeletal structure of bridges, skyscrapers, and other constructions of the modern age. Iron and steel have long played an important, if secondary, role in the economic life of Carbon County. The small forges and charcoal iron operations that dotted the landscape of the modern-day county have already been discussed.

In the twentieth century, the great mills of the Bethlehem Steel Corporation at Bethlehem attracted many Carbon County residents in search of jobs. The proliferation of the automobile meant that these people could return home after work. When the economic pull of such other industries as Allentown's Mack Trucks and Western Electric was added, the result was the transformation of the county into something of a "bedroom community" — one in which many people's jobs were situated at the other end of a lengthy commute, and they returned home in the evenings only for rest and recreation.

From around the turn of the twentieth century, though, Carbon County had its own giant smokestack industry, and a brand new town to go with it. The industry was zinc; the town was Palmerton. While its plants certainly were every bit as imposing as those of the steel industry, zinc could not otherwise be called a high-profile industry; in fact, it is doubtful that many people outside the field of metallurgy could have named any uses of the metal. This made it different from either the products of Bethlehem Steel, where so many county residents traveled to work, or from the output of the anthracite mines, Carbon County's other, and much older, heavy industry. Steel was used for building; anthracite was used to heat homes and to power industries. But what good was zinc?

Though it cannot be described as the sole or main ingredient in anything, zinc is an extremely versatile and important metal. It and its by-products are now used, or have been used in the past, in an enormous range of products and processes. It was, and to a lesser degree still is, virtually everywhere. Many of the uses of zinc are tied in with the steel industry. Galvanizing, the process of coating iron and steel with zinc to prevent rust and corrosion, is one of its most important uses. Galvanized pipes, culverts, roofing, steel girders, cables, buckets, and garbage pails continue to be common everywhere.

Elements found in zinc ore after the zinc itself was separated out are key ingredients in spiegeleisen ("looking-glass iron"), also called "spiegel iron," or simply "spiegel." First made in Prussia in 1850, which accounts for its German name, spiegeleisen is an alloy containing manganese, carbon, and iron. It was refined from zinc residuum in blast furnaces and was used in the production of steel, primarily as a deoxidizer and recarburizer.

Zinc oxide was used in the manufacture of a wide variety of weather-resistant paints and pigments, as well as in vitreous enamels, in pottery glazes, and in certain types of colored glass. Solutions of zinc oxide also were used to treat tree diseases, and to make medicinal ointments for humans. In the days when natural rubber was an indispensable ingredient in tires, boots, and the like, zinc oxide also was used to strengthen the rubber.

In wartime, luminescent zinc pigments lighted planes' instrument panels, and zinc oxide-based paints were used for camouflage purposes. In addition, metallic zinc was used in the alloys that went into the making of shell casings, and zinc oxide was one of the main ingredients in smoke-screen compounds. These were among many military adaptations of the metal.

In 1943, to conserve vital copper, the United States government began coining zinc-coated one-cent pieces, now interesting items in the hands of coin collectors around the country. Today, almost all Americans are in daily, if indirect, contact with zinc, for the metal is the base for the clad "pennies" that have been in use since 1964.

This by no means exhaustive discussion of zinc and its uses serves as a background in assessing the role of the zinc industry, not only in the life of Carbon County, but in American life in general.

Historical Background

Such metals as copper, gold, silver, and iron have been known by humanity for millennia. However, it was not until the twelfth century A.D. that the separate existence of zinc was recognized. The industry to exploit this belatedly understood mineral was therefore late in developing, not only in Europe, but also in the United States. Much of the early history of the American zinc industry, and in particular of the New Jersey Zinc Company, the founders of Palmerton, is tied up with a deposit of zinc ore in the Franklin-Sterling area of New Jersey, some fifty miles northwest of what is now New York City.

This deposit, containing what has been called the purest zinc ore in the world, had been known to Europeans since the seventeenth century. Around 1640, mining experts from New Amsterdam, the Dutch colony then centered on Manhattan Island, explored the area; but they seem to have been baffled by the nature of the ore. While most zinc ores are associated with heavy metals such as cadmium, copper, and lead, this deposit was relatively free from such metals. Instead, it was associated with manganese and iron — a rare mixture indeed, and one that was to take two centuries to learn how to work.

Around 1760 the land containing the deposit passed into the hands of a colorful figure — William Alexander. Although he claimed a British peerage and even called himself "Lord Stirling," Alexander served in Washington's army during the American Revolution, and rose to the rank of major general. He was one of many who attempted to develop the zinc deposit on his property. The puzzle eluded him, though his estates did become a major source of iron.

In 1848, Colonel Samuel Fowler acquired title to the deposit, and began to assemble a group of experts to solve the challenge of working the ore. Thus was founded the Sussex Zinc and Copper Mining and Manufacturing Company, which after several changes of name became the New Jersey Zinc Company.

A metallurgist named Samuel Wetherill made an important breakthrough while working for the new company; he discovered a way to make zinc oxide directly from the New Jersey ore. Wetherill later left and became general manager of a new company, called variously the Lehigh and Pennsylvania Zinc Company or the Lehigh Zinc and Iron Company, and situated in South Bethlehem, Pennsylvania.

The early years of the American zinc industry were marked by competition among many entrepreneurs, dispersed facilities under many owners, and conflicts over patents. But by the last decade of the nineteenth century New Jersey Zinc was fast becoming the dominant power in the field. The company or its subsidiaries acquired in rapid order the Passaic Zinc Company, Wetherill's Lehigh Zinc and Iron Company, the Mineral Point Zinc Company, the Empire Zinc Company, the Bertha Mineral Company, and the Friedensville Zinc Company. Still more facilities were added or developed later.

Two prominent trademarks were to remain among the relics of New Jersey Zinc's historical origins. One was the horse's head that appeared on an early New Jersey coin and on the seal of the state, and which now appears on the seal of the town of Palmerton. The other was "Sterling," a designation for high-quality metallic zinc which commemorates the name of the New Jersey mines where this fabulously rich ore was mined.

From 1892 until 1912, the burgeoning company was headed by Stephen Squires (or Squiers) Palmer, whose name was to be attached to Palmerton, but of whom disappointingly little is known. Born in 1853, 1854, or 1856 — no one seems certain even of the year — he was the son of David Palmer, cashier of the National City Bank of New York. As a young man he became a clerk in the well-known New York mercantile firm of Moses Taylor. In 1892 Palmer was elected president of the New Jersey Zinc and Iron Company and oversaw its expansion and consolidation into the New Jersey Zinc Company. Following his resignation as president in 1912, he served as chairman of the board until his death in January, 1913.

Palmer presided over a company whose labor, social, and even environmental policies were remarkable for their time, as will be seen. Under the circumstances, it would be interesting to know to what extent these policies mirrored his own ideas. Unfortunately, this information seems lost beyond recovery.

Considering that the best-known legacy of zinc manufacture in Palmerton is its status as a Superfund environmental clean-up site, the assertion that the environmental policies of the New Jersey Zinc Company were "advanced" may seem ludicrous. But no one knew decades ago about long-term buildup of pollutants in the soil and atmosphere, nor about their lingering effects on health and the ecosystem. As the noted historian Lance Metz has pointed out, all smokestack industry was polluting by its nature.

But New Jersey Zinc appears to have recognized that there was a sound business reason for attempting to minimize pollution and waste: to do so was to maximize profits. In its anonymously written 1924 corporate history, *A Record of Accomplishment, 1848-1923*, two striking examples of its efforts to control waste are pointed out with pride. One is the use of material from the separation of ore for road building in New Jersey; the other is the treatment of smoke at Palmerton to eliminate a "nuisance." Elements in the smoke were used to manufacture sulfuric acid, which became an important company product.

How, then, can the environmental outcome be accounted for? Did the company and its successors lose interest in controlling the problems of waste materials and emissions?

Many such questions may no longer be possible to answer. It does seems evident, though, that New Jersey Zinc should be credited with attempting to do something about pollution at a time when few other companies concerned themselves with the problem.

(Above) Looking north from Lehigh Gap, showing the railroads on both sides of the river and the large boatbasin in the canal.
(Below) The wagon of George Kuhl, confectioner from 641 Hamilton Street, Allentown, attracting a small crowd at Lehigh Gap in 1886.

Early views of the area that became Palmerton after the coming of New Jersey Zinc.
(Below) On the far right, at the top of Marshall's Hill (known then as Eddy's Hill), is the grand home built in 1881 by Elisha G. Marshall, a former brigadier general in the Union Army, for his bride, Janet Rutherford. Her family, a branch of the Rutherford, New Jersey, Rutherfords, owned paint-ore mines and processing mills in the area. The marriage was said to have been troubled. Gen. Marshall left the area, but his wife continued to live in the hilltop mansion with her Great Danes. Although not entirely unfriendly, she had few visitors and became known as "the hermit of Lehigh Gap." Mrs. Marshall closed her home in 1911, leaving to seek treatment for cancer. She died on October 30. Her estate was worth $1.75 million.

In addition to its early environmental concern, the company had a concern for the welfare of its employees that was far in advance of its time, at least for most American companies. From the beginning of its corporate history, it took care to provide health, educational, housing and recreational opportunities for its employees, on a scale that workers for most other companies could only envy.

Bethlehem Steel, that other large regional smokestack employer, provides an instructive contrast to New Jersey Zinc's social policies. In 1911 "steel" was hit by a strike, which it broke with the aid of the Pennsylvania State Police — then known as "Cossacks," because the role of the mounted officers was invariably to defend the interests of management against the aspirations of workers. In the wake of the strike, and only then, did Bethlehem Steel executives discover the wisdom of corporate intervention to improve their workers' lives. Armed with this new insight, the company began to provide clinics and recreational opportunities for employees and their families. Though the new policy was successful in staving off further serious labor unrest for decades, it looked, under the circumstances of its adoption, suspiciously like co-option.

New Jersey Zinc, on the other hand, seems to have pursued enlightened policies from the very beginning of its corporate existence, without the immediate incentive of labor strife. Perhaps the zinc company had no higher goal than the steel company — to prevent labor trouble. But to anticipate, to do what was possible to defuse stressed labor relations before problems arose, somehow seems more graceful than to wait, and to respond to a challenge only after the fact. Though the policy may be called paternalistic, paternalism is not without virtues.

Birth of a Town

It was in Palmerton, built from the ground up to manufacture zinc, that the zinc company's social policies were possibly to find their fullest expression. The town was founded in the wake of the consolidation of the zinc industry that had taken place in the last decade of the nineteenth century. The expanded New Jersey Zinc Company found itself with smelting facilities scattered through New Jersey and Pennsylvania. For the sake of efficiency, a decision was made to consolidate all such operations at one point — a point that must, among other things, have excellent transportation and access to a reliable fuel supply.

The search for such a location led to a tract of land just on the Carbon County side of the Lehigh Gap. Perhaps the selection was aided by Samuel Wetherill, a New Jersey Zinc Company board member and son of the former head of the Lehigh Zinc and Iron Company. Wetherill owned land in the area from 1883 until his death in 1890.

The chosen site ran from the village of Lehigh Gap, whose antecedents predated the American Revolution, to another village some two or two and a half miles up the Lehigh River. This village was called Hazard, after Erskine Hazard, Josiah White's partner in the Lehigh Coal and Navigation Company. The terrain between the two settlements was rocky or swampy, and the population was sparse.

Perhaps most important, the tracks of the Lehigh and Susquehanna Railroad, part of the New Jersey Central rail network, ran by the place, making the shipping of ore and finished products easy; and Carbon County's rich anthracite fields were close at hand, able to provide energy for the new industry.

An eleven-mile railroad, the Chestnut Ridge Railroad (later the Chestnut Ridge Railway), angled off across the future location of Palmerton, stretching its full length to Kunkletown in Monroe County. Known as the railroad financed by "two millionaires per mile," because its backers included the likes of J. Pierpoint Morgan, Chauncey M. DePew, and many others among America's richest men, it was built for the purpose of moving fine-quality white bricks manufactured in the Monroe County village to big city markets. There also was talk, for a time, of establishing a resort in the Kunkletown area, but nothing came of it. New Jersey Zinc bought the railroad and later elevated its tracks through the town; for a long time it carried zinc workers to and from work, as well as handling some freight shipments. The men used to play cards on their trips to the plants and back home, huddling around potbellied stoves in the cars for warmth in winter.

The plants in which they worked were not especially large, but they were designed to include the most advanced equipment for their time. What became known as the West Plant was the first to be built; it occupied a site near the village of Hazard, which it soon swallowed up. By about 1910 it had spread over about five hundred acres and employed some two thousand people. It included service and maintenance facilities, as well as units for the manufacture of spiegeleisen, zinc oxide, and slab zinc.

In 1911 a new plant was built east of Palmerton. During World War I it was very much enlarged, primarily to provide supplies of zinc oxide for use in tires. Later, facilities were added for producing the zinc pigments — lithapone and zinc sulfide — as well as rolled zinc, metal powders, luminescent pigments, sulfuric acid, and ferromanganese. New Jersey Zinc also established an important research laboratory in the new town.

As in other heavy industries, life in the plants was hard and dangerous. One long-time supervisor quit his job after many years; when asked why, it is said he explained, "I got tired of having to go to wives and tell them their husbands had been killed." But the work was steady, the pay was good, and the new town in which most of the workers lived offered many advantages to its residents. And this was due in large part to careful planning by the zinc company.

In order to lay the groundwork for Palmerton, two companies had been formed. The Palmer Land Company, with Mauch Chunk's Horace Lentz as its first agent, undertook the job of acquiring the land needed both for the plant and for the town.

By a power of eminent domain that no water company today would possess, the Palmer Water Company acquired the rights to all the waters of the Pohopoco Creek at Parryville, and began the process of laying four miles of thirty-inch pipe to the town, and many more miles of distributing water mains in the new settlement itself. Although Palmerton was officially founded in 1899, the water system was not completed until the spring of 1900. On September 1 of the same year, the sewer system and sewage disposal plant were completed. This was at a time when most American communities did not treat their wastewater at all, but tended to dump it, if possible, into the nearest available stream. The sewage plant had been built under the direction of Harrison N. Blunt of New York, the young engineer under whose direction much of Palmerton was planned. Blunt was assistant to G.G. Convers, who had succeeded Horace Lentz as agent for the Palmer Land Company. Upon Convers' death in 1908, he himself became the company's agent.

The ninety-foot-wide swath of Delaware Avenue is sufficient to show that, from the first, Palmerton was a town its builders intended to have taken seriously. And there was much more than just the sweep of this one street to confirm the impression. For example, architect William E. Stone was commissioned to design the first fifty workmen's houses, the luxurious inn, later known as the Horsehead Inn, at Third Street and Lafayette Avenue, four supervisors' houses and a store building, of which more will be said later.

Within a relatively short period of time there were in the town the first hospital in Carbon County (built in 1908 and enlarged in 1911), schools, a park, and churches, in addition to rows of tidy homes for workers and the more grandiose houses of their supervisors. The latter were situated in what was originally known as "The Reservation," for Palmerton's founders had a sense of social caste.

Housing for workers was good, if sometimes in short supply in the early days. Moreover, New Jersey Zinc employees were encouraged by easy terms to own their own homes. The purchase process was begun by the payment of 10 percent of the cost of a house and lot, and the house plans were submitted to the purchaser for approval. After 35 percent of the cost had been paid, the worker acquired title to the house, while the company carried the mortgage for the remaining 65 percent. The term of such mortgages was five years, and the interest rate a nominal 4.4 percent.

If the buyer could not keep up with the payments he was able, under certain circumstances, to return the home to the company and receive most of his money back, minus allowances for repairs and depreciation. The widow of a buyer could, if she chose, apply to receive back all the payments that had been made, plus 5 percent interest.

There was nothing cramped about the lots on which the workers' houses stood; each one included space for a garden. The company actively encouraged gardening by offering annual prizes for the best examples in town.

New Jersey Zinc went beyond even these efforts to provide a good life for its employees, and for other residents of Palmerton. In 1907 it established what it called a Sociological Department, and set up a Neighborhood House in the town. This was moved in 1911 to a larger building, and placed under the direction of social worker Florence Hughes. Neighborhood House provided a wide variety of social, cultural, educational, and recreational opportunities for residents and their families. The building contained a gymnasium that could double as a theatre, baths, bowling alleys, club rooms with billiard and pool tables, a circulating library, and play facilities for very young children. It was the site for mothers' meetings, shop and home economics training for young people, and for many other programs and events.

One person who took advantage of the opportunity was Styles S. Butz, who had moved to Palmerton with his parents in 1904, and who remained to become one of the town's most prominent businessmen and one of its most important keepers of historical memories. The author is indebted to Mr. Butz, who unfortunately died while this work was in progress, for making available his published articles and unpublished memoirs, which provide valuable insight into life in the town's early days.

Mr. Butz's father, J.S. Butz, did not work for New Jersey Zinc; he was a miller who milled iron ore from the Stony Ridge east of the town into iron oxide for paint. Later, when for health reasons the senior Butz could no longer continue in this line of work, the family founded the Palmerton News Agency.

But Neighborhood House was open to all, company employees' families and other residents as well; and Mr. Butz remembered ever afterward the well-equipped woodworking shop where he spent many hours.

"I got a lot out of that place," he commented.

For many years the zinc company provided still another educational opportunity, one that seems to have been restricted to its own employees. This was a night school on technical subjects related to zinc manufacture. Students bought their own books and paid a nominal tuition fee to be taught by the company's draftsmen, metallurgists, chemists, and other specialists.

Aerial view of the New Jersey Zinc Company's west plant at Palmerton, taken by noted Carbon County aviator Jake Arner, a one-time company employee. The canal has since been filled in and a roadbed laid over it. Courtesy, Byron Arner

From Subdivision to Community

In 1912 Palmerton was formally incorporated as a borough. Its first chief burgess was Dr. John Weaver Luther, who had been physician in charge of the town's hospital since its founding. Dr. Luther was destined to die at sea at the early age of forty-two, while on his way to Savannah, Georgia, to recuperate from an illness.

By the time of his death in 1917, the town he headed was already well established and prospering. It was a "company town" in the best sense of the term. Due largely to examples from the coal regions and from other industrial areas, that term has taken on a pejorative meaning. It has come to signify a town built and run entirely for the profit of the employer, where the workers and their families remained in conditions of near-servitude regarding such necessities of life as work, food, clothing, and shelter; where many could indeed lament, to paraphrase Tennessee Ernie Ford's famous song about a coal miner, that they "owed their soul to the company store." (The county's most prominent coal operator, the Lehigh Navigation Coal Company, the "Old Company," appears to have been considerably better than the average anthracite operator in these respects.)

In Palmerton there were many contrasts to this too-familiar state of affairs. Take, for example, the "company store" itself. New Jersey Zinc saw the need for a store to serve Palmerton residents, since only one store — Prutzman and Gruber's General Store — was within easy walking distance of everyone. Residents who could get there could also patronize Craig's General Store at Lehigh Gap, or Reuben Ash's or Wilson Ziegenfus's stores at Aquashicola, once called Millport.

To fill the need for a more accessible store, the zinc company built a structure for that purpose in 1904 or 1905; its design was by architect William E. Stone. Situated on Third Street across from the park, it was within easy reach of the whole town. Rather than run the store itself, New Jersey Zinc rented it to Easton merchants Person and Riegel. Local residents served as clerks under the firm's appointed manager, Frank Best. Though it was called "the company store," the extortionate atmosphere that characterized too many stores run directly by companies appears to have been absent. The establishment was richly stocked, and very popular. It was taken over later by a Palmerton resident, Harry Bossard.

Other businesses wishing to locate in Palmerton found their paths smoothed, a state of affairs that did not normally apply in a company town. In 1903, for example, the Read and Lovatt Manufacturing Company opened its second silk mill in Carbon County in Palmerton (its first was at Weatherly), and by 1920 the mill had undergone a fifty percent increase in size.

This firm was largely an employer of female labor, but there were many firms employing men as well. From 1917, for example, the Alliance Hollow Cement Block Company of Northampton operated the former B.A. Lichtenwalner Sand Quarry, which was situated on Stony Ridge above Hazard Road. The sand was used not only for the making of concrete blocks, but for building highways and for mine and railway locomotives as well.

Founded in Slatington in 1905 by D.M. Reitz and George B. Snyder, and moved to Palmerton in 1907, the firm of Reitz and Snyder was practically a conglomerate in itself. In addition to being involved in building and contracting, it operated a sawmill, a sand quarry, a cement block factory, a hardware store, a lumber yard, a warehouse, a planing mill, and a garage. As a contractor, it built Neighborhood House in Palmerton, among other buildings, and its contracting services were in demand in many other communities as well. In 1923 this firm employed about fifty men. Styles S. Butz acquired the company in 1948, and from then on it did business under the name of the Butz Building Center.

John E. Light's small Carbon Cement Block Company was opened on Lafayette Avenue in 1908. By 1923 it had five male employees.

The Palmerton Printing Company, job printers and publishers of the Palmerton *Press*, came on the scene in 1912. The company's president was George R. Elliston. The same year J. Tachovsky incorporated the Palmerton Bottling Works, which within ten years employed seven men and was delivering soft drinks from Easton to Wilkes-Barre.

In 1915 the firm of Bondy and Lederer began making cigars in the town. The company soon became a part of the United Cigar Manufacturers' Company, which later changed its name to the General Cigar Company, Inc. White Owl cigars were the brand manufactured locally.

These and many other businesses, most of them smaller, were backed up by many support-type enterprises. These naturally included the Palmer Land and Water Companies, as well as the Palmerton Lighting Company, whose independent existence can be dated from 1912; the Palmerton Disposal Company, which began in 1900 with the completion of the sewage works; and the Palmerton Telephone Company, organized in 1912.

Several financial institutions also grew up during the town's early years. They included the First National Bank of Palmerton (1907); the Citizens Bank of Palmerton (1917); the Palmerton Building and Loan Association (1915), and the Palmerton Savings and Trust Company (1920).

Life in Early Palmerton

The Setting

On good days tall plumes of smoke rose above Carbon County's newest town like feathers touching the sky. On bad days a pall lay over the town, nuzzling the flanks of the Blue Mountain. That was to be expected; that was, in fact, what Palmerton had been built for. It is doubtful that anyone could have predicted the environmental problems that lay decades down the road. It is doubtful, too, that all of them could have been prevented even had they been anticipated, given the technology then available.

If you didn't mind the smoke — and probably very few Palmertonians saw it as anything but a sign of burgeoning prosperity — life in Palmerton must have been reasonably pleasant, and in many ways unusually interesting. It was a place rapidly evolving into a genuine community; and that community included new Americans from many nations.

Melting Pot: National Churches and Organizations

Styles S. Butz remarked that at one time Palmerton was believed to be home to members of more than forty ethnic groups. He remembered an especially large influx of newcomers from Central and Eastern Europe and other foreign countries around 1912; but in fact they began coming much earlier than that. What drew them was what all heavy industry had to offer in those days: jobs for unskilled labor.

The town's church history more than hints at their coming. The first churches in the area — and, once it had been established, inside Palmerton itself — were characteristic of the region; at least some of the same denominations and congregations could have been found in any town within a hundred-mile radius. Thus, in 1896, shortly before Palmerton itself was founded, Trinity United Evangelical Church was built. This was followed in 1902 by a union Sunday School chapel, built jointly by Lutherans and members of the German Reformed Church.

In 1906 St. John's Episcopal Church was dedicated. Made of local stone, it was designed by H.J. Hardenbergh of New York, an architect who must have been related to Henry Hardenbergh, a New Jersey Zinc Company board member and later president of the company. Perhaps the two were the same person, although this seems unlikely. St. John's was founded by Stephen S. Palmer in memory of his wife, and it was often called Palmer Memorial Church.

A Catholic parish church, Sacred Heart, was built in Palmerton in 1908; and by 1912 the German Reformed Church felt strong enough to begin its own congregation, now First United Church of Christ. Meanwhile, the Presbyterians and Lutherans established missions in the town.

Side by side with this growth of the predictable regional variants of religious expression came an explosion of ethnic churches, each one serving the people of its national background who had come to work in the zinc mills. The year 1914 brought the founding of St. George's Russian Orthodox Church, and of a "Hungarian, Slavish, and Vindish" Lutheran Church. (What or who is meant by "Slavish," or Slavic, a very broad term encompassing many Central and Eastern European peoples, is difficult to imagine. "Vindish" or "Windish," a word whose precise origins remain in dispute, is a popular term for Slovenians.)

In 1915 Sts. Peter and Paul Greek Catholic Church was founded. Its name does not imply any connection with Greeks as a national group, nor with the Greek or any other Orthodox Church; rather, it was — and is — an Eastern Rite church acknowledging the spiritual rule of the Pope in Rome. In 1918, before this group had finished building its own edifice, members from the Polish region of Galicia seceded and formed their own congregation.

The year 1917 saw the establishment of what was called the Czechoslovak Church. Presumably its members were either Czechs or Slovaks, yet it affiliated with the Polish National Catholic Church, an insurgent group in the Wilkes-Barre area that split off from the Catholic Church a few years before this time. The Polish National Catholic Church continues to have congregations in Polish communities around the country, but this must be one of the few instances in which it attracted a congregation of non-Polish origin.

In 1918 St. Vladimir Greek Catholic Church, another Eastern Rite parish, was founded. This church served Eastern Rite Catholics of Ukrainian origin.

Sacred Heart Catholic Church was multicultural, serving the religious and cultural needs of some ten nationalities. Among the ethnic associations affiliated with it were Magyar (Hungarian), Polish, and Windish societies; Catholic Sokols, an athletic and cultural group prevalent in Central Europe; and the Sacred Heart Slovak Beneficial Pennsylvania Society. In addition to other, purely social and cultural, functions, groups such as these commonly provided health and burial benefits for members.

There also were a number of other national organizations in town, lacking affiliation with a church. They included the Hungarian Verhovay Society, an organization whose sole function may have been to pay out benefits to its members, and the Slovak Gymnastic Union Sokol, which had its own hall and presented gymnastic exhibitions, lectures, plays, and dances.

There were also the First Windish Fraternal Beneficial Society of America — Palmerton Branch; the fifteen-member Slavish Band, organized in 1913 and led by Andrew Hrusovsky; and the Greek Catholic Union of U.S.A., Fraternal Beneficial Organization, consisting of Palmerton Lodge No. 734, Palmerton Ladies' Branch No. 214, Palmerton Youth Branch No. 423-424, and Palmerton Sokol Branch No. 163.

The South Bethlehem First Hungarian Sick and Beneficial Society of Palmerton was organized in 1904; and the Hungarian Club (officially the Hungarian Immigrant People's Society) began in 1919.

In addition to these mentioned, other sizeable immigrant groups included Mexicans, Spaniards, Portuguese, Italians, and Lithuanians. No doubt many other groups came and went without achieving the numbers necessary to found churches, clubs, or lodges. The early history of the turn-of-the-century immigrants from Central, Eastern, and Southern Europe is now recoverable only in fragments, not only in Palmerton, but elsewhere.

Civic and Service Groups

The various national groups were far from being the only organizations in Palmerton. At the top were those groups whose activities encompassed the whole town, as they worked toward goals that would benefit all the residents.

Organized in 1906-1907, the Citizens Co-operative Association was an outstanding example of such an organization. It was made up of local businessmen and zinc company employees, and its main accomplishment doubtless was its successful drive to bring about the incorporation of Palmerton as an independent borough. This goal was achieved on October 14, 1912.

The CCA was active in many other areas as well. In 1914 it organized the first of its Fourth of July celebrations, with sports, parades, and fireworks. These events, which are said to have drawn 40 to 50 thousand people to Palmerton in some years, in turn generated a demand for a park bandstand, so the organization raised money for that.

It also established the Palmerton Fire Department, though it was not quite up to the fundraising demands of supplying it with a chemical fire engine. It hired Officer Peter Dougherty as the town's first policeman; and it obtained for Palmerton its own railroad station and free mail service. From planting trees to influencing the citizenry against the growth of the liquor trade, there was hardly a civic cause in which the Citizens' Cooperative Association was not involved.

In 1918 this organization was succeeded by the Palmerton Board of Trade, which took a similar activist stance in getting Delaware Avenue lighted and paved, and in dealing with highway improvements in the area and with the housing shortage that had already developed in the town.

Among the groups rendering service to the community on a more specialized level were the Palmerton Hospital Auxiliary and the American Red Cross Sanitary Training Detachment No. 1.

The Palmerton Hospital Auxiliary was an organization of women dedicated to aiding the work of the hospital in every possible way. Perhaps its most substantial achievement was the funding, in 1919, of a residence for students at the school of nursing, which had been founded in 1910. The group also made numerous, substantial donations of supplies and equipment to the hospital.

The American Red Cross Sanitary Training Detachment No. 1 was chartered in December 1916 by the Red Cross. As its name implies, it was the first group of its kind in the country, and may indeed have been the only one. Originally organized in the zinc plants to take care of on-the-job emergencies, the detachment consisted of men who were trained in first aid. As it began expanding its services into the community, it added many other skills. Each member had to pass a rigorous, two-year Red Cross course covering such subjects as first aid, elementary anatomy and physiology, and elementary nursing. The detachment annually spent a week in camp, combining recreation and further training.

When a severe epidemic of "Spanish flu" struck worldwide toward the end of World War I, a subject which will be discussed more fully in the chapter on the county in America's wars, the men of the Red Cross Sanitary Detachment served in the dangerous role of nurses, both in Palmerton and in Franklin Township. When Franklin Township was hit by a typhoid epidemic in 1922 it again asked the Sanitary Detachment's help, and seventeen men responded. All participants received medals from New Jersey Zinc in recognition of their services.

Special Interest Organizations and Lodges

In addition to the groups whose goal was community service for its own sake, many special interest groups and lodges sprang up in Palmerton. Quite a few of these also concerned themselves with civic betterment, though it was not their chief reason for being.

For boys and girls, there were the Boy Scouts and the Campfire Girls; for women, the Concourse Club, which soon became a member of the General Federation of Women's Clubs. Within a few years the men of the town formed an Exchange Club. And a local branch of Chautauqua, the informal educational network that was so popular in the United States in the late nineteenth and early twentieth centuries, offered lectures and other educational opportunities for Palmertonians of an intellectual bent.

The town and its surroundings also were home to a number of patriotic organizations. These included the Washington Camp, No. 601, Patriotic Order Sons of America (1901; Daughters of Liberty, Pride of Palmerton Council No. 199 (1908); Sons of Veterans, Corporal John Sterling Camp, No. 47 (1907); and the Robert Mader Post No. 269 of the American Legion, with the post's associated American Legion Auxiliary for women.

There were other lodges with more purely social objectives. They included the American Commandery No. 308, Knights of Malta; Palmerton Chapter No. 86, Order Knights of Friendship; two local lodges of the Independent Order of Odd Fellows; the women's May Rebekah Lodge No. 50 of the Independent Order of Odd Fellows; the Po-Hon-Achee Tribe, No. 49, Improved Order of Red Men; and the John W. Luther Chapter, No. 365, Order Eastern Star.

Sports buffs early founded organizations that served their interests. The Palmerton Athletic Association was organized in 1907. Soon there were also a Palmerton Tennis Association, the Palmerton Rod and Gun Club for hunters and fishermen, and the Blue Ridge Country Club, which offered the pattern usual for such organizations: golf plus social opportunities. Among the young people, the all-American sport of baseball thrived; and a young Irish mason named Jack Kelly introduced basketball into the town.

Band music was a central part of small-town American culture in the late nineteenth and early twentieth centuries, and Palmerton was no exception; a number of band organizations were prominent in its early days. The Slavish Band led by Andrew Hrusovsky has already been mentioned. There were as well the Lyra Band and the Palmerton Band and its offshoots.

Organized as an octet in 1901, the Lyra Band soon expanded into a full-sized band, which played for picnics, parades, dances, and concerts. Its best-known director was Dr. Hans von Berg, a graduate of Heidelberg University and a chemist who for a time headed New Jersey Zinc's lithopone division. To the average Palmertonian, the doctor was far better known as a cornetist and band director.

Dr. von Berg returned to his native Germany around 1909, but never entirely lost touch with his former band members. Following World War II, member Charles Klein received a letter from him saying he was living in a bombed-out Berlin basement but still had his cornet, and that he would very much appreciate some music. Klein passed the letter on to Claude Hay, then a prominent Palmerton-area orchestra leader. Hay sent a package of music, and received an appreciative response from von Berg.

By 1911 the Lyra Band had disbanded. The Palmerton Band was organized in that year, with Stewart A. Prutzman as its original leader. The band quickly developed a Boys' Band, to serve as a feeder for the adult band, and a Prep Band for beginners. Later, when the local high school had a band of its own, that group took over training functions on an informal basis, and the Palmerton Band's two younger offshoots were disbanded.

Until the 1960s coal silt was dredged from behind dams on the Lehigh River and brought to the zinc company in Palmerton to be used as fuel in the furnaces. Boats brought it by canal until 1942; after that it was transported by truck.

(Top) Dredging operation near Lehigh Gap.

(Left) Private and LC&N boats moored in front of the spiegeleisen furnaces.

(Below) A steam-powered tug boat and a scow loaded with coal silt docked near the dam at Lehigh Gap.

Working for "The Zinc":
Mark Pastir

When Mark Pastir was growing up, Palmerton was very much a "company town" but one whose atmosphere was far removed from that of its counterparts in the coal regions. Many coal operators tended to offer their workers little more than ramshackle housing, with tenancy at the whim of the company, and a gouging company-store system that often left miners and their families deeply in debt.

By contrast, the New Jersey Zinc Company at Palmerton provided help for workers who wanted to own their own homes, and offered as well a wide range of health, educational, and social benefits and niceties that would have been the envy of almost any American worker in the early part of the twentieth century.

Years later, Pastir retained a vivid memory of one of the niceties sponsored by the zinc company. This was the annual community picnic, held at Kunkel's Grove near the East Plant. Anyone could attend — no questions were asked — and those from the town who wished to go could ride out on the Chestnut Ridge Railroad free of charge.

Soon after he graduated from high school in 1935, the young man went to work as a laborer in the East Plant. In so doing, he was following in the footsteps of his Slovak immigrant father, who also was a company employee. But he doubtless had little choice. The '30s were the years of the Great Depression, and only the zinc company was making a concerted effort to provide young people just out of high school with jobs.

Postcard view of a shift change at New Jersey Zinc's West Plant in Palmerton in the 1940s. Courtesy, Raymond E. Holland Collection.

As a laborer, Pastir did whatever was required of him. He could be used just about anywhere, and his job might include working at the spiegel furnaces, general cleaning up, and dumping or loading railroad cars. After a few months of this he was moved to construction, and had a hand in building a giant vertical retort. Then he went to the rolling mill.

At that point he was tapped for an apprenticeship in electricity. This was a great learning opportunity, since the company had its own transmission lines, and offered the chance to work on everything from institutional to residential wiring. Many years later, he still considered himself lucky to have had the apprenticeship offered to him. "A lot of the people hired at the same time I was got with a department and stayed there," he remembered. The company did offer advancement to those it considered qualified, but by definition not everyone could advance.

Pastir spent the rest of his zinc company career with the electrical division of the service and maintenance department. During World War II he went to volunteer for military service, but was given a deferment because his job was considered vital to the defense effort.

He did not look back on his entry-level job as laborer with any enthusiasm. "It was hard work," he said. In those days there were no forklifts or front-end loaders; you did it all by hand. "I didn't enjoy that work *per se*, but I appreciated being able to learn a trade." To better his company-taught skills, he also took Pennsylvania State University extension courses in Allentown for five years.

Like workers everywhere, zinc employees enjoyed a chance to get together with friends after work, and they all had favored spots for socializing. Pastir was no exception.

"I frequented a lot of clubs," he remembered. "My favorite was the [Slovak] Sokol Club on Lehigh Street. It had bars, bowling, card playing, basketball, volleyball, gymnastics, and so on."

In 1946 and 1947, when close to three thousand men worked in the zinc plants, Pastir became an organizer in a successful drive to unionize the plants under the United Steelworkers.

"At the time there was not fair treatment of all workers," he explained. "There was a lot of favoritism, and a lot of people in the plants actually were abused because they were limited in education and not too sharp.

"The supervisors at the lower levels felt they had to be domineering. The mistreated workers tended to be older, and to have large families.

"Top management were good people, but I think they were mostly not aware of what was going on. The victims were afraid to complain.

"It surprised a lot of people that I got involved," Pastir reflected, "I was doing my job, and was well taken care of. But I said, 'I don't want to be treated like that when I'm older.'"

Former New Jersey Zinc Company employee Mark Pastir reminiscences about the years he spent working for the company. Photo by Joan Campion.

The vote on the union was unique because it had to be adjudicated by the National Labor Relations Board. At issue were five contested votes.

"The count was so close that one of those five votes had to be for the union," Pastir said. "It was."

No strike was involved in organizing the plants, but there was a strike around 1948. He could not remember all the details.

"At the time, union workers at steel plants were striking for an increase of 18½ cents an hour; and we struck, too, for the same amount. It seemed high to me.

"In the end we settled for something. I forget what."

In 1953 Mark Pastir left the employ of the New Jersey Zinc Company. After that he was in business for himself, and also worked for Prince Manufacturing Company in Bowmanstown, and for a regional Coca-Cola plant in Hamburg, Pennsylvania. Following retirement, he settled in Palmerton.

Rough edges and a Charismatic Bricklayer

Like any new town, Palmerton in the early days had some of the aspects of a frontier settlement. Loneliness was sometimes a problem, as it is whenever all the people in a place are originally from somewhere else and have not yet had time to make the connections that will bind them into a new community.

The town was unfinished and full of rough edges. Sizeable areas of it were, in those first days, pure swamp. One such area, south of Lehigh Avenue and east of Third Street, was called Bakavaros ("Frog Town") by the Hungarian residents, and no doubt various other things, not all of them printable, by residents of other national origins. A rough plank bridge led across it, but it did not significantly diminish the chance of an accident on a dark night, or under the influence of one too many drinks.

Building went on constantly, and to do the building workers were hired from wherever they could be found in the region, sometimes from considerable distances away.

Thus, in 1910, there came to town a young Philadelphia bricklayer, to work on building the east plant of New Jersey Zinc. He was of Irish extraction, his name was Jack Kelly, and to the boys of the town he was a fabulous, charismatic figure because of his great athletic ability and his rippling muscles. It was Kelly who introduced the comparatively new sport of basketball to the town, organizing games in a room above the company store. Thus, he may have made a lasting impact on Palmerton's sports culture, for Styles S. Butz and his friends saw Kelly's demonstration, and no doubt it influenced their view that Stephen S. Palmer High School should have a basketball team. Basketball was to become a very important sport in Palmerton, in some ways even more important to the high school's reputation than football.

John B. "Jack" Kelly's real sport, however, was rowing; he has been called the greatest oarsman in history. In 1919 and 1920 he won 126 consecutive single-scull competitions, and he was a star of the Antwerp Olympics. Only the Diamond Sculls of England's famous Henley Regatta kept him out, because, as a bricklayer who worked with his hands, he was accused of being a "professional." This bit of classism and snobbery was avenged, however, when Kelly's son Jack, Jr., won the Diamond Sculls not once, but twice. By this time Jack Kelly, Sr., was the head of Kelly Construction Company of Philadelphia, and the Kellys were rich.

Jack Kelly, Sr.'s, own accomplishments were destined to be eclipsed by the accident of his having a beautiful daughter. She was named Grace; and she went on to become a famous movie star and, later, Princess Grace of Monaco, dying an early, tragic death.

Twenty-five Years of Palmerton Business

Local histories funded by advertising provide readers with an intriguing, intimate look at the past. Spread before us, we can see the names of the places where our ancestors shopped, and the now often quaint-seeming goods and services they bought there.

The 1923 history of Palmerton, compiled to commemorate the twenty-fifth anniversary of the founding of the town, shows us that a wide range of businesses existed after a comparatively short period of time. Among the advertisers in the book were the following: Howard E. Pettit, women's clothing; E. Hawk, confectionery; John Ruzicka, shoes and notions; T.J. Snyder, undertaker and embalmer; the Palmerton Hotel; Charles E. Hellmuth, an Aquashicola furniture dealer; F.W. Diehl, baker; and Beer's Variety Store, offering ice cream, sodas, candies, household specialties, and bargain prices to boot.

There also were the Hotel Snyder, John F. Miller, proprietor; Milkowics' Meat Market, owned by L. Milkowics; Mrs. William Behler, groceries and provisions, of Hazard Road; Miss Mary S. Faust's The Grafair Shop, millinery; H. Brobst and Son, artificial fishing flies; Fried's Express, whose owner, W.F. Fried, specialized in freight hauling; and Ruzicka and George's Zinc City Garage, which among other things was the local Nash car dealership.

Harry Leshe, tailor, would make you a suit or alter one you already had, while Frank Vido, Shoe Repair, was ready to help you put your best foot forward at all times. F.E. Berger sought to paint your house, hang wallpaper, and perform other decorating functions; and Ray Souerwine of Ray's Electric Shop was eager to wire the house for lighting.

Ladies could shop at Miss Louella Lewis's The Ladies Shop, and be driven there and back by Hagenbuch's Taxi Service. G. L. Snyder offered insurance and notary public services. Roth's Garage was the local dealer for Gray automobiles. Warren Minnich invited your patronage of his Upper Millport Hotel; and H.J. Stofflet, barber, would be glad to give you a trim before you went there — or anywhere else, for that matter.

Some business combinations of the era appear strange to our eyes. B. Kaslovsky and Son is one example; besides being bakers, the Kaslovskys were dealers for Paige and Jewett automobiles. A.D. Kresge's Willard Storage Battery Service Station made a specialty of recharging and repairing automobile and radio batteries; and Greenzweig Garage had the dealerships for Durant, Star, and Chevrolet automobiles.

In addition, there were Charles W. Ziegenfus, insurance; the People's Furniture Store; Mooney's Meat Market and the Martin Nemecek Hotel, both in Aquashicola; Paul Pupak, who dealt in men's apparel; and A.A. Costenbader and Eugene George, who each had a plumbing and heating business.

J.A. Maurer ran a wholesale beverage business, while D.M. Browell was the proprietor of a popular movie house, the Park Theatre. There also was a Park Restaurant, but nothing suggests it had any business connection with the theatre.

It cannot be deduced, from its ad, what Fernbrook Park had to offer Palmertonians; but W.A. Buck made the range of his offerings abundantly clear. Buck had a store and also sold farm equipment, and was a funeral director on the side.

Other advertisers included Charles Horlacher, wholesale and retail beverages, who carried the Pur-Ox Soft Drinks line; Charles W. Kline, dealer for Willys-Knight cars; W.B. Snyder and sons, meat market; E.C. Deisher Motor Company, dealer for Hudson and Essex automobiles; Harvey S. Rader, auto accessories, and E.W. Borger Shoe Repair.

The Up-To-Date chose not to explain its business specialty, but it sounds very much like a clothing store. Prince Manufacturing Industry of Bowmanstown took an advertisement touting its presence and its paints, while "Jimmy" Mereyeas, "The Fruit Man" of Slatington, obviously did not want his Palmerton patrons to forget him.

Also present on the pages of the 1923 history were J.S. Costenbader, dry goods and groceries dealer of Aquashicola; Homer Kern, The Variety Store; Charles W. Smith's Sanitary Barber Shop; H.W.R. Detwiller, a tire dealer; C.B. Goodrich, Jeweler; P.M. Osterhout's United Stores, evidently another variety store; and — yet another strange combination to modern eyes — J.S. Ziegler, undertaking and embalming, and auto equipment.

In addition, there were J.G. Heintzelman's meat market; photographer John Mankos; J.S. Butz's Palmerton News Agency (owned by the father of Styles Butz, who was so helpful in providing information on Palmerton for this work); Jacob Frable, contractor and builder; Simon Sherman, men's clothing; B.W. Shipe, hardware; Alex Gergar, smokers' supplies and variety store; and Fred Mendsen, women's hosiery and shoes and children's clothing.

Stemler's Hardware Store may still be seen on Delaware Avenue, though it has changed hands, and its name also has undergone some changes. Mrs. Kline's General Merchandise of Hazard is long gone, as is Hazard itself — and, for that matter, the majority of businesses advertising in 1923.

The list of those businesses continues: Clayton Green, barber; the Palmerton Electric Supply Co.; Nothstein's Meat Market; Heimbach's Garage (the local Ford dealer); the Mauser Mill Co.; the Palmerton Supply Company, purveyors of food and fuel; S.V. Noll's Lehigh Valley Transportation Co., which ran buses; Constantine Brothers, quick lunch and confectionery; and R.A. Snyder, wholesale fruits and produce.

The Gordos Brothers did heavy hauling, while the Garin Brothers ran a pool parlor which also sold general merchandise. The Colonial Theatre was a rival to the Park for the patronage of movie goers.

A.J. Vlossak sold business machines, office furniture and fixtures, while W.E. Reamer was the proprietor of the Palm Drug Company. Justice of the Peace F.A. Seip also made collections and dealt in insurance, bonds, and real estate.

The Golden Anvil Hotel took out an ad in the history, as did Charles E. Basler's Basler Hotel. They were joined by J.A. Mooney & Co., a kind of general store; Shindel's Jewelry Store; Dr. R.S. AuRand, optometrist and optician; T.A.Y. Hodgson Texaco; Homer L. Kern, General Merchandise; and John C. Schaefer, dealer in coal, sand, cement, and plaster. (Schaefer, also a county commissioner, made his ad do double duty by including a pitch for re-election. His fellow commissioner, Adam Berger, also had an ad, in which the sole product plugged was Berger's own candidacy.)

A.A. Lester promoted his ice house, music teacher W.H. Schafer his lessons; and the Carbon Electric Company its products. Jesse S. Ziegenfus of Aquashicola was selling livestock feeds; and the Stemler Motor Company of Bowmanstown (S.E. and L.W. Stemler, proprietors) was pushing the sale of Buick and Dodge cars.

Back in Palmerton, it was possible to shop for clothing at Philip Brothers, Men's Clothing and Furnishings, or at the Harrison Store of New York, which specialized in women's clothing. Costenbader's Drug Store was the last such store represented in the 1923 history; and Palmerton Garage, the Studebaker dealership, the last of the automobile dealers.

There is romance in such a commonplace, prosaic list as this. To read it is to be carried back to a simpler time, when ice wagons and farmers with produce went door to door, and when a hot summer evening might end with a stroll to the local soda fountain for an ice cream cone.

That way of life is gone now, as truly "historical" as the Battle of Gettysburg — but, of course, a lot more pleasurable to remember.

Carbon County
in America's Wars

Indian Wars and the American Revolution

The series of dynastic wars between England and France in the first two-thirds of the eighteenth century was fought out in part on the North American continent; but for many years these American offshoots of essentially European conflicts left the region of Carbon County untouched. Only following Braddock's defeat in 1755 did war hit home in this sparsely settled area, with the Gnadenhuetten Massacre, the Frederick Boyer captivity, and a series of bloody but almost forgotten Indian raids on outlying farms and outposts.

As far as the future county was concerned, the Revolutionary War — the first "American" war, strictly speaking — was another such conflict. It had a thunderous echo near at hand, in the form of the Gilbert family captivity, but for the most part it took place far away.

At one point many of America's most prominent political and military leaders — men like John Adams, the Marquis de Lafayette, Count Casimir Pulaski, and John Paul Jones — gathered in Bethlehem, just a few miles south of the Lehigh Gap. It was feared that the British, having taken Philadelphia, were coming in pursuit of these prominent rebels. But all this can have had little impact north of the gap, if only because there were so few inhabitants on whom to impact.

The closest important military encounter — and it certainly did not compare to battles like Brandywine or Trenton — was the so-called Wyoming Massacre of 1778. In this battle, Col. Zebulon Butler, the commander of the Forty Fort stockade, lost control of his forces. They insisted on leaving the stockade, and many were slaughtered by British-sympathizing Tories and the Indians allied with them. The event sent shock waves up and down the frontier, just as Braddock's defeat once had done; but it had no serious effect on the outcome of the war.

Despite its remoteness from the main scenes of action, there are mementos of the Revolution on the Carbon County landscape to this day. In Beaver Meadows there stands a monument to Lt. William Wilson, an officer in Washington's army. He was the father of William Hart Wilson, who is regarded as the town's first settler.

In a separate, secluded Beaver Meadows cemetery lie the actual remains of several Revolutionary War soldiers. Among them are Daniel Washburn, Ephraim Ladd, and James McGarvan.

Washburn, whose mother was a descendant of settlers who came on the *Mayflower*, was only fifteen in 1778; yet he took part in the Wyoming Massacre and was one of its last survivors. In 1846 he recorded his memories of the event on paper. He died the same year.

Ephraim Ladd (1748-1836) was a member of Lt. Ezekiel Olcutt's Company, Connecticut Militia. As such, he aided in the relief of Boston early in the course of the Revolution. In 1829 he and his wife moved to Beaver Meadow, where they spent the rest of their lives. Ladd evidently was among those land-hungry Connecticut men who sought acreage in the northern part of what is now Pennsylvania, in territory once claimed by Connecticut. This claim was to precipitate the series of small wars known as the Yankee-Pennamite Wars.

About McGarvan little appears to be known, except that he was born in 1734 and died in 1830. It is said that the remains of ten other soldiers were removed from the Revolutionary War burial ground and placed in the Citizens' Cemetery.

In the central part of the county, on a hillside just south of Normal Square, is the grave of Peter Nothstein, another Revolutionary War veteran. Nothstein enlisted in the Pennsylvania Militia in 1775 and served for the duration of the war, rising to the rank of lieutenant. He seems to have been a daring and resourceful soldier; during the débacle of Washington's Long Island campaign, Nothstein evidently was one of those who escaped capture by the British by tying his flintlock to his back and swimming across an inlet of Long Island Sound. Following the Revolution he moved to what is now Mahoning Township, where he died in 1804 at forty-six — not a very advanced age even for those times. Historian Fred Brenckman, though, refers to him as an "aged patriarch."

The highest-ranking Revolutionary War veteran associated with Carbon County was Gen. Thomas Craig. Craig was originally from Craig's Settlement, or the Scotch-Irish Settlement in East Allen Township, south of Lehigh Gap. Like the rest of the county's prominent Revolutionary War veterans, his local ties date from after the war.

In 1776 he was commissioned a captain in Col. Arthur St. Clair's Pennsylvania Battalion. He took part in the American campaign into Canada, and by September 1776 was colonel of the Third Pennsylvania Regiment.

Brave and impetuous, Craig fought in the battles of Brandywine, Germantown, and Monmouth, and also in the siege of Yorktown, which led to the surrender of the Earl of Cornwallis and final American victory in the war.

Craig is credited with aiding Lydia Darrah, a Quaker woman with secret sympathy for the American cause, in preventing a surprise attack upon Washington's forces at Whitemarsh. The attack, so the story goes, was planned in the Darrahs' house during the British occupation of Philadelphia. Having overheard it all, Lydia Darrah slipped out on the pretext of buying flour. She encountered Lieutenant Colonel Craig, to whom she told the British plan. The subsequent attack was aborted as a result.

Craig's last military appointment was as Major General, Seventh Division, Pennsylvania Militia. He moved to the Lehigh Gap area in 1789, and kept an inn there for some time. His last few years were spent with a daughter in Allentown, where he died and was buried in 1832.

Craig left behind him a formidable social reputation. "Having quitted the tented field, he sought excitement and pleasure amid the lilacs and roses with the blonde and brunette beauties of old Northampton," noted Fred Brenckman, who as usual does not give us a source for this tantalizing bit of information.

Doubtless it was a phase that passed. The general, after all, lived to be ninety-two, and had plenty of time to modify his ways.

An interesting feature of Carbon County's Revolutionary War connection was the settlement, after the war, of a group of Hessians in the Quakake Valley.

"Hessians" was the generic term for German mercenary soldiers hired by King George III to fight his rebellious American colonists. They were hated and feared by the Americans; but they were not as formidable as they seemed. Their own lives were hard, miserable, and circumscribed. Attracted by the lures of religious, political, and economic freedom, as well as by the easy availability of land in the "enemy" country, many of these soldiers deserted or found other ways to remain. Often they were helped and encouraged by the German settlers already in the country, who were soon to be known in this region as the Pennsylvania Dutch.

The Quakake Valley group of settlers included Col. Jacob Hartz, Daniel Gerhard, Daniel Heil, John Faust, George Kless, John Wetzel, and Jonathan Winter.

The Yankee-Pennamite Wars

Many generations of Pennsylvania schoolchildren must have been puzzled by a particularly nagging question from their state's early history. That question is: Why did George Washington, colonel in the Virginia militia, accompany British General Edward Braddock on the latter's ill-starred expedition into western Pennsylvania in 1775? The answer is that Washington, and the governor who commissioned him, believed he was helping to defend Virginia, not Pennsylvania territory.

When seventeenth-century British officials, sitting in far-off Whitehall, divided the territory of North America among their chosen colonial proprietors, they were not always careful to avoid overlapping boundaries. One result was that parts of what is now Pennsylvania were claimed by Virginia, Maryland, and Connecticut. These conflicting claims were settled, in part, through mini-wars and battles, like Lord Dunmore's War with Virginia and Cresap's War with Maryland. The Maryland border also was stabilized by the surveying of the famous Mason-Dixon Line, the traditional boundary between North and South in American history.

The real trouble Pennsylvania had was with Connecticut. Had the struggle here come out differently, the state would have lost the northern two-fifths of its territory, including Carbon County's own Kidder Township.

Settling the issue on this northern front required a whole series of small wars. Known as the Yankee-Pennamite Wars, these conflicts began in the eighteenth century and spilled over into the early nineteenth. The "Yankees" in the equation were, of course, the Connecticut settlers. The "Pennamites" were those who traced their claims to the land to the Penn family, proprietors of Pennsylvania.

The trouble originated with the fact that Connecticut received its charter in 1662, well before William Penn was granted proprietary rights to Pennsylvania. The Connecticut charter granted that colony land from sea to sea between the 41st and 42nd parallels, with the exception of territory already occupied by "any Christian prince or state." This excluded New York, then a Dutch colony; but it meant that the Connecticut land claim could be considered valid west of the Dutch holdings.

At first the Connecticut authorities seemed uncertain of the status of these lands to the west, and made no attempt to encourage settlement there. But by the 1750s, Connecticut residents were pressuring their colonial government to open up the western claim.

In 1753, a private land speculation company called the Susquehanna Company was formed and chartered. The following year, at the Albany Conference in upstate New York, the company's leaders purchased land in the Wyoming Valley from the Iroquois Indians.

Since the Iroquois had promised to sell this land only to the Pennsylvania government, the legality of this new arrangement was questionable. Nevertheless, the Susquehanna Company at once began promoting settlement by Connecticut residents in the Wyoming Valley.

The Indian raids of the late 1750s delayed large-scale settlement for a time. Following the end of the French and Indian War in 1763, though, several hundred families from Connecticut moved to the Wyoming region. The Penn family obtained a court order in London, requiring Connecticut to curb further occupation of the land in dispute. Moreover, in 1768, at Fort Stanwix, the Penns got the Iroquois to repudiate their earlier sale of the land to the Susquehanna Company, and to sell it to them instead. This was known as the "Old Purchase" treaty: but it did not settle the issue among whites.

The Susquehanna Company offered a five-mile-square plot of land to any group of forty Connecticut residents who would settle in the Wyoming Valley and defend the land against claimants from Pennsylvania. Under these provisions, Forty Fort was settled in 1769.

Simultaneously, the Pennsylvania government was encouraging Pennsylvanians to go to the disputed region and hold it against the newcomers from Connecticut. This set off the first Yankee-Pennamite War, a series of raids and counter-raids that lasted from 1769 to 1771, and that ended inconclusively.

A few years later, in 1774, the Connecticut government stirred up the situation once again by formally recognizing the Wyoming settlements, and creating there a Connecticut county with the inflammatory name of Westmoreland. For some time, indeed, the five thousand Connecticut residents of the new county sent delegates to the Connecticut legislature.

The second Yankee-Pennamite War broke out in 1775, when Connecticut settlers established the town of Muncy. An uneasy truce reigned during the American Revolution, as both sides combined against the common British foe.

Following the war, Pennsylvania appealed to the Articles of Confederation government to settle the land dispute with Connecticut. The resulting Trenton Decree of 1782 confirmed Pennsylvania's title, but added that the rights of individual Connecticut settlers should be sustained. Disagreements over this settlement resulted in the Third Yankee-Pennamite War.

Fortunately, this proved to be the last in the series. An 1807 statute once again confirmed the rights of the Connecticut landholders in the Wyoming region, but granted their Pennsylvania rivals cash compensation. With that, the long conflict ended.

The imprint of the Connecticut settlers remains in the Wyoming Valley. Its most visible symbols are the buildings remaining from this period which have been preserved at historic sites — buildings with a pronounced New England aspect, such as the Forty Fort Meeting House, the Sweatland Homestead, and the Denison House.

The War of 1812

Although it was the war of "the rockets' red glare," inspiring Francis Scott Key to write the verses of our national anthem, the war of 1812 is largely forgotten by Americans today. It was America's second military encounter with England, the mother country; and the terms on which it ended were not especially favorable to the United States.

And so, if we remember anything about the war beyond "The Star-Spangled Banner," we remember the British burning of Washington, D.C.; but we tend to forget that the burning came about in retaliation for the American burning of York (now Toronto) in British Canada. Above all, if we are thinking about this war, we remember the Battle of New Orleans, fought after the war had ended, which catapulted Gen. Andrew "Old Hickory" Jackson to fame, and later to the presidency.

The War of 1812 impinged fairly heavily on Pennsylvania. The British blockaded Philadelphia for a time; Gov. Simon Snyder called up fourteen thousand men. At the western end of the state, Commodore Oliver Hazard Perry cobbled together a fleet with the aid of some naval architects, and defeated the British in a battle on Lake Erie. Perry's victory was important; it guaranteed continuing American control of what was then called the Old Northwest.

Carbon County's best-known connection to this war was Col. John Lentz of the Pennsylvania Militia. Lentz enlisted in the war at the age of nineteen. Originally from Lehigh County, he moved to the Carbon County area and became a hotel keeper and a key figure in the politics surrounding the establishment of the county. When the Civil War broke out, Lentz volunteered again, but was turned down because of his age. Nevertheless, at the time of the Battle of Gettysburg he formed a company to march in defense of the state. He died in 1875, aged eighty-two.

Young Samuel Horn of Carbon County was a drummer boy during the War of 1812. He served in the Battle of Lundy's Lane, under a regimental commander named Colonel Winfield Scott. Horn later became a member of the Stockton Artillerists and fought in the Mexican War. There his commander was, once again, Winfield Scott, now the general commanding the American advance on Mexico City.

The significance of this war to Carbon County was profound. Trees in the vicinity of Philadelphia had long since been cut down and used for fuel and building; when British blockades prevented coal from Virginia from being delivered to the city, efforts to ship anthracite down the Lehigh and Delaware rivers increased, leading in turn to increased experimentation in ways to use the hard coal. Although use of soft coal resumed when the war was over in late 1814, the stage had been set for commercial development of Carbon County's vast anthracite reserves.

The Mexican War

President James Knox Polk was a politician with an overriding idea. The idea was known in its time as Manifest Destiny; today it is called in many quarters by less flattering names, such as imperialism. What it amounted to was that the United States should push westward to the Pacific Ocean, since it was the nation's "manifest destiny" to rule over the entire expanse of the North American continent between the Atlantic and the Pacific.

A great many obstacles stood in the way of this ambitious agenda — not only vast plains, mighty rivers, inhospitable deserts, and towering mountain ranges, but whole peoples. There were numerous Indian nations, the British settlers of western Canada, and Mexicans.

Whether Polk's political philosophy is liked or deplored today, he was an amazingly successful president in terms of doing exactly what he set out to do. When he left office after four years, the present boundaries of the continental United States had been pretty well established, and most of his campaign promises had been kept. Probably no other president, before or since, can make that claim.

It took a certain amount of saber-rattling; and in fact it took more than that. It took the Mexican War. This is another conflict that, like the War of 1812, has been largely forgotten. It is hard to see why; this is, after all, the war in which the Marines came to the Halls of Montezuma. It is almost overstocked with colorful incidents and characters — characters who, in many cases, were to make a deeper impression on history later. There was the corpulent and flamboyant general-in-chief, Winfield Scott, who had already been a highly ranked officer in the War of 1812, who later ran for president, and who, at the beginning of the Civil War in 1861, was still on active duty as army chief of staff.

There were two other generals, Zachary Taylor and Franklin Pierce, soon to be presidents of the United States themselves. Capt. Robert E. Lee was there, and Lt. Ulysses S. Grant, and many other young soldiers who were to be the generals on both sides during the nation's looming Civil War. Another officer in the war was Jefferson Davis, the future president of the Confederate States of America.

Few incidents in American military history are more dramatic than the storming of the fortress of Chapultepec. Yet the American people do not, as a rule, remember the adventure of 1846–1848. Perhaps there is indeed some subconscious question in the public mind regarding the ultimate justice and necessity of the war, as has been suggested by more than one historian. Or perhaps the citizenry simply is exercising its inalienable right to forget.

To this brilliant and deadly war, Carbon County sent its first organized military company, the Stockton Artillerists. They drew their name from Commodore Robert Field Stockton, a friend of Asa Packer, who was the builder of New Jersey's Delaware and Raritan Canal and commander of U.S. naval forces in the Pacific during the Mexican War era.

After several false starts, and with the financial and moral support of Asa Packer, the eighty-four members of the company found themselves in New Orleans and on their way to Mexico. During their long journey southward they had stopped off in Pittsburgh, where they had become members of the second Pennsylvania Regiment.

Soon they were in Vera Cruz, Mexico, where they received a warm welcome in more than one sense. The day after their arrival, with the temperature hovering around 109 degrees Fahrenheit, they were under fire for the first time.

Then, following the redoubtable General Scott, they were on the march for the Mexican capital.

Scott's success in this endeavor was by no means a foregone conclusion. At least one soldier of considerable reputation considered the American general and his forces doomed. That soldier was the aging Duke of Wellington, the conqueror of Napoleon. When Scott succeeded in capturing Mexico City, Wellington proclaimed him "the greatest soldier of our time."

Carbon County's Stockton Artillerists played a distinguished role in the campaign. Capt. James Miller, for example, wounded though he was, joined better-remembered soldiers like

U.S. Grant and future Confederate general James Longstreet in the daring and successful final assault on Chapultepec fortress.

But the price was high. Twenty-three members of the company were killed in combat. Others died of wounds or disease, in some cases falling victim after they had returned home. Their ranks were reduced, in the end, to less than half of their original number.

A Letter From Mexico

Thomas Crellin was a boy when his parents moved their family from England to the United States in 1823. The Crellins located in Mauch Chunk, then a boom town with many opportunities. Following the early death of their father, Thomas and his brother John went to work for the Lehigh Coal and Navigation Company. There they made friends with young Robert H. Sayre, who later became a prominent associate of Asa Packer in the building and management of the Lehigh Valley Railroad, one of the founders of the Bethlehem Iron Company, forerunner of Bethlehem Steel, and president of the board of trustees of Lehigh University.

The Crellins were engaging letter writers, as was their friend Sayre. Several of their letters have been preserved on microfilm in the archives of the National Canal Museum, Easton. One of the most interesting of these so-called "Crellin letters" was written by Thomas to his sister Elizabeth on April 27, 1846. As a member of the Stockton Artillerists, Thomas was serving in the Mexican War. The letter gives a description of the battle of Cerro Gordo, and of the living conditions of the troops from Carbon County. What follows is an excerpt:

> We left Vera Cruz and marched four days (approximately 40 miles) to a place called Cera Gorda [sic] where we was attacked by Santa Anta [sic] with 20,000 men. It was a pass and it would be impossible to get through it without being cut to pieces. We held up 3 miles from this place until all our forces got together and then we commenced on them and it lasted about two hours and was pretty hot work while it lasted. I never knew what it was like to be in an engagement before. There were three wounded in our company. The Mexican balls are principally made of copper which makes wounds something bad. We have a first rate physician who takes good care of the men. I was over the battleground the next day and a harder sight I never saw our dead and wounded were taken care of immediately, but the Mexicans both dead and wounded was laying there. It was a terrible sight to see indeed, we took a great many pieces of artillery, muskets and ammunition. Also a great many prisoners among them was General LaVega. Scott has released them all but the officers. Them he has sent back to Vera Cruz. We then marched for Gallapa [Jalapa] and it took two days to get there they did not resist but gave up at once. The two Pennsylvania Regiments camp close together. We live pretty well. Have fresh beef occasionally. We draw flour and make shortcakes.... We sleep in little huts of brush to shelter us from the hot sun and heavy dew. The country here is considered very healthy. We don't know how long we will be here but it is rumored we will not go any further but if we do it will be to the city of Mexico which is 200 miles from here. I am in hopes we will be home soon.

Rumors of the health of the Mexican countryside proved grossly exaggerated, at least where Thomas Crellin was concerned. He soon contracted a raging case of malaria, and it nearly killed him. He spent the rest of the war as an invalid, and when at last he was able to return home to Mauch Chunk his brother noted that he looked skeletal.

But Crellin survived the war and recovered from his illness, and these are things that cannot be said for all his comrades of the Stockton Artillerists.

The Civil War

Despite imposing Civil War monuments in towns like Jim Thorpe and Weatherly, this first modern war was widely unpopular in the coal regions. The coal miners, largely Irish at that point, felt in many cases that the liberties they were being asked to defend were not ones in which they themselves shared. Many of them feared, too, that if the Negro slaves of the South were freed, they would be brought north and hired to take over the miners' jobs for even lower wages than the miners themselves were getting.

In Hazleton, in neighboring Luzerne County, and in Cass Township, Schuylkill County, there were draft riots when conscription was introduced in 1863, though these were dwarfed by similar demonstrations in places like New York City. The federal government also sent troops to Columbia County, which was strongly Democratic, to quell the so-called "Fish Creek Insurrection." In a gross miscarriage of justice, forty well-known citizens were arrested and held in Fort Mifflin. The "insurrection" appears to have been nonexistent; but this harsh move by the government reveals the deep anxiety felt in Washington over discontent in the Pennsylvania anthracite region.

There seems to have been no disturbance in Carbon County large enough to be called an anti-draft riot. But there was disaffection nevertheless; and Carbon County miners appear to have joined those from Luzerne and Schuylkill counties in going on strike and shutting down the mines. The Lincoln administration found it necessary to base troops in Schuylkill County for the duration of the war. Those were commanded by Carbon County's Brig. Gen. Charles Albright, later chief prosecutor of the so-called Molly Maguires.

In 1862, at a July 4th celebration, the young miner John "Black Jack" Kehoe spit on the American flag. The unpopular celebration organizer, a mine foreman named F.W. Landon, was attacked and stoned that night, and died of his injuries the next day. Kehoe was later executed for Landon's death, although in the end he received a posthumous pardon.

On November 5, 1863, a mob of men with blackened faces broke into the home of mine owner George K. Smith and murdered him. Smith had been a staunch proponent of military conscription.

In Penn Forest Township, in the Hunters' Hotel on the way to White Haven, a Union Army recruiter was shot dead. His killer was never found. And forty-five men from the now-defunct village of Northern Liberties near Mauch Chunk enlisted in Mr. Lincoln's army; but one man, it is said, registered his dissent by signing up as a Confederate.

But for the most part, the men from the anthracite region did serve, and served with great heroism. It was miners from Schuylkill County, for instance, who undermined and blew up one of the Confederate forts at Petersburg (the so-called "Petersburg Mine"), though the opening they thus provided for Union forces was squandered by incompetent generalship.

In the early stages of the war, the Lehighton Fairgrounds saw an encampment by Pardee's Rifles (Company A, Twenty-eighth Regiment, Pennsylvania Volunteers). Entirely supplied and equipped by Hazleton coal baron Ario Pardee, this force was led by Captain Ario Pardee, Jr., who later rose to the rank of brigadier general. It was passing through on its way to Philadelphia to join the regiment of Col. John W. Geary.

Carbon County, of course, had military units of its own, as did every county in those old militia days. (The modern Pennsylvania National Guard was not organized until the 1870s.)

Thus, before the Civil War, Mauch Chunk had the Cleaver Artillerists, later the Anderson Grays; the Hibernian Guards or Irish Infantry; and the dark-green-clad German Jaegers (the word means "hunters") who, as might be expected, were riflemen. In Summit Hill there were the Carbon Guards, and in Beaver Meadow the Lafayette Guards. The "Lafayettes" were named for the great French hero of the American Revolution, but they were garbed like American troops of the War of 1812.

Lehighton and Mahoning Township both contributed men to the Scott Rifles, named after Mexican War hero General Winfield Scott. There even was a cavalry company from Towamensing and Lower Towamensing; it was commanded by John Craig, a grandson of Gen. Thomas Craig and himself later a colonel in the Union Army.

Despite local disaffection with the war, Carbon County sent over two thousand men to serve with United States forces. This was at a time when its total population was just over twenty-one thousand.

All in all, the county supplied soldiers for twenty-two companies. Eli T. Connor, the twenty-nine-year-old commander of the Anderson Grays, was the first to respond to the Union's call for troops. He opened a recruiting office and enlisted three full companies of young men within twenty-four hours. They were attached to the Sixth Regiment, commanded by Pottsville's Col. James Nagel, and served in the disastrous early encounters of the war at Harper's Ferry and on the upper Potomac. After three months they were discharged; however, many reenlisted for three years or the duration of the war.

Although originally signed on for three months, the next Carbon County company in fact accepted a service term of three years. It became an important component of Company F, Forty-second Regiment, originally organized in Harrisburg as the Thirteenth Pennsylvania Reserves. This regiment became famous as the Bucktail Rifles.

Company F also was called the Irish Infantry. It was captained by Dennis McGee, its first lieutenant was Hugh Mulligan, and its roll was replete with other Irish names — because most of the Irish did do military service, often serving with great distinction.

The Bucktail Rifles went on to show their mettle in many of the major battles of the Civil War. These engagements included Bull Run, Chancellorsville, Gettysburg, and the Wilderness Campaign, among others.

In addition to these initial units, twelve to fifteen more companies, or their equivalent, were raised mainly in the county. They included two companies for the Twenty-eighth Regiment, four for the Eighty-first Regiment, one for the Eleventh Regiment, and one for the Fourth Pennsylvania Cavalry.

There also were portions of companies for the Fifty-third Regiment, the Eleventh Infantry, and the Eleventh Cavalry. The equivalent of about another company was scattered among other units.

When Confederate Gen. Robert E. Lee first moved north, a move which was checked at Antietam, many more men from the county volunteered. In 1862 two additional companies were recruited in the area for the 132nd Regiment.

Some four hundred more county men responded when Lee and his forces invaded Pennsylvania and were repulsed at the bloody Battle of Gettysburg in July 1863; old Col. John Lentz, veteran of the War of 1812, raised a company to meet this emergency. In 1864, more than two hundred additional men volunteered for one year.

The service record of young men associated with the public school at New Mahoning, Mahoning Township, deserves special mention. No fewer than thirty-seven men from the vicinity of this small crossroads village enlisted, most of them connected in some way with the school. This was at a time when only twenty-one voters lived in the district.

Years after the war, one of the survivors caused a tablet to be erected in memory of his friends and comrades. The plaque was erected in 1908 at the New Mahoning School, and has since been moved to the Mahoning Elementary School. The names on it are: Oliver F. Musselman, Otto Stermer, Joseph Eames, John Miller, John Callahan, and William Nothstein, all listed as having been killed in battle or having died of wounds, and Henry Snyder, William H. Fulton, Joseph Ackerman, Samuel Eberts, William Stermer, Nathan Stermer, D.W.C. Henline, Thomas Musselman, Jacob Nothstein, Daniel Houser, Thomas Strauss, Reuben Reinsmith, Robert Sinyard, William Sendel, Ammon Fritz. Also Josiah Musselman, Daniel Kressley, Stephen Fenstermacher, Peter Eberts, David Eberts, William Eberts, Henry Zellner, Jacob Strauss, Aaron B. Miller, Moses Neyer, Aaron Snyder, Elias S. Hoppes, John H. Arner, and James F. Kressley. Joseph Fulton and James R. Swank are listed as teachers.

Navies were just beginning to go to coal-fired steam rather than sail power, and the anthracite of Pennsylvania was a valuable asset — which, above all, is why the federal government found it necessary to guard against disaffection in the coalfields. That disaffection proved, as we have seen, to be broader than it was deep; but this was not something the government could take for granted in advance.

When John Ericsson's innovative ironclad U.S.S. *Monitor*, with its revolving gun turret that made it look, as people said, like "a cheese box on a raft," clashed with the Confederate ironclad *Virginia* (formerly the *Merrimack)*, the engagement was an historic one. It pointed the way to future navies composed of ships of metal, totally dependent on engine power rather than on wind power. It is said that, when the *Monitor* steamed to meet the *Virginia*, its fuel was relatively smoke-free anthracite from Spring Mountain in Carbon County.

For some decades anthracite would continue to be a valuable defense commodity, powering both ships and the industries that built the ships and cast the guns. In the last analysis, though, its contributions to victory would not be enough to save the hard-coal industry.

Letters From the Front: James Hughes in the Civil War

James Hughes of Junedale was just eighteen years old, and not even an American citizen, when he enlisted in Company B, 147th Pennsylvania Volunteers, on August 17, 1861. Born in Wales, he was not naturalized until 1868, several years after his war experience had ended.

The young man may have been influenced by economic considerations, as well as by feelings for his adopted homeland, when he decided to become a soldier. His parents were separated, a situation more common in the nineteenth century than is generally realized, and he was living with his mother. In an era in which women were not expected or encouraged to work outside the home, her lot must have been a hard one.

Hughes was already working as a miner; but that was a notoriously underpaid job, and one in which there were likely to be long periods without work or pay. Volunteers for the army were supposed to receive a three hundred dollar bonus, and that was a sum large enough to be of genuine help in the family's situation.

We may assume, too, that one of his motivations for enlisting was a sheer sense of adventure. He was, after all, a young man. As it turned out, he was also a lucky young man.

His regiment saw some of the hottest action of the Civil War. He survived, when many of his comrades did not.

Hughes could not write. Like many other soldiers, he kept in touch with his family through letters dictated to officers, some of them barely more literate than he. A number of his letters have been preserved by his great-granddaughter, Maxine Eisenhower of Hazleton. Despite their poor spelling and lack of grammar and punctuation, despite the knowledge that they are, in a sense, second-hand communications, it is possible to hear in them a real voice — the voice of the average, hard-driven, hold-fast, heroic soldier of the Civil War.

He seems to have come under fire for the first time at the Battle of Antietam in 1862. This represented Confederate Gen. Robert E. Lee's first attempt to carry the war into the North. Lee was repulsed, but at enormous cost.

Following the battle, the young Junedale man dictated a letter to his mother.

Whoever took his dictation choose to preface the letter with the conventional phrase, "I take my pen in hand once more..." The letter is reproduced exactly as it was written.

Louden Heights Va

Sept. the 28th — 62

Dear Mother I take my pen in hand once more to drop you a few lines to let you know that I am well at this time & hope this will meet you & all the rest of you in good health. I received your letter Some time ago & was glad to hear from you the reason I did not wright sooner was be caus we was on the march for Six weeks & could not rite as wee was not long enough in one place. after we crossed in to Maryland we was on the move all most every day wee heard the rebels was crossing in to maryland wee gave them all the chance they wanted & when they started for frederick city wee then be gan to move pretty fast in persuit, but when wee got to Frederick they had left & had gone to what is called the South mountain hear they had made a Stand McClellan attacted them a sharp battle ensued but wee put them to flight captureing some eight hundred prisoners & a couple of pieces of their artilery I was not in this battle our army followed them to the Antietam creek here they got reenforcement & was determined to try us again whitch they did to their Sorrow our forces attacted them on Wednesday the 18 the battle commenced at day light & lasted til dark our brigade was engauged in this battle we went in at five o'clock & was engaged six hours during whitch time we engagued & put to flight Some three rebel brigades & captured three of their flags at one o clock a nother brigade took our place & relieved us we lossed a good many men but they lost at least five to our one after this battle they crossed in to virginia they had told the rebels private they was a going in to pennsylvania & when they got their they should rob and tak evry thing they could get but they did not get so far as they escepted they are now in virginia verry mutch disheartened at getting whiped & chassed back so quick since the last battle wee have moved to harpers ferry our division holds possession of Louden heights the rebels are reported to be in force at winchester I think we will move on them soon I received a letter from my father a bout the same time I received yours he said he had heard I had sent money to Mauch chunk bank & said if I would send him my money he would put it is safe ceeping I sent no money to any one but you & I think your carr of it as safe as anuone else wee are looking for the pay master evry day now and when I receive my money again I will send it to you our regiment was all ways wanting a fight

me with the rest & I am not anseious to see a nother it is a Horrible Sight to
walk over a battle field sutch as the last one in maryland their is where wee
see the horror of war william wiely is here he is well he send his best respects to you I have nothing more to right at preasant but I will remain
your affectionat son till death.

James Hughes

The writer of the letter then added an admiring personal postscript, which Hughes may
or may not have been told about:

Mrs. Hughes any old lady Should be proud to have a Son in the army as
braive as your Son is he fought like a hero

Hughes was stationed near Washington, D.C., at the time of the Battle of Gettysburg;
thus he missed the titanic struggle on the soil of his own state. But the news of Meade's defeat
of Lee must have come in by telegram, because already on July 3, 1863 — the last day of
the battle — the young man sent a reaction to it:

Cattic [?] Station, July th 3r

Dear Mother

I received your welcom letter Some time ago but have been unable to give
you an answer untill now for we have been marching every day Since I was
glad to here that you was Still in good health as this leves me at Present.
Dear mother I Suppose you have herd about the grait Battles that we have
fought in Pennsylivania we fought hard for three days and gave the rebels
the worst whipping Ever they got and Chased them Back to Virginia again
and I don't think they will trouble the People of Pennsylvania any more we
took a great many Prisoners and canon and Small arms and I fell thankfull
to god for his kind mercy in Protecting me through Every Battle and I hope
he will continue his goodness towards us. and I hope that this crull war is
about at an end So that we may Enjoy a Peaceful home once more. I had a
letter from Sister Mary the Same day that I got yours they weir all well. I
have received no letter from Father this to months. I must Come to a Close
with my kind love to you all the mail is about to Start and I have little time
to write no more at Present But remains you

Son James Hughs
Co. B 147. PV
1St. Brigade 2nd division
12 Corps Washington Dc

The 147th Pennsylvania Volunteers were with Gen. William Tecum-
seh Sherman on the famous (or infamous) March to the Sea through
Georgia in 1864. A Hughes letter from conquered Atlanta takes full
account of his surroundings, and of his anti-Confederate fervor. But
much of the letter is devoted to money matters; his mother may have
had special difficulties at this time. We learn here that several years
after the start of the war, the promised $300 enlistment bonus still had
not been paid to Hughes and his comrades:

*James Hughes, Carbon County's oldest surviving Civil War veteran, outside
his home in Junedale.* Courtesy, Maxine Eisenhower.

Atlanta, Ga. Sept 17th/64

Dear Mother — I am glad that I can Say that both of your last letters as well as the one you wrote to Col. Craig [apparently the reference is to fellow Carbon Countian Col. John Craig] came to my hand a few days ago — You need not trouble yourself about the local Bounty at all. I must share the fate whether I get it or not with the rest of the Company. No man in our Company has yet received the Local Bounty and when and where they get it I will also get. Efforts are now being made to get it from the place of our Enrollment and that is at Coalmont, Huntingdon County, Pa. The Directors of that place have agreed to pay us at a given time to Secure our credit — When it will be paid to us I cannot say yet but it is morally certain that if they do claim us for their credit which they can do unless we are specially credited elsewhere They are bound to pay us according to the State law which voted each volunteer who are credited to their respective places of Enrollment Three hundred Dollars. According to that very act we will be paid. but in Such a case of course we may have to wait a year or more as the money would have to be collected through taxation. But the prospects are that they will have to pay us voluntarily before a great while. Capt. Moore is not with the Company and has not been since last May when he was wounded.

But he is arranging with the aforesaid Directors of Coalmont to get our Bounty and of course I will get my credit there. I will See in a few days what will be done regarding the matter and if things are not satisfactory I will write to him for a Certificate and Send to you to obtain my Bounty where you think best. But there is not the least doubt but what it will be get some day If you are out of money why inform by return mail and as we are daily expecting our Government pay and in case that we are paid I will send you by Express or any other way I can. I would like to hear how my Cousin John Smith likes soldiering by this time, send me his addrys when you again write. I have had but one letter from Philip Harris since I was at home and not one from Lemuel Morgan. We are now Encamped within the town of Atlanta Ga. which place we captured on the last day of August. A Heavy Battle was fought on the right and South of the City and our army proved victorious compelling the rebels to retreat and leave us in possession of the City. We took a great many prisoners and munitions of war with but slight loss to our gallant Army. Atlanta is a pretty large town and it is called a City. The rebels had it well fortified so much so that five different lines of Breastwerk were thrown up around the town with forts here and there dotting their defenses. But we overcame all these and drove them from the city and we will drive them clear out of their Confederacy if they give us nother year longer to fight them. we are at present resting from our long and weary Campaign in order that we may get paid clothed and well fed so as to begin a fresh fall Campaign against the rebels to drive them still farther in the direction of the gulph [Hughes likely means the Gulf of Mexico] they they may all drown I am quite well and happy and have nothing to complain about but am as content and happy as a gay Summer Lark.

Respectfully your
Afectionate Son
James Hughes
Co. "B" 147th Regiment PV
2nd Div. 20th

Following the war James Hughes returned to Junedale, where he married and had a family. He died in 1920, having survived longer than any other Carbon County Civil War veteran. We may never know whether he finally received his three hundred dollar bounty payment.

Interlude: The Spanish-American War and Afterward

The Spanish-American War of 1898 was the culmination of a long-standing feud between Spain, which then held an empire including Cuba and Puerto Rico as well as the Philippines, and the United States. James Knox Polk's idea of Manifest Destiny was still powerful, and in the minds of many prominent Americans, such as Theodore Roosevelt, expansion beyond continental North America was the next logical step.

When the battleship U.S.S. *Maine* was blown up in the harbor of Havana, Cuba, on February 15, 1898, with the loss of many of her crew, the United States blamed Spain for the incident. President William McKinley issued a call for volunteers.

Theodore Roosevelt, who was soon to succeed McKinley as president, called this "a splendid little war." It featured such dramatic episodes as Admiral George Dewey's destruction of the Spanish fleet in Manila Bay in the Philippines without the loss of a single American; and the similar feat in Havana harbor, where admirals Sampson and Schley destroyed the opposing fleet with only one man wounded and no fatalities for the United States. The war also was memorable for Roosevelt's own charge up San Juan Hill at the head of his personally recruited Rough Riders.

At least, these colorful and bloody episodes gave the Spanish-American War a certain notoriety at the time. Like the War of 1812 and the Mexican War, it has receded into the mists that hide forgotten conflicts.

The whole thing lasted around six weeks. Carbon County was a little slow in gearing up for the show, and missed it.

Under a second call for volunteers, Dr. William H. Clewell recruited some one hundred twenty-five county men. They were attached to the Ninth Regiment of Col. Charles B. Dougherty of Wilkes-Barre. Clewell became a lieutenant in his own company, while Robert S. Mercier, also of Wilkes-Barre, served as captain.

About thirty Panther Valley men joined Col. Theodore Hoffman's Eighth Regiment at Tamaqua. Both Clewell's and Hoffman's men were shipped off to camp; but the war was over before they could be sent into combat. It was, perhaps, the county's most fortunate war.

The Spanish-American War left the United States with a far-flung empire, including the Philippines. Many Filipinos, though, wanted to be free not only of Spain, but also of the United States. Under the leadership of Emilio Aguinaldo, they staged an insurrection that in June 1904 claimed the life of a Carbon County man. He was Capt. William H. Wilhelm, a Regular Army officer, who was born in Mauch Chunk in 1867, graduated from Lehigh University in 1883, and from West Point in 1888. Before being sent to the Philippines he was stationed in the American West and in Cuba.

This Carbon County soldier sitting on a horse-drawn artillery caisson reminds us that World War I was the last to be fought with cavalry units for both combat and supply. Eastern Pennsylvania supplied thousands of horses, sold to dealers who shipped them to Europe starting long before the United States entered the war. Courtesy, George Harvan

World War I

In Europe, in the last years of the nineteenth century and the first decade of the twentieth, a system of alliances and counter-alliances had been built that boded ill for the peace of the world. The final arrangement pitted the German Empire and the Austro-Hungarian Empire, long ruled by the Hapsburg dynasty, against England, France, and the Russian Empire of the Romanoffs. The two sides built up their armaments, jockeyed to win advantages from each other, and challenged each other in farflung colonial territories in Africa and elsewhere.

All Europe was a tinderbox, awaiting only a spark to set it off. In Sarajevo, Bosnia, in 1914, that spark was supplied by a young Serb named Gavrilo Princip, when he fired a shot at the heir to the throne of the Austro-Hungarian Empire. Within minutes the heir, the Archduke Franz Ferdinand, and his morganatic wife were dead; and war, if not truly inevitable at that point, was made so by the ensuing round of ultimata, threats, and miscalculations.

The roar of "the guns of August," 1914, was not to cease for more than four years. When at last there was silence, it was the silence of death. A whole generation of European manhood had been all but wiped out in the trenches of France and the massive battles that raged on the eastern front. The royal houses that had seemed so permanent a part of the European scene just a few years before — Hapsburgs, Hohenzollerns, and Romanoffs — were gone, too, for the most part, packed off into exile or, in the case of the Romanoffs, murdered.

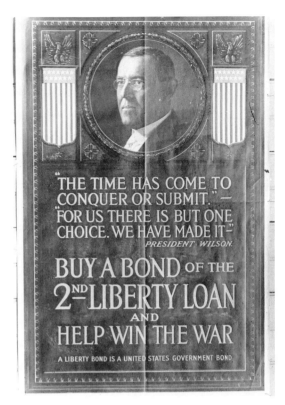

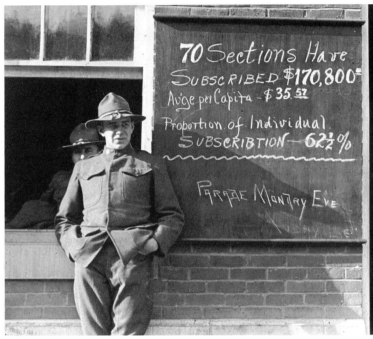

(Above) Poster for the Second Liberty Loan drive, which took place in October, 1917. Posters for subsequent drives featured such hard-sell, emotional icons as "The Kaiser, the Beast of Berlin" treading on a helpless child, or a gold-star mother wrapped in the stars and stripes. All citizens were expected to give a certain quota to the war effort through bonds. The drives were accompanied by rallies and parades, featuring popular speakers and stage and movie stars who toured the country to help raise money. These photos were taken by a Carbon County photographer by the name of Shaeffer who worked at Lehigh University. *Courtesy, George Harvan*

At first President Woodrow Wilson refused to involve the United States in the distant struggle, describing the country as "too proud to fight." In 1916 Wilson ran for re-election on the slogan, "He kept us out of war." It was close indeed; but he won.

German attacks on neutral shipping eventually became at least the pretext for American intervention. From late 1917 through the Armistice of November 11, 1918, American doughboys played a key role in breaking out of the years-long stalemate of trench warfare in France, and bringing victory to the Allied cause.

Pennsylvania's Twenty-eighth Division gained renown in this war; and as usual Carbon County supplied its share of manpower to the war effort. The names of those who did not return — names like Dolon, Shoemaker, Garland, Dietrich, and others — often were attached to local posts of the American Legion, founded in 1919 in a foredoomed attempt to guarantee that the so-called "war to end wars" they had just been through achieved its announced objective.

Foreshadowing the vast social changes that were to occur in the United States during the twentieth century, the Lehigh Navigation Coal Company hired three or four young girls to work as slate pickers in the Nesquehoning breaker during World War I, apparently because there was a shortage of young men. One of these "breaker girls" was Susan Skladony, later

(Above) Carbon County draftees at the Terminal Station in Allentown, leaving for training camp. While many served in Europe, many Carbon Countians served at home. Miners and railroad workers were considered essential war workers.

(Opposite) Carbon County troops being mustered in at the Fairgrounds in Allentown, site of the closest large army encampment.
Shaeffer photos, courtesy of George Harvan

Mrs. Stephen Watto. Her daughter, Mary Watto Zabroski, said her mother seems to have found the work surprisingly congenial. "She always bragged about it. She must have really loved it, the way she talked."

Bethlehem Steel also was among the regional industries hiring women during the war. The trend was to continue, and to be greatly accelerated, during World War II; and women's relative economic freedom during these times of crisis in turn helped lead to their greatly expanded, while still far from perfect, role in modern life. At the southern end of Carbon County, the New Jersey Zinc Company won a letter of commendation from the U.S. War Department for its contribution to the war effort.

Women of the Red Cross marching in the parade welcoming Palmerton's men home from World War I in 1919. Courtesy, Raymond E. Holland Collection

World War I cost more than eight million military deaths. Horrifying as that total is, it was not the end of the large-scale dying of this tragic decade. October 1918 brought an epidemic of so-called Spanish flu, which killed twenty million people worldwide, including more than half a million Americans. One hundred and five Panther Valley area employees of the Lehigh Coal and Navigation Company died, as did Lansford nurse Anna Gluck, who caught the disease while nursing a victim at a Pottsville hospital.

On October 23, 1918, James J. Boyle's *Mauch Chunk Daily Times* reported that nearly fourteen thousand Pennsylvanians had died of the flu since October 1, and an additional number in excess of five thousand from flu-related pneumonia.

Survivor Mike Donegan, now deceased, described the course of the disease to Jack Yalch, a writer for *The Valley Gazette* of Lansford: "You'd get sick, run a fever of 105 or 106, and that was the end," said Donegan. "There were no wakes and no church services. They took them right to the cemeteries."

By the end of November the disease had pretty well burned itself out, leaving an exhausted human race to face the double burden of its self-inflicted war losses and the vastly greater losses inflicted by nature.

Palmerton Women in World War I

In all of America's wars women have played a role — peripheral and unofficial at first, but ever-increasing in its scope, complexity, and official recognition.

A few women also were known to have disguised their gender, and to have fought as soldiers in early conflicts; but these were rare exceptions. Even rarer was a personality like Anna Ella Carroll of Maryland, a Union pamphleteer of great talent who also has been revealed as an important strategist for the cause of the North in the Civil War.

Women were more usually nurses, a traditional role for them, and one with important outcomes for society. Out of the crucible of Civil War nursing, for example, Clara Barton forged the American Red Cross.

World War I marked the United States Government's first large-scale attempt to make systematic use of women in a wartime situation. Women telephone operators, not in the armed forces but under contract, served abroad. There were about three hundred female Marine reservists, called "Marinettes," over twelve thousand female yeomen in the Naval Reserve, and about three hundred in the Coast Guard. These women performed clerical and administrative duties, freeing men for combat. Only the U.S. Army refused their services.

The largest group of women in uniform were the members of the Army and Navy Nurse Corps, some twenty-two thousand Army nurses and fourteen hundred Navy nurses. Formed around the turn of the century as a reluctant response to the inefficiencies of contract nursing during the Spanish-American War, they worked in many dangerous situations, and as a group were much decorated.

Several of these nurses came from Palmerton Hospital, then the only hospital in Carbon County. They included Mabel Silliman, Bertha M. Carson, Ada James, Lottie Lewis, and Rose Meyers. Their service, and that of others like them, helped pave the way for a wider role for women, not only in the armed forces, but throughout American society.

World War II

Following its brief encounter with the world during World War I, a disenchanted United States withdrew into isolation with the election of Warren G. Harding as president in 1920. When the Great Depression struck in 1929 it helped to ensure that Americans' thoughts would be concentrated on their own considerable internal problems, at the cost of the rest of the world.

But from 1932 the country had a new, activist president, Democrat Franklin D. Roosevelt, who did his best to solve those internal problems. And, by the late 1930s, events abroad — the imperialist expansion of Japan and the European designs of Germany's leader Adolf Hitler — made a new foreign war seem more and more likely.

That war exploded in 1939, when Hitler marched into Poland. Roosevelt, who had a broader sense of the United States' place in the world than did many of his contemporaries, did his best to aid the British in what seemed to be a hopeless struggle against Nazism. But not until December 7, 1941, when Japanese forces launched a surprise attack on the United States naval base at Pearl Harbor, Hawaii, was America committed to the defeat of the Axis powers, Germany, Japan, and Italy.

Pennsylvania contributed mightily to the success of the war effort. Many of the key American military, air, and naval leaders of this conflict were Pennsylvanians, including Army Chief of Staff Gen. George C. Marshall; Gen. Henry H. "Hap" Arnold, commander of the Army Air Force; his second-in-command, Gen. Carl "Tooey" Spaatz; Maj. Gen. Lyman Lemnitzer; Maj. Gen. James M. Gavin, the daring commander of the Eighty-second Airborne Division, a former enlisted man from the coal regions who jumped into battle with his men; and Adm. Harold Stark, first chief of naval operations and later commander of U.S. naval forces in European waters.

Once again Pennsylvania's famous Twenty-eighth Division, the Pennsylvania National Guard, was in the thick of things, though it did not go into action until late July 1944. Its German foes called it the "Bloody Bucket" division, possibly for its red Pennsylvania keystone arm patch; possibly, too, for the ferocity with which it fought, and for its ability to take punishment.

The division needed all its collective force of character, all its determination, to stand up to what was hurled at it. After a month's fierce fighting, the Twenty-eighth entered Paris. On September 11 it became the first American division to enter Germany in substantial force; its casualties in the Huertgen Forest were very heavy.

The Twenty-eighth was moved to a "quiet" sector in December 1944. Almost immediately, on December 16, it found itself in the path of the desperate German offensive known as the Battle of the Bulge. It resisted fiercely and was smashed, but was later reconstituted and joined the Seventh Army of fellow Pennsylvanian Gen. Alexander M. Patch. The survivors returned home to Fort Indiantown Gap in August 1945.

Not all Pennsylvanians served with the Twenty-eighth of course, although that division may stand as an example of Pennsylvania's fighting qualities. Carbon County men — and women, for in this war nobody's contributions could be overlooked — served in every branch of the armed services, in every part of the world. Many were among the thirty-three thousand Pennsylvanians who died in the course of the conflict.

Carbon County was there from the very beginning, at Pearl Harbor. Palmerton soldier Ramon Carazo was among the county residents who came under attack at "Pearl"; he lost his left arm in the encounter. He returned home in late June 1942, following a long convalescence during which he met King Peter, the young, exiled monarch of Yugoslavia.

Carazo, who was given a hero's welcome and a parade by his home town, was quoted as saying, "I was willing to give more, but the Army said 'No.'"

Fellow Palmertonian Alex Gaydos was less lucky. He was reported missing after the Japanese bombed Clark Field in the Philippines on December 27, 1941. Gaydos never came home. Later his name was joined with that of World War I victim Robert Mader in the name of the Palmerton American Legion post, which became the Mader-Gaydos Post.

Lansford sent more than sixteen hundred young men and women into the armed services during World War II; of these fifty-two died. Palmerton contributed about the same number of soldiers, sailors, airmen, and the auxiliary service people, mostly women, who backed them up.

Other towns in the county sent proportional contributions of manpower and woman-power; but Nesquehoning is said to have won special recognition from Robert Ripley, creator of the then-popular newspaper feature "Ripley's Believe It Or Not." Ripley, it is said (though the author has been unable to track this down and confirm it), claimed that Nesquehoning had the highest proportion of residents in the armed services of any town in the United States. Some two hundred of the Nesquehoning contingent came from just one church — the Italian parish of Our Lady of Mount Carmel.

From Weatherly and Beaver Meadow to the Lehigh Gap, Victory Gardens flourished everywhere, as those who stayed at home threw themselves into the war effort. Scouts and other groups collected tons of recyclable scrap — aluminum, rubber, paper, glass, and other materials — as a contribution to national defense.

A hometown newspaper, the *Service Star*, was published by volunteers for service personnel from Palmerton and vicinity; and students from the Stephen S. Palmer High School sold enough war bonds to pay for not one, but two warplanes. (This is not the reason why Palmerton Area High School teams are today called the Blue Bombers; according to Warren Siegmond, the "Bombers" name predates the war.)

At the other end of the county, coal production had begun to rise in the late 1930s, in anticipation of coming trouble abroad. During the war the Lehigh Navigation Coal Company

A defense worker labors in the Lansford shops of the Lehigh Navigation Coal Company during World War II. *Photograph by Walter Strauss*

turned to its older miners to keep up the production pace, for over one thousand (1,058) of its younger employees were in uniform and scattered around the world. Perhaps no one could foresee it, but this was to be the last major war in which Pennsylvania's anthracite industry would play so major a part.

In Palmerton, women moved into many of the New Jersey Zinc Company's office jobs to replace men in the military, although they did not work in the plants. Bethlehem Steel had its Rosie the Riveters, just as it had had women working in its plants during World War I; but the zinc company had no exact counterparts.

The women who were employed locally in defense-related jobs were far more numerous than they had been during World War I, and they were only a small manifestation of a much larger nationwide phenomenon. Philip S. Klein and Ari Hogenboom, authors of *A History of Pennsylvania*, indicate that, during the war, one-quarter of all war workers were women; so were almost half of all other workers. Handicapped workers filled a small niche in war production; and many unskilled African-American laborers got the training they needed to take over skilled jobs. In Pennsylvania this upgrading was aided by the Fair Employment Practices Committee and the state Department of Public Instruction's War Production Training Program.

In Lansford, jubilant residents celebrate the end of World War II. Photo by Walter Strauss

When atomic bombs were detonated over the Japanese cities of Hiroshima and Nagasaki, they not only brought about a speedy end to the war in the Pacific, they ushered in a new and terrifying era in warfare and its technology.

In the last analysis, though, that may prove to be less significant than the fact that so many previously overlooked groups — women and minorities — had helped to win the war, and knew that they had done so. The clock could not be turned back, nor the past undone — at least, not on a permanent basis. Although only echoes of the struggle for greater equality may so far have reached conservative Carbon County, that struggle continues. In terms of its impact on American life, it is perhaps one of the most enduring legacies of the twentieth century, and in particular of World War II.

Korea, Vietnam, and Beyond

By the time the curtain was rung down on World War II, it was evident that the Soviet Union and the Communist Bloc states posed a new threat to democracy around the world. When, in the late 1940s, a successful revolution led by Mao Zedong placed China squarely in the Communist alignment, the bitter attacks and recriminations that followed in the United States made and destroyed political careers, and had repercussions that are felt in American political life to this day.

Following a policy laid out by distinguished diplomat George F. Kennan, successive United States administrations attempted to "contain" the Communist threat by engaging in a limited warfare against it whenever it appeared to threaten a vital interest of the West. The overall policy was known, not illogically, as "containment."

Its first major test came in the early 1950s. When troops from Communist North Korea invaded South Korea, President Harry S Truman ordered American troops into action on the Korean peninsula. There they were joined by contingents from many other members of the United Nations.

The ante was upped considerably when Chinese Communist troops poured across the Yalu River to join their North Korean allies. The bitter war that followed was fought to a draw; South Korea remained out of Communist hands, and an uneasy truce has prevailed between the two Koreas to this day.

As usual, Carbon County sent its contribution of men to what became known as the Korean Conflict; and many died in Korea. But the public, still worn out by the horrors of World War II and not comprehending the significance of a faraway Asian peninsula, often greeted the returning soldiers with indifference — at least, in many parts of the country; Carbon County has long been noted for its respect for veterans.

If the Korean Conflict was fought to a "tie," Vietnam, the trauma of the '60s, was lost altogether. Veterans returning from that war were sometimes greeted, although very seldom in Carbon County, with a hatred and contempt they surely did not deserve.

What can be said of these two military encounters, one a stalemate, the other lost? Writing in a letter to the editor of *American Heritage* magazine, Attorney William Manske of Oshkosh, Wisconsin, offered a broader view of these traumatic national experiences, in the aftermath of the collapse of the Soviet Union:

> It now appears that the policy of containment worked. Because it did work, I think it is time we took a new look at the Korean War and the Vietnam War and view them not as wars but as battles in that longer Cold War.
>
> ... Our neglected Korean War veterans and our tortured Vietnam War veterans should be encouraged to see that their participation in those battles was part of an overall Cold War plan that was successful. We could then, at last, afford them the gratitude that their service and sacrifice earned them.

Manske may be premature; there still are countries that call themselves Communist, including China, Cuba, and North Korea. But the Soviet Union, once the core of Communism, is gone; and his healing suggestion deserves acceptance.

The wars of the future will not likely be against Communism; indeed, in the Persian Gulf War we have already had our first post-Communist conflict. Two things may be counted upon: America will continue to become involved in wars from time to time; and Carbon County soldiers, sailors, pilots, and nurses will always be there.

Race Street in Jim Thorpe. Pen and ink drawing by David Price, based on his watercolor of the same scene. Used with the permission of the artist.

The Artistic Experience:
Carbon County Arts

Human nature appears to require art in its various forms, to satisfy a need to understand existence, and to impose order and beauty on life. As far as we can tell, the arts have been used since prehistoric times for these very pragmatic purposes.

But it was millennia before humankind had the leisure and the security, not to mention the economic means, to elevate artists to professional status. Long before there could be a Michelangelo, an artist with a career, there were anonymous cavemen placating the gods of the hunt by painting images of game animals on the walls of caverns. Long before Beethoven, there were drummers beating out the rhythms of ritual dances, or the sound of the lone human voice raised in song or chant.

When professional artists and musicians did arrive on the historical scene, they naturally congregated in cities. There, they could find people wealthy enough to pay them for their productions. From Athens to Florence, from Paris to New York, artistic greatness is bound up with the greatness of cities.

By urban standards, a place like Carbon County was and remains a place of which not much could be expected artistically. And yet, some interesting art and music were created in the county. Artistic expression and the chance to encounter it have greatly increased in recent decades, thanks to the influence of a few key people.

Folk Artists

A number of the county's finest artists were never formally trained, nor were they professionals in the strict sense. They were what used to be called "primitive" artists. The trendy, but equally disparaging, term for them today is "outsider" artists. Such men and women paint or create out of a deeply felt inner need. They do not know "how" to draw, in the conventional sense. Since they have little or no notion of perspective, which is one of the bases of the Western visual arts tradition, their works do not look "real." But there is more than one way to organize reality for seeing. The works of folk artists are often very well organized indeed, according to their own plan. At their best, their productions are vibrant, bursting with color and life. The works of many such artists are prized today by museums and collectors.

No fewer than four of America's finest folk artists of the twentieth century have their roots, or spent most of their lives, in Carbon County. They are Justin McCarthy of Weatherly, who painted a wide variety of subjects; Lamont Alfred "Old Ironsides" Pry of Mauch Chunk

"Train in Stroudsburg" by Jack Savitsky. From a gallery postcard, courtesy of Mary Louise Savitt.

(Jim Thorpe); Charles "Charlie" Dieter of Little Gap; and John "Jack" Savitsky of Lansford, also known as "Coal Miner Jack." All are featured in Chuck and Jean Rosevak's *Museum of American Folk Art Encyclopedia of Twentieth Century Folk Art and Artists.*

Justin McCarthy (1892–1977) was the scion of what was once the wealthiest family in Weatherly; his father was a newspaper publisher. The family, however, was dogged by tragedy, notably the death of a young son, and by financial reverses. When McCarthy's father died in 1908, the family's financial ruin was complete.

McCarthy lingered on in the old family home for most of the rest of his life — first with his mother, who lived until 1940, and then alone. He survived in part by selling vegetables from the family garden, and he sold his paintings on a similar informal basis. The paintings were displayed at local crafts shows as well; and so McCarthy was discovered by East Stroudsburg artist and collector Sterling Strauser. Strauser assisted and underwrote McCarthy, and promoted his work. He performed similar functions for Pry, Dieter, Savitsky and other folk artists; the artists he took under his wing in this way became known collectively as "the Strauser group." Justin McCarthy died in Tucson, Arizona, where he had gone seeking improvement in his health.

Lamont "Old Ironsides" Pry (1921-1987) loved circuses, and specialized in wonderfully evocative circus scenes. His nick-name, "Old Ironsides," is said to have stemmed from his amazing recovery from injuries sustained as a member of the Army Air Corps, when he crashed while on a routine flight during World War II.

Pry spent the last years of his life at the Carbon County Home for the Aged in Weatherly, now known as Weatherwood. There he encountered Charles Dieter (1922-1986), who had lived at the home since his mother died when he was forty-seven years old. Dieter evidently found it difficult to cope with the demands of everyday life, but that fact did not interfere with his artistic vision. He and Pry both were enrolled in the art class Mary Brown Thompson taught at the county home, but by her standards they were difficult students. She said of them, "I couldn't teach the boys. Those two boys had their own way of doing things."

Jack Savitsky (1910-1991) was born in New Philadelphia and spent most of his life in Lansford. He worked as a coal miner, but the closing of the No. 9 Mine plus his own work-related ill health led to his early retirement. At that point his son, newspaperman Jack Savitt, suggested that he take up painting. It proved to be an inspired suggestion. Savitsky painted various subjects, but he is best known for his works depicting coal mining and life in the coal regions.

"Formal" Art

Possibly the only person associated with Carbon County to achieve world renown was the abstract expressionist painter Franz Kline. Kline, who lived from 1910 to 1962, was in fact not born in the county, but in Wilkes-Barre. Following the suicide of his father, he attended Girard College for a time, then moved to Lehighton to be with his remarried mother.

He then attended Lehighton High School, where he illustrated his class yearbook and was noted as an athlete. His teachers recognized his talent; and one of them, mathematics teacher Daniel I. Farren, had definite ideas about what the young man should do with his gifts. Farren, who went on to become the long-time principal of the high school, recalled years later, "I used to tell him, 'Franz, you should go into commercial art. You could make a fortune.'"

But Kline preferred a career in fine art. He made his contribution as a member of the school of painters known as abstract expressionists which also included such notables as Jackson Pollock, Willem de Kooning, and Mark Rothko. Perhaps his best-known work still in Carbon County is an early panoramic mural of Lehighton, above the bar of the Shoemaker-Heydt American Legion Post in that town.

Franz Kline's sense of humor is evident in these caricatures from "Gachtin Bambil" 1931, the yearbook of Lehighton High School. The sketch on the right represents junior high students, the one below left represents juniors, and the one below right represents seniors. On the following two pages is Kline's review of the school year 1930-1931. Courtesy, Raymond E. Holland Collection.

Within the past several decades many artists have chosen to make their homes in Carbon County. For this development, Kline is in part responsible. As a teacher and as a friend, his influence on other artists was profound; and at least two of the Carbon County residents, Edward Halter Meneely and Joel LeBow, have ties to him.

Edward Halter Meneely was born in 1927 in Wilkes-Barre, also Kline's birthplace. He and Kline became friends during the 1950s, when he was living, studying, and working in New York City. His paintings and sculptures have been widely exhibited, both here and abroad. Works by Meneely are part of the collections of many museums, including the Metropolitan Museum of Art, the Museum of Modern Art, and the Whitney Museum of American Art, all in New York City; University College, Dublin; and the New University of Ulster, Coleraine. He now lives in Weissport.

"Belief Reborn" by Joel Lebow. Used by permission of the artist.

Joel LeBow, now of Jim Thorpe, received his bachelor of fine arts degree from the University of the Arts, Philadelphia, where Kline was one of his teachers. He is a gifted watercolorist, whose works in this apparently modest medium can be monumental in size, and in the past few years he has taken to doing large works in acrylic on canvas. His work has won numerous awards and, like Meneely's, is in many collections.

At the time this was written, LeBow seemed to be an artist in a state of rapid evolution. He appeared to be most interested in expressing a spiritual point of view, what has been called "his perceptions and certitude of a multi-layered, multi-dimensional universe."

Japanese-born Shozo Nagano studied at the Kanazawa Fine Art University in his native land, as well as the Art Students League and Pratt Institute in New York City. He came to Jim Thorpe in 1980. Nagano paints in acrylics on shaped canvas, and makes heavy use of draped human figures, flowers, and geometrical shapes. Among the collectors of his enigmatic works have been noted author James Michener, as well as actors Cary Grant and Steve Martin.

"Self" by Shozo Nagano. Used by permission of the artist.

Watercolorist and printmaker David Watkins Price, also a Jim Thorpe resident, was a 1990 winner of the F. Lamont Belin Art Scholarship. Using the scholarship funds, he created "Standing Stones," a series of works depicting eighteenth and nineteenth-century stone houses in the Pennsylvania landscape, and his emotional and spiritual reactions to them. He, too, is a much-collected artist. His pen-and-ink drawing of Race Street is used as a frontispiece to this chapter.

Eva Cutler is a fiber artist and fashion designer. She has a deep love for fibers and their diverse natures, and observed of her work, "Textiles and other fabrics became my palette, thread my brush." Born in Budapest, Hungary, in 1925, she survived the Nazi Holocaust and came to the United States in 1946. As this was written, she had lived in Jim Thorpe for around eight years.

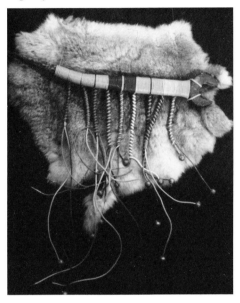

Sculptor and painter Harold Nothstein, a native of Lehighton and a graduate of the Rochester Institute of Technology, has had a shorter career than most of the artists discussed here. His work is made largely of cast-off materials and "found objects," and it evokes both the "rust belt" modern history of Carbon County and the culture of the American Indian that came before it. Nothstein himself is part Lenni Lenape. He has exhibited at the Sordoni Art Gallery of Wilkes University, Wilkes-Barre; the Allentown Art Museum, Kutztown University, and Allentown's Mayfair.

"Ceremonial Wrench" by Harold Nothstein. Used by permission of the artist.

Music

Like the visual arts, music is one of the most ancient forms of human expression. It is also one of the most varied, including in its range everything from the sound of the unaccompanied voice or ceremonial drum to that of a full symphony orchestra — or, for that matter, of an electronic synthesizer.

Carbon County must always have been a musical place — at least in an amateur way. Many of the immigrant groups that came here, such as the Welsh and the Irish, were famous for their musicality. Later comers were just as competent, and formed polka bands, tamburitzan groups, and other performing groups. There was a time when the upper and lower parts of the county, in particular, must have rung with hymns, fiddle tunes, folk songs, and dances from a score of countries.

Later, American popular music gained prominence, and the region from Flagstaff to Lakeside and Lakewood Parks in neighboring Schuylkill County became noted as a center of Big Band music. Two prominent musicians of the Big Band era, brothers, were born in Coaldale, just over the Schuylkill County line. They were Tommy and Jimmy Dorsey, and they were probably the most famous musicians the Carbon-Schuylkill region has ever produced.

In the late 1940s and early 1950s, David Wendell Guion might have been regarded as the county's classical musician-in-residence. He was not a native of the region, but was born in 1895 in Texas. No doubt in part because of this accident of birth, he was known as "the cowboy composer."

His credentials, though, were serious. He had studied at London's Royal Academy of Music; and, during a stay in Vienna, Austria, he had received piano instruction from the noted Polish pianist Leopold Godowsky. He had taught at Southern Methodist University, among many other institutions.

His large-scale compositions are numerous. They include "Shinganli," described as "a primitive African ballet" by the *International Cyclopedia of Music and Musicians* (New York, 1956). There are also a number of suites, including "Mother Goose," "Southern Nights," "Sheep and Goat Walking To Pasture," and "Alley Tunes."

Guion lived for a number of years along Wild Creek in Carbon County. The author has been unable to learn when he arrived, when he left, or where he went afterward. It is known, though, that he lived until 1981.

Guion's musical reputation has vanished almost without a trace. If he is remembered at all today, either in Carbon County or elsewhere, it is for something he definitely did not write. He was interested in American folk songs, and made transcriptions of many of them, including the familiar "Home On The Range." It was an amazingly successful transcription. County residents who remember him at all believe he actually composed the song, rather than merely created a setting of it. According to local stories, their belief was shared by no less a personage than President Harry S Truman — who, to Guion's disgust, used to call him up and ask him to sing it. The Presidential attention must have been anything but flattering to a man who aspired to have his whole body of creative work taken seriously.

Concert halls and opera houses and the music they present have, for generations, been far removed from most of the people of Carbon County, both geographically and experientially. This state of affairs appears to be changing to some degree, thanks in part to the efforts of newcomers to the county.

Artist Joel LeBow and his wife Helena, manager of the couple's Hazard House Gallery in Jim Thorpe, may have been the county residents most responsible for bringing about the establishment of the Laurel Festival of the Arts, held annually in the county seat since 1990. The festival originated when the LeBows met Marc Mostovoy, founder and conductor of the Concerto Soloists of Philadelphia, and two of his colleagues — violist Richard Fleischman and bassoonist David McGill. The three musicians were looking for a place to hold a summer music festival and the LeBows helped convince them that Jim Thorpe was the goal of their search. The Mauch Chunk Historical Society then undertook the volunteer effort needed to turn the festival from a dream into a reality.

While it has offered other musical fare, the festival has traditionally concentrated on chamber music. And, while the majority of the performers come from out of town, the festival also has offered scope for local musicians whose chief interest is classical music. One of these is Randall D. Perry, founder of the Bach and Handel Chorale of Carbon County and former director of music at the Episcopal Parish of St. Mark and St. John. Although the Chorale was still relatively new at the time of the first Laurel Festival, it had already achieved sufficient excellence to justify its being invited to perform.

Increasingly, Carbon County has become a place where residents may experience the full range of the arts, from the most popular to the most exalted. This means a fuller, richer life, both for those who live here and for those who visit.

The Changing Economic Scene

In the early days of the twentieth century, Carbon County's economic future seemed to rest unshakably on twin pillars — anthracite coal and zinc — with the railroads and the Lehigh Navigation as indispensable auxiliaries to the two great industries.

For some time the textile industry, in the form of silk mills in particular, provided employment for many of the women and young people of the county. This industry was to disappear within a few decades; but it was replaced by the garment industry, which sewed clothing on a contract basis for manufacturers based for the most part in New York City. Although individual garment shops might employ only somewhere between a dozen and a couple of hundred people, the garment industry was to grow to become, in the aggregate, the second largest source of employment in the county.

Whatever happened in other areas of economic life, it must have seemed unlikely that those two pillars, anthracite and zinc, could ever be shaken. Few could have anticipated that the anthracite industry would be effectively finished by mid-century, and the canal and railroads with it; or that the zinc industry would be a ghost of its most expansive self several decades thereafter.

The Slide

The Great Depression of the 1930s affected different parts of the county differently. Worst hit, probably, were the coal mining areas. There, people hunted and fished for food, started gardens, illegally picked up chunks of coal for fuel from culm banks, and ran up credit purchases at their neighborhood grocery stores. Many of the helpful grocers were forced out of business as a result. Miners were lucky if they got two days of work per week. The employer of most of them, the Lehigh Navigation Coal Company (the "Old Company"), was in no financial position to help them out. Besides, relationships between company and workers were traditionally adversarial.

At the other end of the county, the Depression laid a much gentler hand on Palmerton. Every young man whose family had lived in the area for a reasonable length of time, and who had graduated from Stephen S. Palmer High School, was guaranteed a job in one of the plants of New Jersey Zinc if he wanted one. The zinc and zinc products that were produced under the full-employment policy seem to have been warehoused if they could not immediately be sold.

New Jersey Zinc's policy was worthy of a great and fabulously wealthy company; which, at the time, it was. But, like anthracite, zinc's days as a source of economic power were numbered. Soon after coal had ceased to be an important factor in the county economy, zinc, too, had shrunk to a small part of the overall economic picture.

Unlike zinc, the anthracite industry was visibly in trouble even before the Depression. In 1923 it reached a post-World War I production peak nationwide, mining in excess of 77,000,000 tons. However, such competing fuels as prepared bituminous (made up of 60 percent anthracite and 40 percent bituminous, or soft coal), gas, and oil were beginning to cut into traditional anthracite markets. Even military uses for coal, whether anthracite or bituminous, were diminishing. In the decades following World War I, the world's navies, including the U.S. Navy, began a rapid conversion to the more convenient oil.

The coal-powered generating plant of the Pennsylvania Power and Light Company in Hauto was a landmark in Carbon County for decades. It was finally shut down in 1969, and razed between 1975 and 1978. Courtesy, PP&L

The demand for anthracite declined steadily in the years after 1923. At the height of the Depression about a third of anthracite miners were unemployed, while the earnings of those who were still employed dropped substantially. Labor troubles became intense in the Panther Valley by 1933.

The mines of the Panther Valley were noted for their labor unrest, and thus presented special problems for local anthracite users. In the late 1940s, although the Lehigh Navigation Coal Company produced only six percent of the anthracite industry's output, lost time due to strikes by its workers amounted to ninety percent of the total time lost by the entire industry.

The strikes often were wildcat strikes, and they tended to come at the worst times of the year, such as the dead of winter. As a result, many local users naturally became nervous about the reliability of hard coal as a fuel.

The miners of the Panther Valley were almost all employees of the LNC and devoted members of District 7 of the United Mine Workers of America. They could be so recalcitrant to the will of the national union, though, that District 7's charter was finally revoked and its officers were appointed by the national leadership. But W. Julian Parton, a mining engineer who spent much of his career with the LNC, and who served briefly as it president in the 1950s, noted that even this move by the national leadership did not quell the labor turmoil.

From 1927 to 1940, the Old Company failed to earn a profit; from 1930 to 1940 it racked up losses totalling nearly ten million dollars. That was a sum far more impressive in those days than it may seem today.

One of the main issues between the LNC and its labor force was that of work equalization. The workers were seeking exact equalization of working time at all collieries, even though this was bound to have a negative effect on efficient management. In 1935, without the approval of the UMWA's national leadership, an Equalization Committee was set up in the Panther Valley to pursue this aim.

Parton blamed the local labor leaders and their allies, such as editor James "Casey" Gildea of the *Coaldale Observer*, for pushing for equalization. It is true that Gildea's efforts made him popular enough to win two terms in Congress; but it is difficult to believe that he and the miners were anything but sincere.

Work was scarce. There were no "fallback positions" such as unemployment compensation or other jobless benefits. It seemed better to the men for everyone to have some work, however limited, than for some to be without the basic necessities of life. From his point of view Parton was right; but the miners just as certainly were not wrong.

In 1936 the Lehigh Navigation Coal Company agreed to a contract providing for equalization, as well as for a seven-hour workday for eight hours' wages. Given the company's financial difficulties, the wage concession appears to have been far more unwise than the surrender on the issue of equalization.

In 1937, coal production dropped to 2,223,886 tons. At its peak, it had amounted to five million tons.

But temporary help, in the form of trouble on the world scene, was on the way. Hitler's saber-rattling in Europe, coupled with Japanese expansionism in the Far East, made it clear even to many of the less discerning that war was coming. Even before the war broke out, the demand for anthracite increased as a result of the threat.

World War II erupted on September 1, 1939, as Hitler hammered Poland. The United States would not join the combatants until December 8, 1941, the day after the Japanese attacked the American naval base at Pearl Harbor in Hawaii. Nevertheless, the intervening time saw America move increasingly to a wartime footing.

The Lansford Breaker, No. 6 Colliery, in 1929. It was shut down by the Lehigh Navigation Coal Company in June of 1954 and reopened temporarily under the management of the Panther Valley Coal Company later that year.

The demand for anthracite remained high during the war years, and management proceeded on the assumption that it could hold the markets it had temporarily regained during the emergency. Worker demands were made on the same assumption — which, unfortunately, proved to be false. Overburdened, the Old Company ceased mining coal in the Panther Valley in 1954. Thirty years later its parent company, the famous Lehigh Coal and Navigation Company, went out of existence.

At this point, the New Jersey Zinc Company had yet to reach its high point in terms of employment. That milestone was attained only in 1968, when the company provided some three thousand jobs. But the glory days of the zinc industry, too, were almost over.

In the late 1940s, the plants at Palmerton were organized by the United Steel Workers. Paying union-scale wages perhaps made it somewhat harder for New Jersey Zinc to compete in world markets, although the company economized to some extent by closing down such amenities as the Community House. This does not seem to have been an action taken in retaliation for unionization; many of the social services had outlived their usefulness. Where workers had formerly had few opportunities for recreation and education beyond those offered by the company, by the late 1940s more such opportunities were available to them.

What caused the decline of New Jersey Zinc was not unionization, but something far more fundamental: the decline in the quality of available ore. As we have seen, making effective use of the "Sterling" ore from the mines at Franklin, New Jersey, had presented unusual technical difficulties. Once this problem had been solved, though, this ore was the richest and purest in the world. One of its greatest virtues was that it contained only very small quantities of such dangerous heavy metals as lead, mercury, and cadmium.

For decades, the New Jersey mines must have seemed inexhaustible; but of course they were not. By the 1950s the ore from the Franklin mine was depleted. That left the company with the mine at Ogdensburg, New Jersey, as its main source of ore. But Ogdensburg was not nearly as rich as Franklin; and by the 1980s it, too, had run out of ore. To continue production in Palmerton, it was necessary to bring in ores from Friedensville in the lower Lehigh Valley, as well as from other sources farther afield. But these ores had higher concentrations of heavy metals and other impurities than those from Franklin and Ogdensburg. This fact compounded a pollution problem that had been growing in the Palmerton area, especially on the Blue Mountain.

New Jersey Zinc had always made efforts to control pollution. For example, the company had controlled emissions of sulfur dioxide from its plants, and constructed sulfuric acid plants. The problem thus became a product, and a profitable one.

But the mountainside above the East Plant had never come back following a devastating forest fire during World War I; and the buildup of heavy metals in the soil presented a new pollution problem, less easily dealt with than sulfur dioxide emissions. In the mid-1970s the company put $130,000,000 into the plants, and spent $20,000,000 to reduce emissions. It also started to revegetate the cinder heaps and the slopes of the Blue Mountain. At this point the federal Environmental Protection Agency and the state Department of Environmental Resources stepped in to assess the situation, as a result of which Palmerton was designated a Superfund cleanup site. It is only within the last several years that permission has been granted to resume the revegetation effort.

In the meantime, the name New Jersey Zinc Company had ceased to exist. Gulf + Western Industries acquired the company in 1966, and in 1981 private investors and company executives bought large portions of the old firm from its new owners. Among the facilities they acquired were Palmerton, Depue (Illinois), and Ogdensburg (New Jersey).

Later a company called Great Lakes Carbon, with corporate headquarters in New York, was bought. In 1987 St. Joseph Resources was added, and the Zinc Corporation of America was formed.

As of 1992, ZCA and Horsehead Industries Resource Development Company, which recycles zinc from waste, were operating in Palmerton, under the eyes of the Environmental Protection Agency and the Department of Environmental Resources. Attempts to revegetate the Blue Mountain had resumed. The zinc industry was still providing some 400 jobs in the county, but 175 of those were due to be cut in the near future.

As is usually the case in such situations, the citizenry of the town was bitterly divided. Old-line residents tended to favor attempting to save jobs at all costs, while newcomers seemed more concerned about what they saw as grave environmental danger to themselves and their families. ZCA and Horsehead hinted more than once that they might withdraw from Palmerton.

The outcome of this situation cannot yet be predicted. It can only be said that moderation has trouble thriving in such circumstances.

The Lehigh Canal and the Railroads

As soon as Asa Packer's Lehigh Valley Railroad had pushed its way up the valley into Carbon County, the Lehigh Navigation was, in effect, obsolete. Yet traffic on the canal was a long time in dying out — decades, in fact. This was despite the fact that the Lehigh Coal and Navigation Company came to own its own railroads — among them the Lehigh and Susquehanna, leased to the Central Railroad of New Jersey, which in spots ran parallel to the canal.

Shipping coal by canal possessed several fundamental drawbacks, especially when compared with trains. The canal was, of course, unusable in the wintertime. Trains, on the other hand, could continue to operate through all but the very worst winter weather. The canal was extremely vulnerable to massive damage during floods, and could be closed for months while sections were repaired. Unlike railroads, canals could not, at least in Carbon County, go directly to the breaker for coal to be loaded onto boats. Most significantly, a single train could pull far more freight, and much faster, than a canal boat could carry.

So the tonnage on the canal fell with each passing decade. In 1932 shipments of mined coal ended. But they would have ceased decades earlier if there had been a railroad line along the Delaware River in Bucks County. It was only after trucks took over hauling coal by road that the canal fell into disuse — until then, the large coal dealers in Morrisville, Yardley, and Bristol along the Delaware Canal had no other way to be supplied.

The railroads, too, had their troubles. Just as anthracite was being challenged as a fuel by oil and gas, so railroads were being challenged by trucks, cars, and airplanes. The LC&N's Lehigh and New England Railroad, for example, which had carried a great portion of the output of the Lehigh Valley's portland cement industry, suffered when the cement began to be shipped in trucks.

Following World War II, peacetime production resumed in America's automobile factories. Many more families now could afford their own cars, and passenger traffic on the railroads dropped off. The trend was accentuated by national policy, which in the 1950s emphasized the building of roads and highways. One of the key reasons for this policy was the perceived threat from the Soviet Union. It was believed that an enlarged highway system would make possible the easier evacuation of cities and a faster response by the military in the event of a nuclear attack.

The Packerton yards, the large repair and maintenance yards of the Lehigh Valley Railroad, were closed down in 1972.

(Above) Train crews and officials on three steam locomotives at the yards during busy times.

(Below) Grass grows among the unused tracks of the once-giant complex.

Locally, there was a special reason for the decline of rail transportation. Much of the freight the local lines carried was still anthracite. As the market for hard coal declined, so did the viability of the railroads that served Carbon County.

The Lehigh and New England Railroad was the first to go out of existence; it abandoned service in 1961. In the 1970s, in an attempt to remain viable, the Lehigh Valley Railroad absorbed the Pennsylvania operations of the Central Railroad of New Jersey. A few years later the LVRR itself was absorbed by Conrail.

Passenger service on both the Central and the LVRR had ceased some years prior to the demise of the railroads themselves.

The Rise and Decline of the Garment Industry

Until comparatively recent times, there was no such thing as mass-produced clothing; every garment had to be hand-tailored to its wearer. The introduction of mass production of ready-to-wear clothing in the latter part of the nineteenth century offered certain advantages to the customer. It took far less time to go into a store and buy an outfit from a rack than it took to get fitted for a handmade one — and much less time than it took to make one.

Labor costs were lower, too, because many items of a standardized size could be turned out in the time it used to take for one individualized garment — especially when many people joined in the manufacturing effort, each one sewing only a particular part of the garment. Many of these savings were passed on to the purchaser.

So the modern garment industry was born. But at first many of its benefits, to manufacturers and customers, were achieved on the backs of workers.

The industry was concentrated initially in major cities, particularly in New York. Many of the workers were immigrants, and perhaps the majority of them were women. They labored in what became known as "sweat shops," crowded, unsanitary, overheated in summer, close to unheated in winter. Whether they were paid by the hour or on a piecework basis (so much per completed unit), their wages were minimal, as a rule too little to provide for even a decent level of subsistence.

The Triangle Shirtwaist fire of the early part of the twentieth century offers a lasting memory of the remorseless profiteering and exploitation of workers that marked the early days of the garment industry in New York. Employees were trapped behind locked doors when fire broke out in their garment shop, located on the top floor of the Triangle Building. Scores died as a result, either burned to death in the shop, or killed as a result of leaping from windows.

It is not surprising that, in an industry in which such horrors could occur, trade unionism made rapid strides among the workers. The unions that grew up included the Amalgamated Clothing Workers (ACW) and the International Ladies Garment Workers Union, or ILGWU. (The "Ladies" in its title was really "Ladies'"; the membership could, and did, include men, but all its members were engaged in making women's clothing.)

The ILGWU, in particular, was noted for its progressive policies and practices. It ran a resort for workers in the Poconos, and offered many educational opportunities to members.

Gradually the contract sewing part of the garment industry began to disperse over the landscape, and many sewing shops opened in Carbon County. The county provided an ideal location for such shops. It had an intelligent and industrious population of employable women, some of whom had formerly been employed in the silk mills that had once been part

The W.F. Hofford silk mill in Bowmanstown later became the last surviving contract sewing shop of *Wilmer Fashions, Inc. Courtesy, the Merluzzi family.*

of the local scene. It had excellent train connections to New York, important in moving merchandise. In the waning days of train transportation, Interstate Dress Carriers, or IDC, was established. With its local terminal in Lehighton, IDC transported finished garments directly to New York's garment district.

Sweated labor as it had been known in the city was much less common in the Pennsylvania contract sewing shops. One reason for this was the activity of the unions, the ILGWU in particular. An effort was made to see that sewing contracts went to union shops with union standards. A visit to a typical local garment factory today reveals a clean, well-lighted, well-ventilated work area, far removed from the horrors of the early days on New York's Lower East Side.

For decades the garment industry has been, in the aggregate, the second largest industrial employer in Carbon County. It still is, although now the leading industry of the county is not anthracite mining, but tourism.

But it is clear that the garment industry cannot continue its important economic role for long. To discover why this is so, let us examine the experience of the Merluzzi family of Lehighton.

For a long time, the Merluzzi family name was virtually synonymous with garment making in Carbon County. Peter Merluzzi, the family patriarch, came to Philadelphia from Italy early in the twentieth century, when he was a very young man and already an apprentice tailor. He soon moved to Lehighton, where he got a job with a tailoring firm. Later he opened his own shop. He kept at it until about 1930. It was not easy, and not only because the Great Depression had just struck the country and the world.

"It wasn't so much the Depression, as the fact that clothing was being factory made," recalled one of his sons. "There was less need for tailoring."

Peter Merluzzi understood the trend, and had the wisdom not to resist it. He went to work for a prominent Lehighton entrepreneur named Franklin Drumheller, and later moved to Loomtogs in Summit Hill. There he opened and managed the plant.

Around 1933 or 1934, Merluzzi started the Model Mill on the top floors of the Baer Silk Mill in Lehighton. In 1939 he went into partnership with Lewis "Lew" Williams of Lehighton, and founded Wilmer Fashion Company, Inc. Later he bought Williams out. Eventually Merluzzi had mills in several towns in Carbon County. He was instrumental in bringing Interstate Dress Carriers to Lehighton, and with it the hundred or so jobs IDC generated.

The Italian immigrant became a prominent Lehighton resident, and was a key figure in the founding of Gnaden Huetten Memorial Hospital. After he died in 1972, the family continued in the garment business until the end of May, 1992. At that point, the last mill of Wilmer, Incorporated, (the firm's final name) was closed forever. At a meeting with family members in the now-empty shop in Bowmanstown, Wilmer president Frederick Merluzzi stated, "Unless there are some drastic changes, I don't think there is a future in the garment industry."

What went wrong? The answer is: Everything, yet nothing the shop owners or their workers could easily have prevented. At the heart of the matter is the fact that American clothing manufacturers began shipping their work offshore, to Asia in particular, so they can get it done at the lowest possible prices. What was left tended to go into revived illegal sweatshops in New York's Chinatown, where it was done for a pittance by Asian immigrants.

In the case of Wilmer, Incorporated, even the fact that it was affiliated with the ILGWU came to hinder rather than help; whatever work filtered out into areas like Carbon County began to go to non-union shops.

The contract sewing business worked by having the owners of the shops bid on particular jobs, based on their estimate of what the cost for labor and materials would be. But the manufacturer-jobbers began to be extremely demanding to work with. Instead of showing an understanding of the shop owners' economic limits, the jobbers offered work at a "take-it-or-leave-it" price, which often did not cover the cost of making a garment.

Workers were hard to find, too. As Richard Merluzzi, Frederick's brother, pointed out, very few young people graduated from high school and took a job in a garment shop. One reason was that there were many more opportunities for advanced education and training than there formerly were.

Around 1984, some 93 dress shops, or mills where dresses are made, belonged to the Allentown local of the International Ladies Garment Workers Union. By 1989 there were just three left. Wilmer, Incorporated, was the last ILGWU dress shop in Carbon County. Now there are none.

Frederick Merluzzi bitterly laid part of the blame for the situation on Pennsylvania laws and regulations, as well as on such other factors as the shipping of work abroad. "Between Workmen's Compensation and unemployment rates, a lot of people can no longer afford to be in business in Pennsylvania," he said.

Peter Barter and Frank DePaulo, Sr., owners of sportswear manufacturer Fernbrook and Company, had an advantage over the Merluzzis in the early 1990s: They were still in business, although they could not guarantee for how long. DePaulo estimated that, of the former fifteen hundred mill owners in the district, only sixty were left. He observed that three thousand jobs have been lost in northeastern Pennsylvania as a result.

Fernbrook and Company once had twelve plants with two thousand employees. In 1992 the firm was down to three plants in Carbon County and one in Neffs, Lehigh County, and four hundred employees. And DePaulo predicted gloomily, "I don't think you'll find these plants running in two years."

Unlike the Merluzzis, DePaulo was bitter about the unions, although he echoed Frederick Merluzzi on the subject of Workmen's Compensation. "The unions take 17 percent; Workmen's Comp is out of sight," he asserted. "Between them you cannot survive. Where do you find justice?"

Peter Barter, DePaulo's senior partner, was more philosophical than DePaulo, but no less pessimistic. "You have to scramble for contracts," he said. "A lot of the people we worked for are either out of business or sending work abroad. "We've been fortunate; I don't think we've ever had to lay off anyone for any long period of time. But we have had to close factories."

Barter went on, "I don't think we have that much time. I would go five years; we will be here until the end. We gave it all we had; we really did do well for a while. What hurts most is knowing you can't bring another generation into the business."

He added one last disturbing thought: "Years ago we provided a second income for families; now a lot of our employees have to work to support themselves. I don't know what would happen if they had nothing. I think our industry has been hurt the worst."

(The conversations with the garment shop owners and operators were conducted in the late summer of 1992. Frank DePaulo proved wrong in his prediction that the Fernbrook company would not be running in another two years; in 1997, two of the three Fernbrook plants that were running in 1992 still were operating, although the plant at Neffs in Lehigh County had closed.

Contacted again, DePaulo said the two Fernbrook plants still employed about 375 workers. But, although his firm still had a corporate existence, he saw no reason to change his prognostication of impending doom.

"The handwriting is on the wall," he said.)

Other Industries

Communications

One prominent aspect of today's communications industry may have originated in the anthracite region of Pennsylvania. The mountainous terrain of the area blocked out television signals, and so someone developed the idea of placing antennae on the ridges and delivering the signals to homes by cable.

Thus cable television, which now serves a large portion of the United States, was born. Eventually, as home satellite dishes become more common, it may become less popular; but for now it owns a considerable share of public access to television.

Although there is some dispute, it is likely that John Walson, an appliance and television dealer in Mahanoy City, Schuylkill County, was the originator of the cable television concept; he is so accepted by the Smithsonian Institution. Walson had a strong business incentive to do some thinking about the reception problem: it was causing him to lose potential sales of television sets.

When he erected an antenna on a nearby mountain top and connected it by cable to the sets in his store, people jammed the street outside to catch a glimpse of the pictures on the small screens. Walson persuaded nearby residents to buy sets and hook onto his cable, and Service Electric Cable TV came into being.

Historian Richard Hoben believes cable television originated in Lansford; but John Walson's claim seems more valid. There was, though, a very early cable venture in Lansford, and also one in Lehighton — there, the principals included one-time borough manager George Hein and prominent merchant Mahlon Kistler.

But it was a Palmerton resident, the late Claud Reinhard, who turned cable television into a paying proposition in Carbon County. Reinhard took the lead among a group of thirty or so television enthusiasts who organized the Palmerton TV Signal Corporation in 1951. He, and many others who invested in the idea, became millionaires as a result.

Over the years, the Palmerton TV Signal Corporation grew into today's Pencor Services, Incorporated, a diversified communications company still headquartered in Palmerton. Among its holdings are Blue Ridge Cable Television, the Palmerton Telephone Company, Pencor Cellular Communications, ProLog, a regional Internet service provider, and the *Times-News* newspaper, which is located in Lehighton. The *Times-News* germinated from a small publication for cable television subscribers, to which were added in the course of time the Mauch Chunk *Daily Times*, the Lansford *Evening Record*, and the Tamaqua *Courier*, plus several weeklies in Lehigh County.

The Kovatch Corporation

Still more diversified is the Kovatch Corporation of Nesquehoning, which is noted for its customized trucks and other vehicles, but which also has significant real estate holdings and holds local franchises for many makes of automobile. John "Sonny" Kovatch is the president of this firm, although his brother Joseph enjoys equal status. At this point the firm is the largest single corporate employer in the county, accounting for about six hundred jobs.

The Kovatch Corporation purchased Hamm Chevrolet and Cadillac in Lehighton, and changed its name to K Chevrolet and Cadillac. It also gained the local franchises for American Motors Corporation, Jeep, Renault, Buick, Fiat, and International Trucks.

Beginning in the late 1960s, the Kovatch Corporation started winning government contracts. At first the contracts were for rebuilding and reconditioning everything from marine engines to jeeps and trucks. In 1981 it landed a contract to produce eight hundred and forty 5,000-gallon tanker trucks for the U.S. Air Force, working from components including Mack Truck cabs and chassis. The Nesquehoning firm's job was to assemble the tankers, which included mounting the tanks and installing the pumping and electrical systems. The total value of the U.S. Air Force contract was $66,000,000. At the same time, Kovatch contracted to produce ninety additional tankers for the government of Egypt.

The company has become especially well known for its manufacture of customized fire trucks; indeed, it might be said to be a pioneer in the post-mass production era forecast by such writers as the futurist Alvin Toffler.

John and Joseph Kovatch entered the field of real estate in 1963, when they purchased 1,600 acres of the Hauto Valley and began development of Lake Hauto Valley Estates. They also took over the former Bright's Department Store in Lansford and converted it into a mini-mall containing numerous shops and a restaurant.

John Kovatch owns the land on the outskirts of Nesquehoning on which stands the cogeneration plant run by Panther Creek Partners. The function of this plant is to convert fifty-year-old banks of fine waste coal into electrical energy.

The environmental impact of some of the activities of the Kovatch brothers has been criticized by such local environmental leaders as Edward G. Gildea, editor of the Lansford monthly, *The Valley Gazette*. When the cogeneration plant of Panther Creek Partners was proposed, Gildea pointed out that, while the burning of waste coal might possibly reclaim some land for building and reduce wind-borne pollution by coal dust, it also is known to contribute to acid rain, and thus to the demise of forests, streams, and lakes. In short, fine waste coal has all the environmental disadvantages of prime coal straight from the mines. The Lansford editor gained considerable public support on the cogeneration issue, and the citizens of Lansford voted overwhelmingly against the plant. It was built anyway.

Gildea also campaigned against a proposed housing development to be located on the Broad Mountain by the Kovatch brothers. If completed, the project would involve hundreds of individual lots and a golf course, all located very near the reservoir and feeder streams of the Lansford-Coaldale Water Authority. Despite a possible threat of serious water contamination, the development was approved by the county. Some roads were bulldozed in the affected area and a pond constructed, but no houses were erected. Reached in July, 1997, Joseph Kovatch of the firm said he believed no further work had been done on this particular development.

Whatever may be said of the environmental consequences of the Kovatches' activities, the firm appears to be prospering in economic terms. In a job-hungry area, it is hard to win points for the environment over a company that has produced jobs in such abundance. Perhaps someday it will be understood that even more jobs can be created in new industries whose impact on the environment is less damaging.

Wos-Wit Foods

Originating in Mahoning Township, though now located in Schuylkill County, Wos-Wit Foods represents an interesting if small-scale attempt to turn tradition to economic account. Its specialty was, and continues to be, jarred relishes, dressings, preserves, and other foods from the Pennsylvania Dutch heritage. The recipes were adapted from traditional family versions by John E. Kresge, the firm's founder.

Kresge was a musician and music teacher. During his career he taught in Mahoning and Franklin Township schools, served as music director of several country churches, including St. John's Lutheran Church of Mahoning Township, gave private lessons, and founded a variety band that played on many public occasions in the Mahoning Valley and elsewhere. His wife, Dorothy, taught in Mahoning township schools. Together, they tried to maintain a large part of Dorothy Kresge's father's farm. The time was the late 1930s — still the era of the Great Depression — and economic survival was not easy.

Some time before acquiring the farm, John Kresge had begun preserving Pennsylvania Dutch corn relish, which his wife took to the local farmers' market and sold on Saturdays. One day, at the market, Dorothy Kresge encountered a state inspector, who told her the relish needed to have a label and a name. She was convinced that the Kresges' small enterprise was doomed; but when she reported the news to her husband he promptly designed a label featuring Pennsylvania Dutch motifs.

The name was more difficult. Their first choice was "Wos Du Wit," which is Pennsylvania Dutch for "What you want." But they felt it would be too long. Finally they settled on "Wos Wit," which means "What do you want?" The eager purchasers of the products either did not know about the strange name or, if they were Pennsylvania Dutch, did not care about its strangeness.

Wos-Wit Foods remained located on the Kresge farm on Route 902 west of Lehighton for many years. In a small way, it prospered, growing to employ fourteen or fifteen workers. Toward the end of his life Kresge gave the business to the employees, reserving only the first $5,000 of yearly profits for himself.

Unfortunately, the employees lacked the skills and knowledge required to keep the business thriving. Soon after his death in 1983 it was sold, and was moved out of the county not long afterward. Its products remain on the market today, and its existence remains a tribute to the entrepreneurial spirit of its founder.

Electronics

The electronics industry is a comparative newcomer on the county scene, and one that to date probably has not developed to its full potential. With its intelligent, industrious workforce and its easy access to East Coast markets and shipment points for Europe, the county would appear to have much to offer as an East Coast Silicon Valley, while hopefully avoiding some of the environmental problems of the California original.

Located on Fritz Valley Road south of Normal Square, Mahoning Township, GTI Electronics is owned by George T. Isleib, who moved to Carbon County in the early 1970s from Tamaqua, and has lived and worked in the Lehighton area ever since. GTI Electronics manufactures equipment that will bring in satellite imagery; among its customers are schools, the Department of Defense, NASA, and NOAA, the National Oceanic and Atmospheric Administration.

Lehighton Electronics, Incorporated, was founded in 1963. It is a developer and manufacturer of high-quality special test and control equipment, and of printed circuit boards and assemblies.

The Resurgence of Tourism

The story of Mauch Chunk's re-emergence as Jim Thorpe, the jewel in Carbon County's tourism crown, has been discussed elsewhere in this work. There are many aspects of tourism, though, besides sightseeing and antiquing in quaint old towns. Skiing, hunting, fishing, camping, and other outdoor activities also are part of the mix; and in this outdoor adventure category the county these days offers something for nearly everyone. Beltzville State Park and Mauch Chunk Lake Park have ample facilities for swimmers and boaters, while the new Lehigh Gorge State Park is a delight for hikers. There are numerous trout streams, and a vast acreage of state game lands for hunters. Those with a highly developed sense of adventure may enjoy a whitewater trip down the Lehigh River.

One of the key corporate players in the field of tourism is the Blue Ridge Real Estate Company, spun off, as will be recalled, in the final breakup of the Lehigh Coal and Navigation Company. Blue Ridge no longer owns its original resort, Split Rock Lodge (now Split Rock Resort). To compensate, though, it is the owner of two prime skiing resorts, Jack Frost Mountain and Big Boulder. The latter is the site at which artificial snow was first introduced into the country; it was developed by John Guresh.

Split Rock Lodge and Club on Lake Harmony opened in February, 1942. With thousands of acres of land and over 50 miles of stream leased from the Lehigh Coal and Navigation Company, the club was able to offer its members exceptional fishing and hunting.
George Harvan photo

At Big Boulder the company has constructed an artificial lake, which, according to company president Gary Smith, is free of many of the problems of such older natural lakes as Lake Harmony. For example, sewage disposal was planned from the start, reducing the possibility that Big Boulder Lake will become seriously contaminated.

At this writing the Blue Ridge Real Estate Company continues to hold 13,000 acres of land, a large part of which is a contiguous parcel running from Jack Frost Mountain in the north to Big Boulder in the south. Approximately three hundred homes have been built at each ski area, and the homeowners have the option of making their homes part of a rental program.

"Skiing had its really great days in the 1980s; in the past three or four years it has declined somewhat," Smith admitted. Yet, of all the business leaders interviewed by this writer, he was one of the most sanguine about future economic prospects. His company has about eighty full-time employees, a number which rises during the ski season to around eight hundred; and he estimates that about twelve hundred are employed in Carbon County during the season. This total would include those employed at Blue Mountain Ski Resort near Little Gap in the southern part of the county.

But it was on the basis of real estate development that Smith expressed the greatest confidence: "We are primarily a second-home market, and we've been providing first class housing in the range of $150,000 and up. Some we built ourselves, and we also invited others in.

"A lot of companies have been filing for bankruptcy in the Poconos, but our company is strong. The second home market has come apart over the last couple of years, but it's a cyclical thing and it will come back.

"We're preparing for a turnaround in the economy. It's weak but it's not dead."

Jim Thorpe merchant Thomas McBride, proprietor of the tourist-oriented Treasure Shop, shared Gary Smith's optimism about the continuing potential of tourism and of tourist-related industries. McBride noted that in July and August of 1992, a year of economic woes,

Whitewater rafting on the Lehigh River represents today's new emphasis on adventure tourism as part of Carbon County's economy. Raft trips through the Lehigh Gorge have become a popular summer activity for both residents and tourists. Courtesy, the Walbert family

his own shop's business was up fifty percent over the previous year, and that other Jim Thorpe merchants reported similar excellent results. "We had to read the newspapers to discover there was a recession," he commented.

Future Prospects

It is difficult at this point to share the optimism of such leaders as Agnes T. McCartney of the Carbon County Tourist Promotion Agency, Gary M. Smith of the Blue Ridge Real Estate Company, and Jim Thorpe merchant Thomas McBride regarding the continuing economic clout of tourism in Carbon County. The industry seems vulnerable both in economic and environmental terms. The Great Depression of the 1930s wiped out what was left of early tourism. A catastrophic economic downturn might produce the same effect again.

Assuming that a trend toward global warming really exists, a question on which the scientific community is still divided, it could easily wipe out the ski industry, as well as the whitewater sports industry.

In the event of such calamities, of course, not only Carbon County would suffer. Assuming that the worst can be avoided, it seems advisable to have a coherent plan for the future of this beautiful but devastated region. The closest thing to such a plan seems to be the suggestion put forward by Edward Gildea of *The Valley Gazette* that the county seek a role as a retirement haven. Jobs then would be generated providing the services the elderly need.

Such a vision may be incomplete, but it is neither dreary nor far-fetched. A function as a retirement haven could be part of a larger plan that might include a large, continuing role for tourism, an increased role for environmentally sound, low-impact industry, and a limited place for agriculture — although it is clear that farming is unlikely to regain its former importance in the county. (Not that agriculture ever had much but local importance, due to the rock-ribbed terrain. Farmers in a few relatively fertile spots like the Mahoning Valley often were able to raise much of their families' food, but Carbon County never had a big agricultural surplus to sell to neighboring areas.)

Like the United States as a whole, Carbon County is at an economic crossroads. The solutions of the past no longer work; the industries and businesses of the past either no longer exist, or no longer generate the jobs they once did.

On the other hand, the situation provides an opportunity for fresh ideas and new solutions. Intelligent planning is likely to be the key to a better future for the people of the county, and for all Americans.

Agnes McCartney

Agnes T. McCartney, founder and former executive director of the Carbon County Tourist Promotion Agency, began her career as a secretary in state government. She went on to put her organizational and human relations abilities to work for Carbon County. In the process, she and such colleagues as Joseph L. "Joe" Boyle managed to write a new chapter in the county's economic life, reviving tourism as a key provider of jobs and income.

During her state government career, McCartney held such important posts as secretary of the Board of Finance and Revenue and secretary to then-Secretary of the Commonwealth (later Governor) David Lawrence. She continued to regard Lawrence as a mentor, noting of him, "He meant business; he taught me a lot."

Her husband, the late Col. Frank McCartney, was State Police Commissioner during the Lawrence administration. When the family moved to Lansford, Agnes McCartney became involved in community affairs and was an activist president of the Lansford Woman's Club. Later she became secretary, then executive director of Carbon County's first-ever planning commission. She remained with the commission for twelve years, and was also active in the Redevelopment Authority, the Housing Authority, and the Recreation Authority. She could see the tourism potential of the county at a time when few others could, and that led her to establish the tourist promotion agency.

"I got involved in tourism because we had a tremendous depression here with the demise of coal," she said. "Buildings were boarded up, and unemployment was at eighteen percent.

"The county did lend itself to tourism. Together with Niagara Falls, Mauch Chunk once was one of the main tourist stops in the United States. We had so much history here that we didn't have to do much work to tap it all."

One problem, at least as far as Jim Thorpe was concerned, was Mauch Chunk Creek. West of the town the creek was an ingratiating mountain stream. But it had been channeled under downtown streets; and in stormy weather it tended to rise, flooding buildings and causing more than one drowning. McCartney was a key part of the efforts to tame the creek. "We formed an authority and pursued construction of Mauch Chunk Lake," she recalled. "We developed a plan for water supply and recreation. My job was to buy the land."

Agnes T. McCartney here displays a chunk of anthracite coal, Carbon County's famous "black diamonds," adorned with the logo of the Old Company, the Lehigh Navigation Coal Company. Photograph by Marigrace Heyer, used with permission

She also was among those authority members who favored a lake for recreational purposes, rather than a mere dam to impound flood waters. Her point of view prevailed, and the county was enriched by Mauch Chunk Lake. The dam breastwork was finished just in time for the devastating assault by Hurricane Agnes in 1972. It did its main job, keeping flooding in downtown Jim Thorpe to a minimum. At that point, the redevelopment of the historic district became possible.

In the two decades that have elapsed since then, with vigorous efforts by McCartney's agency, tourism and tourism-related enterprise have surged to become Carbon County's chief source of employment. And the town of Jim Thorpe has begun to attract national media attention, appearing in major magazines and newspapers and in radio and television segments virtually everywhere.

McCartney felt her role in the development of Mauch Chunk Lake would be her chief legacy to Carbon County. Important as that effort was, though, it could be argued that another of her contributions was still greater: That is an attitude — the belief that, no matter how desperate the situation, large dreams coupled with constructive action can lead to high accomplishment.

Joe Boyle

Joseph L. "Joe" Boyle, journalist and community leader, was one of a small group of outstanding figures who have helped shape modern-day Carbon County, and whose influence will continue far into the future. In part because of him, Jim Thorpe is at present a thriving town that draws thousands of visitors annually, rather than two decaying boroughs named Mauch Chunk and East Mauch Chunk. And, to a large extent, the new prosperity of the county seat has percolated throughout the county.

Born in Mauch Chunk in 1915, Boyle was the son of James and Annie (Boyce) Boyle. His father was the publisher of the Mauch Chunk *Times*, later the daily Mauch Chunk *Times-News*. The younger Boyle began working for the paper while still a student at Mauch Chunk High School, and returned to work for it after graduating from Mt. St. Mary's College, Emmitsburg, Maryland, in 1937. During World War II he served in the U.S. Army.

After his father died in 1957, Boyle and his sister Gertrude Apfelbaum co-published the family paper, with him as editor. When the paper was sold to Pencor Services and moved to Lehighton in 1968, he became the first editor of the new Lehighton *Times-News*.

He had long recognized that the towns of Mauch Chunk and East Mauch Chunk were in desperate need of revitalization, and in the early 1950s he was one of the leaders who pushed to bring the body of famed American Indian athlete Jim Thorpe to the area, and to unify the two towns under Thorpe's name.

It may seem an improbable prescription for municipal revival; but it apparently worked. There are many who assert that today's famous and relatively prosperous county seat could not have come about without the unification and name change.

Boyle won national and local recognition for his efforts. He was mentioned in *The New Yorker*, *Forbes* magazine, and *Sports Illustrated*. Once, a National Public Radio reporter followed him on his daily rounds.

The Jim Thorpe Olympian Booster Club named him Man of the Year, and in 1985 he won the Shamrock Award of the Panther Valley Irish-American Association. He was a member of the Jim Thorpe Sports Hall of Fame, and on the day before his death he was inducted into the Carbon County Sports Hall of Fame.

"He bore his fame well," commented Jim Thorpe resident Patrick Conway. "It speaks highly for his character."

Though he was first and foremost a newsman, Boyle's service to the community was far from limited to his professional role. For two years he was a Jim Thorpe councilman, and he ran unsuccessfully for county commissioner in 1975. He served for fifteen years on the Carbon County Planning Commission, and was secretary of the Jim Thorpe Industrial Development Board and the Carbon County Recreation Authority. In addition, he was past president of the Jim Thorpe Lions and Rotary clubs, and was the founder and first president of Men of Marian, a Marian High School booster club. For a time, he also was executive director of the Lehighton Area Chamber of Commerce.

In 1991, after serving the paper in various positions for more than twenty years, Boyle retired from the *Times-News*. Soon afterward, however, he began writing a weekly historical column, "According to Boyle," for the Carbon-Schuylkill-Monroe edition of *The Morning Call*. He looked forward to Carbon County's sesquicentennial observance.

With his camera around his neck, ready for action, "Joe" Boyle appears the consummate newspaperman in this informal portrait. Courtesy, Mrs. Joseph L. Boyle

On May 25, 1992, Memorial Day, Joe Boyle was killed in a freak accident involving a parade float on which he was riding. He was seventy-seven years old.

Managing editor of *The Morning Call*, Roy Heffelfinger, wrote of Boyle, "He epitomized the true journalist who loved his profession, fought tooth and nail for what he believed in, and showed an untiring enthusiasm and dedication to the area."

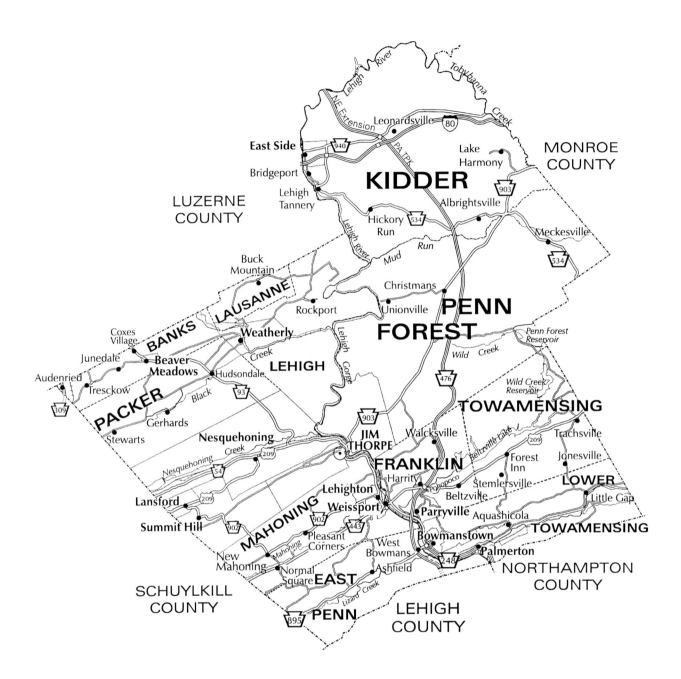

Carbon County's boroughs, townships, and villages.

Towns and Townships
of Carbon County

BANKS TOWNSHIP was erected in 1841, when Carbon County still was a part of Northampton County. It was named after John Banks, president judge of Northampton County from 1836 to 1847. Banks had previously served two terms in Congress (1832–1836), and after 1847 became treasurer of Pennsylvania. A high, plateau-like area atop Spring Mountain, with little arable land, the territory of Banks Township was crossed by the old Lehigh and Susquehanna Turnpike. (See Vince Hydro's article on this famous road; also see the entry for Beaver Meadows.) The future township began to come into its own following the discovery of anthracite there by Nathaniel Beach in 1812. Aside from Beaver Meadow, which later became a borough, the following settlements, all coal towns, came to be located in the township: Jeansville (which straddles the Luzerne County line), Tresckow, Yorktown and its neighbor Audenried, and Leviston, Colerain, and Coolstown, a cluster of mining villages.

BEAVER MEADOWS. As a settlement, Beaver Meadows is considered to date from 1826, when William Hart Wilson and his family settled on the site in what became central Banks Township. The village took its name from the nearby Beaver Creek, and was originally known as Beaver Meadow. It was not incorporated until 1897. Beaver Meadows' main street, Berwick Street, follows the route of the old Lehigh and Susquehanna Turnpike. The town is perhaps most famous as the former location (1834–1842) of the shops of the Beaver Meadow Railroad and Coal Company. Master mechanic Hopkin Thomas, an immigrant from Wales, was credited with many inventions and innovations which benefited both railroading and coal mining. Thomas is credited with successfully adapting anthracite coal as a fuel for locomotives, and with supervising the building of the great 10-wheel locomotive *Nonpareil*. He also designed advanced mine pumps. From 1848 to 1868, Beaver Meadows was the site of a foundry originally built by N.R. Penrose. After several changes of ownership this foundry was relocated in Jeansville, where it became the Jeansville Iron Works. Later still it was relocated to Hazleton, Luzerne County.

BOWMANSTOWN. John Dieter Bowman settled here in 1796. Since the place was on the route of the Lehigh and Susquehanna Turnpike, he opened a tavern in 1808. For years it was known as "the old stone hotel." Around the mid-nineteenth century paint ore (ocher) was discovered in the nearby Stony Ridge; later sand and a fine-quality gray building stone were found there as well. The village became for decades a center for quarrying, and for the manufacture of dry metallic paint. Bowmanstown was incorporated as a borough in 1913.

EAST PENN TOWNSHIP. This township was erected in 1808 from Penn Township (1768), which in its turn had originally been part of Towamensing Township. Other townships established at the same time were Lausanne (Carbon County) and West Penn, which became part of Schuylkill County in 1811. Originally East Penn contained most of now-defunct Mauch Chunk Township (erected 1827) and Mahoning Township (erected 1842, the year before the founding of Carbon County). Modern-day East Penn Township encompasses mostly the north slope of the Blue Mountain and the Lizard Creek Valley. Ashfield, once called Pennsville, is the most significant settlement. It was the site of iron-working operations after 1828, when Penn Forge and Furnace was established there. Such operations seem to have been abandoned before the end of the nineteenth century. Today, East Penn Township appears to be a place of housing subdivisions, although there are still some farms and some light industry.

EAST SIDE. At its erection in 1892, this town was said to be the smallest borough in Pennsylvania. It once was noted for the location there of Sunnyrest Sanatorium. Organized in 1901, Sunnyrest was the first private institution in the state for the treatment of tuberculosis.

FRANKLIN TOWNSHIP. Organized in 1851 from Upper Towamensing (now Towamensing), this township is named after Benjamin Franklin. Originally the economic base of the area was agricultural, with the timber industry and some forges and foundries also being represented. Other small industries could be found in the township, ranging from brick-making firms to contract sewing shops. For many decades, perhaps the majority of employed township residents worked at the Weissport Boatyard of the Lehigh Coal and Navigation Company, making and repairing canal boats, or at the Packerton Yards of the Lehigh Valley Railroad. The canal formally closed in 1932; the railroad yards lingered on into the early 1970s. With the creation of Beltzville Lake and Beltzville State Park in the 1970s, many businesses catering to visitors have grown up, and the township has come to play a vital role in Carbon County's tourism revival. Villages within Franklin Township include Harrity, Walcksville, and Beltzville.

JIM THORPE, the county seat of Carbon County and the current center of its tourism industry, was incorporated in 1954 and named for the noted American Indian athlete Jim Thorpe, who is buried on the east side of town. The present-day borough is composed of two older towns. They are:

> **MAUCH CHUNK**, which was founded in 1818 and incorporated in 1850. As the upper terminus of the Lehigh Canal, it was the shipping point for anthracite on its way from the Lehigh coalfields to markets in Philadelphia and New York. The Lehigh Valley Railroad and the Lehigh and Susquehanna Railroad (leased to the Central Railroad of New Jersey and known locally as "the Jersey Central") later improved access to the coalfields. Although Mauch Chunk was very much an industrial town, its picturesque setting also made it one of the most popular tourist attractions of late nineteenth-century America.

> **EAST MAUCH CHUNK**, which was founded as a kind of suburb to ease the demand for building space in cramped Mauch Chunk. John Burns, the first settler, located here in 1824. The town was incorporated as a borough about thirty years later, on January 1, 1854. Most of the working population was employed at one time either by one of the two railroads, the Lehigh Valley or the Jersey Central, or by the Dery Silk Mill. Glen Onoko, one of the prime tourist attractions of the Mauch Chunk area, also lay on the East Mauch Chunk side of the Lehigh River.

KIDDER TOWNSHIP was organized in 1849. Previously it was a part of Penn Forest Township, the portion of the county that once belonged to Monroe County. Its namesake was Carbon County Judge Luther Kidder. Lumbering and tanning once were its chief industries, but both were destroyed during the Great Fire of 1875. Today, Kidder Township is one of the most important tourism and vacation centers in the entire county. It is the site of much of Hickory Run State Park, as well as of Big Boulder Lake and Lake Harmony, with their attendant resorts. Villages within the township include Bridgeport, Lehigh Tannery, and Hickory Run.

LANSFORD. Based essentially on the patch towns of Ashton and Storm Hill, Lansford filed for incorporation as a borough in 1876, and was incorporated in 1896. It was named for Massachusetts-born Asa Lansford Foster, who made a distinguished career as an entrepreneur in Carbon County. Situated over the so-called Mammoth Vein, possibly the richest vein of anthracite coal in the world, Lansford grew rapidly. It soon contained more than ten thousand residents, and became the most populous town in the county. The decline of the anthracite industry and the end of large-scale coal mining in the Panther Valley led to a rapid shrinkage. Today Lansford residents number about half of those who lived in the town at its peak. It has become a bedroom community, with many people driving to jobs as far away as Allentown and Bethlehem. With such developments as the new anthracite museum in the wash house of the No. 9 mine, Lansford is beginning to share in Carbon County's tourism industry.

LAUSANNE TOWNSHIP, organized in 1808 as a subdivision of Northampton County, was formerly much larger than it is today; its territory once included Mauch Chunk, Banks, and Packer townships, as well as the borough of Weatherly. This mountainous township was one of the earliest coal mining areas in the county. Historian Vince Hydro believes it was named for the village of Lausanne, which was situated within its borders. The village itself seems to have been named for the canton of Lausanne in Switzerland, although no one is certain who bestowed this name on the place, or why.

LEHIGH TOWNSHIP was created in 1875 from Lausanne Township. Its primary industries were lumbering and coal mining. Villages within the township include Rockport and Leslie Run. Today Rockport is a point of access for the Lehigh Gorge State Park.

LEHIGHTON. The first settlement on the site of Lehighton was the ill-starred Gnadenhuetten mission of the Moravian Church, which was built in 1746 and destroyed during the Gnadenhuetten Massacre of November 24, 1755. The future town was laid out in 1794 by Col. Jacob Weiss and William Henry. It was a candidate for designation as the county seat of Carbon County, but lost out to the Lehigh Coal and Navigation Company's effective lobbying on behalf of Mauch Chunk (now Jim Thorpe). Lehighton was incorporated in 1866. It was a center for a wide variety of manufactures, ranging from lace to stoves, but emphasizing textiles and garments. Today a number of garment mills still exist in the town. Blue Ridge Pressure Castings, Incorporated, also is located here, as are the offices of the Lehighton *Times News*, a division of Pencor Services, Incorporated. From 1857 through 1992, Lehighton was the location of the Carbon County Fair, familiarly known as the Lehighton Fair. The popular attraction came to an end when the Carbon County Agricultural Association, which had run it, sold its grounds to the Lehighton Area School District after being threatened with condemnation proceedings. The CCAA subsequently dissolved. Lehighton is the site of one of the county's only two hospitals. Named after the old Moravian mission, Gnaden Huetten Memorial Hospital was built in the 1950s.

LOWER TOWAMENSING TOWNSHIP was established in 1841 from a portion of Towamensing Township. Agriculture was a mainstay of the Lower Towamensing region, although it also had a range of mineral products including slate, ocher, sand, and building stone. The borough of Palmerton once was part of the township. Settlement dates from the eighteenth century; Nicholas Opplinger settled near the mouth of the Aquashicola Creek about 1750, and Benjamin Franklin and his forces stayed at Opplinger's stockade on their way to build Fort Allen in the aftermath of the Gnadenhuetten Massacre. (The name "Opplinger" has survived in early records in a variety of spellings, including "Uplinger.") Villages in Lower Towamensing Township include Little Gap, Walkton, and Aquashicola (formerly Millport).

MAHONING TOWNSHIP. This township was created in 1842 out of part of East Penn. An approximate translation of its Indian name is "creek flowing near a (salt) lick." Mahoning Township has the richest farming land in Carbon County, and for most of its history agriculture was its chief contribution to the economic picture. Nevertheless, many township farmers, unable to live on the proceeds from their farming, sought jobs as coal miners in Summit Hill. Today the township is rapidly becoming a bedroom community, with heavy commercial development on the east end near Lehighton. Villages include Packerton, Pleasant Corner, New Mahoning, Normal Square (formerly Center Square, or Normal), and Mertz's Corner.

NESQUEHONING. Settlement of this coal-region town dates from 1824, when a house was built for Thomas Kelly. It was the second-oldest company town of the Lehigh Navigation Coal Company, after Summit Hill. Yet it was not incorporated until 1963, making it Carbon County's youngest borough. Today, the diversified Kovatch Corporation is the largest employer in Nesquehoning — indeed, in the entire county. The town also is the site of a controversial cogeneration plant, run by Panther Creek Partners, which generates electricity from waste coal. For additional information, see "Nesquehoning" by Vince Hydro, and "The Italians of New Columbus."

PACKER TOWNSHIP. Once part of Lausanne Township, Packer was established in 1847. It was named after Asa Packer, then an associate judge of the Carbon County court. An early center of the lumber industry, it was substantially denuded of trees by the time Fred Brenckman wrote his history in the early twentieth century. The Quakake Valley, which runs through the township, was the primary agricultural region of the northern part of the county. The Tidewater Pipe Company ran its pipeline through the township in the mid-1880s, in an effort to break the Standard Oil Company's monopoly of oil shipments by rail. Tidewater established a pumping station at Hudsondale. Villages in Packer Township include Hudsondale (formerly Hartz's Corner), Gerhards, and Stewarts.

PALMERTON. Founded in 1899 and incorporated in 1912, Palmerton was built as a mill town to serve the needs of the New Jersey Zinc Company. It was designed as a model community, one in which the workers were compensated for their dangerous jobs in the company plants by adequate housing, educational and cultural opportunities, and medical care. Palmerton Hospital was the first, and until the founding of Lehighton's Gnaden Huetten Hospital in the 1950s, the only hospital in Carbon County. While New Jersey Zinc's social policies have been called paternalistic, many people continue to value the benefits they derived from those policies. In recent years, mounting environmental problems have led to the designation of Palmerton as a Superfund cleanup site, and to sharp and bitter divisions among residents.

PARRYVILLE. Incorporated in 1874, this small borough is situated near the mouth of the Pohopoco (or Big) Creek. The first European-stock settler in the neighborhood was Peter Frantz, who arrived in 1780. In the late 1830s, the Pine Forest Lumber Company made its headquarters in the settlement. Daniel Parry was the company's president, and the place was named after him. Originally it was called Parrysville. From 1836 until the freshet of 1841, the town was the southernmost terminus and coal shipping point for the Beaver Meadow Railroad Company. In 1855 Dennis and Henry Bauman (alternate spelling Bowman) established an anthracite furnace at Parryville, which became the Carbon Iron Company. Later it was sold and became, successively, the Carbon Iron and Pipe Company, and the Carbon Iron and Steel Company. In the early part of the twentieth century, it was the only iron furnace in the Lehigh Valley north of the Blue Mountain. At the time of this writing J&R Slaw, Incorporated, was the largest employer in Parryville, with about forty employees in the early 1990s. Owned by Jeanette and Robert Slaw, the firm manufactured precast concrete items including bridge beams, road barriers, and wall paneling for buildings.

PENN FOREST TOWNSHIP. Like Kidder Township, which once was included in its territory, Penn Forest Township formerly belonged to Monroe County. It was attached to Carbon County when the latter was established in 1843, and Kidder Township was set off from it in 1849. The area sometimes was called the Pine Swamp, the Great Swamp, or the Shades of Death. It was a hiding place for Indians during the Indian Wars, and a precarious and uncertain refuge for those fleeing the so-called Wyoming Massacre during the Revolution. From around 1835 until the Great Fire of 1875 wiped out the last vestiges of the industry, it was a lumbering area. Today Penn Forest Township is largely a place of homes and vacation homes. Villages include Albrightsville, Meckesville, and Christmans.

SUMMIT HILL was incorporated as a borough in 1889. It is situated at the site of Philip Ginder's 1791 discovery of anthracite coal atop Sharp Mountain, and in 1818 Josiah White and Erskine Hazard began mining operations there. Later the Lehigh Coal Mine Company's mines were leased to contractors, but after 1866 they were worked directly by the Lehigh Navigation Coal Company. Beginning in 1827, the famous Switchback Railroad carried coal from Summit Hill to Mauch Chunk. After 1846, coal was hauled from the growing Panther Valley community which became Lansford, by way of two planes, to Summit Hill for shipment to Mauch Chunk. The greater richness of the coal deposits in the Panther Valley (the Mammoth Vein) and the building of a direct railroad connection between the Panther Valley and the Lehigh Valley, conspired to reduce the economic importance of Summit Hill and increase that of Lansford. The decline of the anthracite industry affected all the towns of the coal regions. Probably the majority of working Summit Hill residents today commute to jobs out of town, as do the workers of surrounding communities.

TOWAMENSING TOWNSHIP. "Towamensing," the Lenape word for "wilderness," was the name of the Northampton County township organized in 1768, lying east of the Lehigh River and north of the Blue Mountain. Its counterpart on the west side of the river was Penn Township, from which were later formed East Penn, Mahoning, Mauch Chunk, and Lausanne townships, as well as West Penn Township, Schuylkill County. The original territory of Towamensing Township also was divided over the course of time. Chestnut Hill and Tobyhanna townships became part of Monroe County, while Penn Forest, Lower Towamensing, and Franklin townships are part of Carbon County. Towamensing Township once was predominantly agricultural. However, a large portion of Beltzville Lake lies within the township, so that today there is more economic emphasis on tourism and recreation. Villages within the township include Stemlersville, Trachsville, and Jonesville.

WEATHERLY, originally Black Creek, began its existence as a lumbering settlement. Later it became the site of the shops of the Beaver Meadow Railroad Company. When that company was absorbed by the Lehigh Valley Railroad, the LVRR continued shop operations in the town for many years. The settlement was renamed Weatherly in 1848, when a post office was established there. Its namesake was David Weatherly, a clock and watch maker who was a director of the Beaver Meadow Railroad. Weatherly offered to donate a town clock if the place were named after him, but he failed to keep his word. Weatherly was incorporated in 1863. Industries which once were located there include the Roscoe Broad Silk Mill, the Read and Lovatt Manufacturing Company (thrown silk), and the Allen Candy Company. Today the town is perhaps best known as the site of Weatherwood, the county home for the aged.

WEISSPORT. This borough is on the site of the Moravian Church's New Gnadenhuetten mission, built the year before the Gnadenhuetten mission was attacked and destroyed in 1755. Benjamin Franklin built Fort Allen here early in 1756, following the Gnadenhuetten Massacre. Permanent settlement, however, dates from the arrival of Col. Jacob Weiss and his family in 1785. After that the place was known as Weiss's Mill, and after the building of the Lehigh Navigation as Weissport. The town was incorporated in 1867. Formerly many of its residents worked at the canal boatyard, founded by Jacob Weiss's grandson Lewis Weiss, or for the Central Railroad of New Jersey, which ran through the town, or at the Packerton Shops of the Lehigh Valley Railroad.

Note on Mauch Chunk Township: Established in 1827, for the most part from territory formerly belonging to East Penn, the bulk of this township lay west of present-day Jim Thorpe. It no longer exists, its land having been divided among the boroughs of Jim Thorpe, Summit Hill, Nesquehoning, and Lansford.

The Authors

JOAN CAMPION, a native of Carbon County, is a historical journalist. She was born in Weissport; her family moved from the town following the Lehigh River freshet of 1942. She lived and went to school in Lehighton and Mahoning Township, and graduated from Lehighton High School and Cedar Crest College. A previous book, *In The Lion's Mouth: Gisi Fleischmann and the Jewish Fight for Survival,* was published by University Press of America in 1987. Ms. Campion has published several booklets on local and regional history, and has written extensively on arts and musical topics for the former *Globe-Times* of Bethlehem, and for *Arts Alive!* magazine, which is based in the Lehigh Valley. She is the founder of the South Bethlehem Historical Society.

GEORGE HARVAN was born and raised in Lansford, Carbon County. He is a photographer/historian for *The Valley Gazette.* He recently documented the three remaining large anthracite breakers: Huber Breaker at Ashley, Locust Summit near Ashland, and St. Nicholas, west of Mahanoy City. He served as a still photographer with the 5th Army Air Corps during World War II, after which he worked as a media consultant for Bethlehem Steel and as a freelance photographer for the Lehigh Coal and Navigation Company. He has recorded the full range of activities and emotions of the anthracite miner and Pennsylvania's anthracite region. Harvan's work has appeared in numerous publications, including the *Saturday Evening Post, Life, Ford Times,* and many photography magazines. His published works include *Time of the Mollies* and *The Coal Miners of Panther Valley.*

VINCE HYDRO, a native of Nesquehoning, Carbon County, is the Museum Director for the Mauch Chunk Historical Society. He has written articles on local history for the *Times-News* of Lehighton, *The Valley Gazette* of Lansford, and the Canal History and Technology Press. His topics have included the Switchback Railroad, the Room Run Railroad, Mauch Chunk as an anthracite-mining town, the Hacklebernie Tunnel, and the Mount Pisgah drift. He is completing a comprehensive history of the Switchback Railroad, which will be published by the Canal History and Technology Press. He is a regular speaker at the annual Canal History and Technology Symposium. Hydro holds an Associate in Nuclear Engineering Technology from Penn State University, and is currently pursuing a BS in Finance at Allentown College.

MICHAEL KNIES is a Carbon County native from Lansford. His local history writings include the early political and economic problems faced by the Lehigh Coal and Navigation Company, the Beaver Meadow Railroad, and the early development of Mauch Chunk. He is currently working on a history of anthracite coal mining. He has a BA in philosophy, a BA in classical studies, and an MA in American Studies from the Pennsylvania State University, and a Masters of Library Service from Rutgers University. He was collections manager at the archives of Hugh Moore Historical Parks and Museums, Inc., in Easton, Pennsylvania, from 1988 to 1996. Since 1996 he has been the Special Collections Librarian at Weinberg Memorial Library at the University of Scranton.

LANCE E. METZ is a native of the Lehigh Valley and is currently employed as the historian for the National Canal Museum in Easton, Pennsylvania. He is the co-author of several books and many articles on transportation and industrial history. In recent years he has written two books on the Lehigh Valley's portland cement industry. He received his undergraduate degree from Moravian College, Bethlehem, and a graduate degree in history from the University of Maine.

RITA M. PLOTNICKI is currently president of the South Bethlehem Historical Society. Her writings on regional history include the book *Looking Back: A Lehigh Scrapbook*, and short pieces for Lehigh University, Lafayette College, and the Delaware and Lehigh Canal National Heritage Corridor. A former reporter for the Bethlehem *Globe-Times*, she earned a bachelor's degree from East Stroudsburg University, a master's from Hunter College, and a Ph.D. from the City University of New York.

Bibliography

Books and Booklets

A Narrative of the Capture and Captivity of Benjamin Gilbert and His Family. No author given. First edition printed in Philadelphia, 1782; second edition (pamphlet) printed in London, 1790; third edition printed by John Richards, Philadelphia, 1848.

Archer, Robert F. *The History of the Lehigh Valley Railroad, "The Route of the Black Diamond."* Berkeley, California: Howell-North, 1977.

Barrett, Tom. *The Mollies Were Men.* New York: Vantage Press, 1969.

Bartholomew, Ann and Lance E. Metz. *Delaware and Lehigh Canals.* Easton, Pennsylvania: Canal History and Technology Press, 1989.

Bimba, Anthony. *The Molly Maguires.* New York: International Publishing Co., 1950.

Brenckman, Fred. *A History of Carbon County, Pennsylvania.* Harrisburg: James J. Nungesser, Publisher, 1913.

Broehl, Wayne G. *The Molly Maguires.* Cambridge: Harvard University Press, 1964.

Campbell, Patrick. *A Molly Maguire Story.* Jersey City: Templecrone Press, 1992.

The First Hundred Years of the New Jersey Zinc Company: A History of the Founding and Development of a Company and an Industry, 1848-1948. New York: The New Jersey Zinc Company, 1948.

Gillespie, Angus K. *Folklorist of the Coal Fields: George Korson's Life and Work.* University Park: The Pennsylvania State University Press, 1980.

Golden Jubilee Celebrating the Incorporation of the Borough of Palmerton, Pennsylvania, 1912-1988. Nesquehoning, Pennsylvania, 1988.

Greco, Susan. *Diamond Jubilee of Our Lady of Mount Carmel Roman Catholic Italian Parish, 1913-1988.* Nesquehoning, Pennsylvania, 1988.

HAER Inventory, Historic American Engineering Record. Washington D.C.: Department of the Interior, 1979.

Hansell, Norris. *Josiah White: Quaker Entrepreneur.* Easton, Pennsylvania: Canal History and Technology Press, 1992.

Henry, M.S. *History of the Lehigh Valley.* Easton: Bixler & Corwin, 1860.

Historic Resources Study of the Delaware and Lehigh Canal National Heritage Corridor and State Heritage Park. Easton, Pennsylvania: Hugh Moore Historical Park and Museums, 1992.

Hoben, Richard J. *Lansford: The First 100 Years.* Lansford: Centennial Committee, 1976.

_____. *The Story of Lehighton.* Lehighton: Centennial Committee, 1976.

Holm, Maj. Gen. Jeanne. *Women in the Military: An Unfinished Revolution.* Novato, California: Presidio Press, 1982.

Klein, Philip S. and Ari Hoogenboom. *A History of Pennsylvania,* 2nd and enlarged edition. University Park: The Pennsylvania University Press, 1980.

Koehler, Jack. *125th Anniversary of Weatherly Borough Incorporation, 1863-1988.* Privately printed.

Korson, George. *Minstrels of the Mine Patch.* Philadelphia: University of Pennsylvania Press, 1938. Reprinted by Folklore Associates, 1964.

_____. *Black Rock: Mining Folklore of the Pennsylvania Dutch.* Baltimore: The Johns Hopkins Press, 1960.

Kulp, Randolph L., ed. *Railroads in the Lehigh River Valley*. Allentown: Lehigh Valley Chapter, National Railway History Society, 1956-1979.

Lewis, Arthur H. *Lament for the Molly Maguires*. New York: Harcourt Brace & World, 1964.

Livingood, James Weston. *The Philadelphia-Baltimore Trade Rivalry 1780-1880*. Harrisburg, Pennsylvania: Pennsylvania Historical and Museum Commission, 1947.

Mathews, Alfred, and Austin N. Hungerford. *History of the Counties of Lehigh and Carbon, in the Commonwealth of Pennsylvania*. Philadelphia: Everts & Richards, 1884.

Miller, Donald L. and Richard E. Sharpless. *The Kingdom of Coal*. Philadelphia: University of Pennsylvania Press, 1985.

Miller, John P. *The Lehigh Canal: a Very Short History*. Jim Thorpe: Carbon County Tourist Promotion Agency, n.d., but probably 1976.

Opplinger, Carl S. and J. Robert Halma. *The Poconos: An Illustrated Natural History Guide*. New Brunswick: Rutgers University Press, 1988.

Parsons, John, ed. *The Lehigh Water Gap: A Documentary History*. Lehigh Gap Historical and Preservation Society and Museum, 1993.

Parton, W. Julian. *The Death of a Great Company: Reflections on the Decline and Fall of the Lehigh Coal and Navigation Company*. Easton: Center for Canal History and Technology, 1986.

Portrait and Biographical Record of Lehigh, Northampton, and Carbon Counties, Pennsylvania. Chicago: Chapman, 1894.

Powell, H. Benjamin. *Philadelphia's First Fuel Crisis: Jacob Cist and the Developing Market for Pennsylvania Anthracite*. University Park, Pennsylvania: Pennsylvania State University Press, 1978.

A Record of Accomplishment, 1848-1923. A Short History of the New Jersey Zinc Company. New York: The New Jersey Zinc Company, n.d.

Richardson, Richard. *Memoir of Josiah White*. Philadelphia: J.B. Lippincott & Co. 1873.

Royall, Anne. *Mrs Royall's Pennsylvania, or, Travels Continued in the United States*. 2 vols. Washington [D.C.]: Printed for the author, 1829.

Rosevak, Chuck and Jean. *Museum of American Folk Art Encyclopedia of Twentieth Century Folk Art and Artists*. New York: Abbeville Press, 1990.

Rupp, Israel Daniel. *A History of Northampton, Lehigh, Monroe, Carbon, and Schuylkill Counties*. Harrisburg: Hickock and Cantine, printer, 1845.

Shank, William H. *The Amazing Pennsylvania Canals*. 4th ed. York, Pennsylvania: American Canal and Transportation Center, 1986.

Silver Anniversary Celebrating the Founding of Palmerton, Carbon County, Pennsylvania, 1898-1923. Palmerton: Palmerton Printing Company, 1937.

The Story of The Old Company. Lansford, Pennsylvania: Lehigh Navigation Coal Company, 1941.

Thomas, Augusta Dillman (a descendant). *The Bowmans: A History of Hans Dieterick Bauman and His Descendants*. Mahanoy City, Pennsylvania, 1934.

Thompson, Katharine Foster. *Chapter and Verse: The Annotated Diaries of Asa Lansford Foster (1798-1868)*. Wilmington, Delaware, 1992.

Trettel, Josephine A., ed. *Our Town: Beaver Meadows Then and Now*. Beaver Meadows, Pennsylvania: privately printed. 1987.

Wagner, A.E. *History, Government and Geography of Carbon County, Pennsylvania*. Allentown, Pennsylvania, 1910.

Wallace, Paul A.W. *Indians in Pennsylvania*. 2nd ed., revised by William A. Hunter. Harrisburg: Pennsylvania Historical and Museum Commission, 1989.

_____. *Indian Paths of Pennsylvania*. Harrisburg: Pennsylvania Historical and Museum Commission, 1987.

White, Josiah. *Josiah White's History given by himself*. Originally printed by the Lehigh Coal and Navigation Company (n.d.). Reprinted June 29, 1979, by the Carbon County Board of Commissioners in conjunction with the 150th anniversary of the opening of the Lehigh Navigation System Canal.

Yates, W. Ross. *Lehigh University: A History of Education in Engineering, Business and the Human Condition*. Bethlehem: Lehigh University Press, 1992.

Papers:

Baer, Christopher. "White and Hazard and the Lehigh Coal and Navigation Company, 1804-1840." Unpublished manuscript, 1983, in National Canal Museum's Library and Archives, Easton, Pennsylvania.

Bastoni, Gerald. "Episodes From the Life of Canvass White, Pioneer American Civil Engineer." In *Proceedings of the Canal History and Technology Symposium*, Vol. 1, January 30, 1982, 50-85. Easton: The Center for Canal History and Technology, 1982.

Chandler, Alfred. "Anthracite Coal and the Beginnings of the Industrial Revolution." In *Harvard Business History Review*, Vol. XLVI No. 22, 1972.

Dublin, Thomas. "The Equalizaton of Work: An Alternative Vision of Industrial Capitalism in the Anthracite Region of Pennsylvania in the 1930s." In *Proceedings of the Canal History and Technology Symposium*, Vol. XIII, 81-99. Easton, Canal History and Technology Press, 1994.

Hydro, Vince. "Mauch Chunk, Pennsylvania As An Anthracite Town." In *Proceedings of the Canal History and Technology Symposium*, Vol. XI, 69-99. Easton: Canal History and Technology Press, 1982.

Knies, Michael. "Industry, Enterprise, Wealth and Taste: The History of Mauch Chunk, 1791-1831." In *Proceedings of the Canal History and Technology Symposium*, Vol. IV, 17-42. Easton: Canal History and Technology Press, 1985.

Sayenga, Don. "Chain Bridges on the Lehigh." In *Proceedings of the Lehigh County Historical Society*, Vol. 38, 78-89. Allentown, Pennsylvania: Lehigh County Historical Society, 1988.

Theses and Dissertations:

(All in Canal Museum Archives, Easton, Pennsylvania)

Brzyski, Anthony J. "The Lehigh Canal and its Effect on the Economic Development of the Region Through Which It Passed, 1818-1873." Unpublished Ph.D. dissertation, New York University, 1957.

Hartman, Earl J. "Josiah White: A Study of the Lehigh Canal with Relation to the Development of the Anthracite Coal Industry and the History of the Lehigh Coal and Navigation to the year 1870." Thesis, 1938.

Knies, Michael J. "The Development of the Lehigh Coal Field and the Lehigh Coal and Navigation Company: 1791-1820." Thesis, 1989.

Periodicals:

Manske, William, "Cold War Battles." Letter in *American Heritage*, July-August 1992: 8.

"Palmerton Hero Returns Home After Meeting King." In *Zinc*, Volume 21, No. 3, August, 1942: 78-81.

Hazard's Register of Pennsylvania. Philadelphia. July 21, 1832, and various other issues and dates.

The Historical Record, A Quarterly Publication devoted principally to the Early History of the Wyoming Valley, and contiguous territory. Wilkes-Barre, Pennsylvania. 1896.

Newspapers:

"AF contract may bring Nesquehoning 100 jobs," by Vince Moro. In *Standard-Speaker*, Hazleton, Thursday, Sept. 10, 1981: 23.

"Beaver Meadows has tie to Revolution," In *Standard-Speaker*, Hazleton, Friday, Sept. 6, 1991: D-13.

"Chestnut Ridge Line, 11-mile Railroad Palmerton to Kunkletown, Financed by Two Millionaires to Every Mile." In *Call-Chronicle*, Allentown, Nov. 19, 1950.

"Death on the Rails." In *Standard-Speaker*, Hazleton, Friday, Sept. 6, 1991: E-9.

"Disaster" and "Emotional Rescue," by Bob Salitza. In *Standard-Speaker*, Hazleton, Friday, Sept. 6, 1991: B-18.

"Famed Lehighton Mineral Spring Once Was Popular," by Ralph Kraemer, Carbon County Panorama No. 231. In *Call-Chronicle*, Allentown, June 15, 1958.

"Girl slatepickers at Nesquehoning breaker," by Ed Gildea. In *Valley Gazette*, Lansford, March 1992: 13.

"Government contract for area firm." In *Times-News & Record*, Lehighton, Tuesday, Aug. 11, 1970.

"Hazletonians fought bravely in Civil War," by Carl Christopher. In *Standard-Speaker*, Hazleton, Friday, Sept. 6, 1991: D-13.

"King Coal and the early days." In *Standard-Speaker*, Hazleton, Friday, Sept. 6, 1991: B-1.

"Kovatch Brothers Join List of Men Determined to Insure Area's Future." Editorial in *Evening Record*, Lansford, Monday, April 19, 1965.

"Kovatch Rebuilds Jeeps for Peace." In *Times-News & Record*, Lehighton, June 13, 1970.

"Local Civil War soldiers rallied around the flag," by Jim Zbick. In *Times-News*, Lehighton, Saturday, June 13, 1992: 21

"Nathan Beach Started Beaver Meadows' boom," by Bill Berry. In *Standard-Speaker*, Hazleton, Friday, Sept. 6, 1991: A-5.

"Nesquehoning Brothers Purchase 1,600 Acres for Homes, Plants." In *The Morning Call*, Allentown, Saturday, Sept. 28, 1963.

"Nesquehoning firm prepares trucks for use in Nigeria." In *Times-News & Record*, Lehighton, Thursday, Dec. 10, 1970.

"On to Appomatox: Coal region boys fought and died in the bloody war between the states," by Carl Christopher. In *Standard-Speaker*, Hazleton, Friday, Sept. 6, 1991: D-12.

"Palmerton Company Store Filled Community Needs," by Ralph Kreamer. In *The Morning Call*, Allentown, Nov. 13, 1990.

"A place for the Lord: Churches built by pioneers enriched region spiritually and aesthetically," by Dave Seamon. In *Standard-Speaker*, Hazleton, Friday, Sept. 6, 1991: D-16.

"Purchase CONALCO plant; creation of 65 jobs seen." In *Times-News*, Lehighton, Wednesday, March 9, 1977: 1.

"Schools and saloons closed by flu in '18," by Jack Yalch. In *The Valley Gazette*, Feb. 1992: 36.

"Talks aim at reclamation of coal banks," by Ervin Hawk. In *The Morning Call*, Allentown, Saturday, Nov. 1, 1975.

"Tankers for Air Force to be built in Carbon." In *The Morning Call*, Allentown, Tuesday, Sept. 8, 1981.

Mauch Chunk Gazette: 8/8/1840; 7/3/1844; 9/25/1845; 9/28/1845; 8/21/1845; 7/14/1849

Mauch Chunk Coal Gazette: 4/12/1864, and various other issues. Microfilmed newspaper collection at the Dimmick Memorial Library, Jim Thorpe.

Mauch Chunk Democrat, various issues. Microfilmed newspaper collection at the Dimmick Memorial Library, Jim Thorpe.

Carbon County Gazette, various issues. Microfilmed newspaper collection at the Dimmick Memorial Library, Jim Thorpe.

Carbon Democrat: 6/24/1851; 4/7/1855; 1/16/1869; 3/16/1869; 11/28/1876; 3/23/1878

The Lehigh Pioneer and Mauch Chunk Courier: 1/21/1830, and various other issues. Microfilmed newspaper collection at the Dimmick Memorial Library, Jim Thorpe.

Easton Argus: 9/17/1840.

The Valley Gazette: October, 1977; September, 1978.

Weatherly Herald. Series of articles, photocopies, n.d., by Jack Koehler on Weatherly Castings.

Miscellaneous Publications:

Crellin, Thomas. Crellin letters. Manuscript collection in Archives of National Canal Museum, Easton, Pennsylvania.

Holm, Celia. "Women In The Armed Forces." Office of Information for the Armed Forces, Office, Assistant Secretary of Defense (Public Affairs), Department of Defense, Washington, D.C., 1976.

James, Dr. Thomas C. *Deeds to Land at Mouth of Nesquehoning Creek*. Mauch Chunk Historical Society Archives, Jim Thorpe.

_____. *Personal Papers*. Mauch Chunk Historical Society Archives, Jim Thorpe.

Minutes, Board of Directors of the Lehigh Coal and Navigation Company. 2/10/1829; 2/2/1830; 6/7/1831; 9/19/1831; 9/27/1833; 1/27/1835; 4/29/1836; 5/20/1836; 1/9/1844; 11/12/1845; 11/4/1846; 11/25/1847; 10/24/1849; 1/14/1852; 1/17/1856.

Reports of the Board of Managers of the Lehigh Coal and Navigation Company, presented to the Stockholders. Annual Reports. In Archives of National Canal Museum.

Published Archives of Pennsylvania, Ninth Series, various dates. Pennsylvania Historical and Museum Commission.

Weiss, Jacob. *Personal Account Book*. Lehigh County Historical Society collections, Allentown.

_____. *Personal Papers*. Pennsylvania Historical Society, Philadelphia.

Special Sources of Information:

Styles S. Butz, early Palmerton life, early Palmerton schools.

Johnny Gimbor, Glen Onoko.

Maxine Eisenhower, the letters of James Hughes.

Susan Greco, New Columbus.

Helen LeBow, the arts in Carbon County.

Thomas McBride, community histories.

Interviewees:

(All interviews occurred in 1992)

Byron Arner, Peter Barter and Frank DePaulo; William Bechtold, Edmund Flynn and Winston Scherer; Rita Boyle; Arlene M. Haupt; Marie Kovatch; Dorothy Kresge; Marian Kresge; Agnes T. McCartney; Frederick and Richard Merluzzi and Helen and Frank Dise; Mark Pastir, and Gary Smith.

Photographs and Illustrations

Except where otherwise noted, the illustrations in this volume are from the archives of the National Canal Museum (NCM). Many of these are from the Pennsylvania Canal Society collection, which is maintained by the museum.

The Raymond E. Holland Regional and Industrial History Collection, 2020 Hamilton Street, Allentown, Pennsylvania, has generously allowed use of its impressive collection of printed materials. Carol M. Front, curator, assisted in finding suitable illustrations for this publication; Bradley A. Schaeffer, photographer, copied a number of items in the collection for use in this book.

The Jim Thorpe Post Office and the Mauch Chunk Historical Society gave permission to publish the photographs of the Mauch Chunk postmasters. Bradley A. Schaeffer made the reproductions.

The photograph on page 55 of the burned Beaver Meadow breaker is printed with the permission of the Pennsylvania Historical and Museum Commission. It is from the Charles H. Burg Collection in the State Archives, MG-273.

Original photographs for this publication were taken by Joan Campion and Ann Bartholomew.

Individuals who have loaned items from their private collections have been credited in the captions.

Index

Page numbers in italics refer to illustrations; the letter c indicates "caption."

company housing. *See* workers' housing

company stores, 51, 119, 170, 174, 197-198, 209-210

company towns, 3, 35, 41-42, 55, 59, 77, 173, 201-210, 276

Connelly, John, 151

Connor, Cornelius, 169,174,178

Connor, Eli T., 229

ConRail, 4, 85

Constantine Brothers store, 220

Convers, G.G., 207

Conway, Patrick, 271

Cook, Harry E., 92

Cool, William, 157

Coolstown, 273

Coons, Thomas, 181

Cooper, Eliza, *187*

Cooper, John, *187*

Cope, Caleb, 177

Cortright, Nathan, Jr., *187*

Costenbader, A.A., 219

Costenbader, J.S., 219

country clubs, 151, 214, *266*

county commissioners, 220

county courthouses, 67, 174, 175, 179-182

county home, 246, 278

county jails, 175-176, 179, 180

county seat: controversy, 165, 172-182, 275; Easton, 166-167

county status, 165-171

Cox, James, 176-178

Coxe (family), 119

Coxe, Eckley B., 24

Coyle, William, 117

Craig's Settlement, 222

Craig's store, 210

Craig, Allen (Hon.), 24

Craig, John (Col.), 229

Craig, Thomas (Gen.), 222

creeks: Aquashicola Creek, 140, 144; Beaver Creek, 273; Black Creek, 141; Hell Creek, 159; Hell's Kitchen Run, 39; Hickory Run, 141; Lizard Creek, 11; Mahoning Creek, 140; Mauch Chunk Creek, 17, 269-270; Mud Run, 92; Nesquehoning Creek, 73; Panther Creek, 46; Pine Run, 144; Pohopoco Creek, 141, 144, 159, 207; Quakake Creek, 43; Room Run, 22, 27, 73; Sawmill Creek, 140; Tobyhanna Creek, 11; Wild Creek, 159

Crellin, John and Thomas, 227, 228

crime, 52, 55, 95, 228

Cummings, Mary Packer, 34

Cunningham, Bridget (Mrs.), 52

Curran, James, 51

Custard family, 11

Cutler, Eva, 251

Czechoslovakians. *See* Slovaks.

D

dams: Lehigh Gap, *152, 157, 215*; Lehigh Tannery, *14*; at Mauch Chunk Lake, 17, 79, 269-270; Francis E. Walter, 17, 79; maintenance of, 17, 157c, *215*; Packer's, *89*; sluice, 2, 80; wing, 80

Davis, James (Sen.), 104c

Davis, Lincoln, 200

Deisher, E.C., 219

Delaware Canal, 81, 84, 87c

Delaware, Lehigh, Schuylkill and Susquehanna RR, 32

DeLong, D.B., 158c

Democratic Party, 108

DePaulo, Frank, Sr., 262

depressions, economic: caused by decline of coal industry, 269; Great Depression, 253-255, 267

Dery Silk Mill, 3, 274

Detwiller, H.W.R., 219

Devil's Pulpit, 149

Devil's Wall, 3, 149, 150, 210

Diehl, F.W., 218

Dieter, Charles, 246

Dietrich (serviceman), 237

Dimmick, Milo M. (Esq.), 176

Dinkey (Schwab), Emma Eurana, 194

Dinkey, Jacob, 194

Dinkey, Reuben, 194

Dinkey School, *194*

disasters, 92, 117-118

diseases: black lung disease, 99; cholera, 72; influenza, 198, 213, 238; smallpox, 78; tuberculosis, 159; typhoid fever, 144, 213

distilleries, 143

Diver, Michael, 51

Dodson, Abigail, 13

Dodson, Isaac T., 175

Dodson, Samuel, 13

Dodson, Thomas, 13

Dolon (serviceman), 237

Dolonburg, 84

Donahue, John "Yellow Jack," 111

Donegan, Mike, 238

Donner, Samuel, 143

Dorsey, Jimmy, 251

Dorsey, Tommy, 251

Dougherty, Charles B. (Col.), 234

Dougherty, Peter, 213

Douglas, Andrew A., 78

Douglas, Edwin A., 43, 145

Doyle, Michael, 111

dredging operations, *215*

Dreher, Samuel, 110

Drumheller, Franklin, 261

Duffy, Thomas, 111

Dun's, 73

Dunn, Alexander, 23

E

Eadie, J.G., 149

Eames, Joseph, 230

East Hanover, 169

East Mauch Chunk, *18, 89*, 152-156, 196, 270, 274

East Penn Twp., 11, 274, 276, 277, 278; school, 189

East Side Borough, 159, 274

East Weissport, 159

Easton and Berwick Pike, 94

Easton, 43, 166-167

Eberts, David, 230

Eberts, Peter, 230

Eberts, Samuel, 230

Eberts, William, 230

Eckley, 138c

Edison, Thomas, 151

education, 189-198. *See also* schools; higher education

Eisenhower, Maxine, 231

electric power companies, 35, 210, 264, *254*

electric railways. *See* trolley lines

electronics industry, 265

Elliston, George R., 210

emery wheel manufacturing, 159

employee-company relations. *See* labor-management relations

English population, 3, 73

environment-vs-jobs issue, 257, 264

environmental pollution. *See* pollution.

epidemics. *See* diseases

epitaph, miner's, 119

equalization of work, 56, 255

Erb, John, 157

Esser, George, *188*

ethnic groups, 3, 211; Bosnians, 99; Croats, 19, 99, *102*; Czechs, 212; English, 3, 11, 19, 52, 99, 227; Germans, 3, 11, 19, 52, 70; Hessians, 223; Hungarians, 4, 211, 212, 218; Irish, 3, 19, 49, 51, 52-53, 69, 70, 81, 99, 107-109, 120, 228, 251, 270; Italians, 4, 19, 99, 105-106, 119, 212; Jews, 4, 104-105; Lenni Lenape, 9-13, 73; Lithuanians, 212; Mexicans, 212; Moravians, 3, 9-11; Pennsylvania Germans, 3, 11, 81, 95, 99, 223; Poles, 4, 99, 119, 211, 212; Portuguese, 212; cont.